MORALITY AND POWER
IN A CHINESE VILLAGE

This volume is sponsored by
the Center for Chinese Studies
University of California, Berkeley

Richard Madsen

MORALITY AND POWER
IN A CHINESE VILLAGE

UNIVERSITY OF CALIFORNIA PRESS ▪ Berkeley
Los Angeles
London

University of California Press
Berkeley and Los Angeles, California

University of California Press, Ltd.
London, England

©1984 by
The Regents of the University of California
First Paperback Printing 1986
ISBN 0-520-05925-5

Library of Congress Cataloging in Publication Data

Madsen, Richard, 1941–
  Morality and power in a Chinese village.

  Includes bibliographical references and index.
  1. Ethics, Chinese—History—20th century. 2. Confucianism. 3. China—Politics and government—1949–
I. Title.
BJ966.M3 1983   170′.951   83-4887

Printed in the United States of America

2 3 4 5 6 7 8 9

CONTENTS

> We hail from all corners of the country and have joined together for a common revolutionary objective. . . . The Chinese people are suffering; it is our duty to save them and we must exert ourselves in struggle. Wherever there is struggle, there is sacrifice, and death is a common occurrence. But we have the interests of the people and the sufferings of the great majority at heart, and when we die for the people it is a worthy death. . . . Our cadres must show concern for every soldier, and all the people in the revolutionary ranks must care for each other, must love and help each other. (Mao Zedong, "Serve the People")[1]

> We must all learn the spirit of absolute selflessness. . . . A man's ability may be great or small, but if he has this spirit, he is already noble-minded and pure, a man of moral integrity and above vulgar interests, a man who is of value to the people. (Mao Zedong, "In Memory of Norman Bethune")[2]

The above quotations are fragments from two of the three short speeches by Mao Zedong which, it was claimed by Mao's followers in the 1960s and early 1970s, summed up the essence of his moral teaching. The quotations exemplify an ethos of courage, struggle, and self-sacrifice encapsulated in Mao's command to "Serve the People." This ethos deeply impressed many American observers of China, especially in the early 1970s during the beginning stages of America's detente with China. Such American observers were often favorably impressed with what they took to be the positive contribution of the Cultural Revolution to the creation of a morally upright "new man" in China. Thus, in a remark typical of those times, the distinguished journalist James Reston—upon returning from a visit to China in 1971—praised the Chinese Communists for making a "tremendous effort to bring out what is best in man, what makes them good, what makes them cooperate with one another and be considerate and not beastly to one another."[3] By the early 1980s, however, times had greatly changed. The American press now regularly paints a picture of a demoralized China, in which corruption among government officials creates inefficiencies that impede China's economic development.[4] In

1. Mao Zedong, "Serve the People," *Selected Works of Mao Tse-tung*, 4 vols. (Beijing: Foreign Languages Press, 1961–65), 3:177–78.

2. Mao Zedong, "In Memory of Norman Bethune," *Selected Works*, 2:337.

3. CBS Television interview with Eric Sevareid, reported in the *New York Times*, September 1, 1971.

4. Such a portrait of China appears for example in two recent books by Ameri-

China, Mao's moral homilies are not widely propagated any more. And the Chinese Communist Party has officially declared that Mao, at least partly because of his arrogance, made major errors during the last twenty years of his life, the worst error being the launching of the "catastrophic" Cultural Revolution.[5]

What has changed over the past decade, our Western perceptions of public morality in China or that morality itself? To what extent did Mao's ethic of "serving the people" ever have much meaning and resonance in the lives of ordinary Chinese? How do the Chinese think and talk about what it means to be a good person in a good society and has their thinking changed over the past several decades? Have moral commitments had much to do with the tumultuous history of China over the past several decades or can that history be explained mainly in terms of political struggles among various interest groups?

I became interested in these questions, not out of some detached scientific curiosity, but out of a concern arising from my own moral and religious commitments. I began my career as a Catholic missionary, a member of a religious society called the Maryknoll Fathers. I became interested in China simply because, without my having anything to say about it, my religious superiors sent me to Taiwan to study Chinese and work as a clergyman there. While there and in Hong Kong, I became fascinated both by the richness and depth of traditional Chinese culture and by what in the late 1960s seemed to be the morally transforming power and passion of the Chinese revolution. Like many liberal Catholics of my generation, I was rethinking the whole idea of missionary work and coming to see it as a kind of ecumenical dialogue with serious minded non-Christians rather than an effort to "sell" or impose Christianity on non-Christian peoples. I came to define my task as that of a bridge builder who would try to help span the gap between the Western Christian tradition and other systems of belief and conduct, both traditional religious belief systems and modern secular ones. Thus I became interested in trying to understand what someone steeped in a Western Christian tradition might learn about the meaning and purpose of life from people committed to a revolutionary Communist ideology like Maoism.

---

can journalists: Fox Butterfield, *China: Alive in the Bitter Sea* (New York: Times Books, 1982); and Richard Bernstein, *From the Center of the Earth: The Search for Truth about China* (Boston: Little, Brown & Co., 1982).

5. "Resolution on Certain Questions in the History of Our Party Since the Founding of the People's Republic of China," (adopted by the Sixth Plenary Session of the Eleventh Central Committee of the Communist Party of China on June 27, 1981), *Beijing Review* 24, no. 27 (July 6, 1981):10–39.

Although I left my missionary society in the early 1970s, I remain grateful to my old Maryknoll colleagues for teaching me sensitivity to people, to cultures, and to moral issues. Having given up a career as a missionary, I entered graduate school in sociology at Harvard in the early 1970s. This present study is based on my dissertation. Originally I planned to write my dissertation on a topic that would require a careful application of some fairly standard sociological theory and methodology to new Chinese data. But earlier I had written a short paper on "Revolutionary Asceticism in Communist China," which analyzed in a very speculative way certain themes in the development of moral character among Chinese revolutionaries. Professor Daniel Bell suggested that I write my dissertation on the issues broached in that paper. Pursuing such a topic, he suggested, would be much more of an intellectual adventure than the important but relatively "safe" project I had planned. It would be, he said, "like going into an unexplored jungle filled with exotic animals. You would certainly have a very exciting time—but of course you might never come out alive." I accepted his challenge.

The work was both interesting and dangerous because there existed no well-accepted conceptual map for linking the official ideology propagated by the Chinese media with the actual beliefs and conduct of ordinary Chinese citizens. Important books had been written by Western intellectual historians like Stuart Schram and Frederic Wakeman on traditional and modern themes in Maoist ideology, and careful studies were being conducted by a host of political scientists and sociologists on contemporary Chinese social structure. But while the intellectual historians were carefully analyzing ideas, the social scientists were generally discounting the importance of those ideas and explaining actual Chinese political behavior in terms of the pursuit of economic and political interests. The intellectual historians could note that the Chinese Communists' obsession with preaching public morality had its roots in an intellectual tradition going back to Confucius. But in general they could give only vague hints about how that official obsession might affect the beliefs of ordinary Chinese citizens. The social scientists could note the importance of public profession of "correct" thought at all levels of Chinese society, but their methods of analysis led them to discount the importance of that thought. To study the moral basis of local political conduct in China, therefore, I had to look for ways of thinking about the interplay between moral discourse and social life that were not available in the standard literature by China specialists.

I also needed a rich fund of detailed information about the lives of people in China. I needed to know how ordinary Chinese normally talked, gestured, testified, postured, boasted, and, for that matter, lied to each other about the moral basis of their social and political commitments and to understand the economic, social, and political context for moral discourse and social commitment in China. At the time I began my study in 1974, there existed no body of data richly detailed enough to give me the insights I wanted into the relationship between moral discourse and social commitments at China's grass roots. Moreover, it was impossible to go to China to conduct research there. So I went to the Universities Service Centre in Hong Kong to interview emigrés from China.

It was there that I met Anita Chan and Jonathan Unger, at the time both advanced graduate students from the University of Sussex. Having come into contact with a group of young people who had recently emigrated from the same small village in Guangdong Province, they had begun to consider systematically interviewing those people to get an in-depth picture of what life in a particular Chinese village was like. I joined with them on that project, and on the basis of about three thousand single-spaced pages of interview notes drawn from 223 interviews with twenty-six emigrés we eventually collaborated on a book-length study, *Chen Village: The Recent History of a Peasant Community in Mao's China*,[6] which describes in as much detail as possible the complex history of that community from 1964 to 1982. That project also gave me the richness of data needed to form the empirical basis of this book.

The content of the present study inevitably overlaps with *Chen Village,* but its purpose and focus are different. In *Chen Village* Drs. Chan and Unger and I tried to weave a confusing variety of actions carried out by a rich assortment of individuals into a coherent, finely textured story. In this book, I meditate on that story to attempt a systematic argument about moral and political character in China, a kind of extended gloss on the history of Chen Village and on what I have begun to learn from Chen Village about the relationship between moral discourse, social change, and political processes in the recent phases of the Chinese revolution. If one has already read *Chen Village* most persons and events described in this book will be familiar. But I hope this book will help the reader to see some of those persons and events in a new light and stimulate thought about the interplay between the quest for meaning and the search for wealth and power among peasants in China and perhaps even in other parts of the world. If one has not read *Chen Village* perhaps the summaries of village history presented here will produce an appetite for the more detailed account presented in that other book. Needless to say, I am deeply grateful to Drs. Chan and Unger for sharing this data with me and

6. Anita Chan, Richard Madsen, and Jonathan Unger, *Chen Village: The Recent History of a Peasant Community in Mao's China* (Berkeley: University of California Press, 1984). To protect the privacy of the villagers and our interviewees, we altered the names of the village and the people who appeared in our book. I have followed the same practice in the present study.

for critiquing earlier versions of this book. I must, however, accept full responsibility for the interpretations presented here.

Fourteen of our interviewees were former "sent-down youth" most of whom had been sent to the village as teenagers and remained there until the mid-1970s. In the body of this book, I will tell how they were transferred to the village and why they left. Twelve other interviewees were former peasants born and raised in the village. Most of these came to Hong Kong in the late 1970s, although several emigrated in the early 1960s. Our interviewees lived in different parts of the village and occupied a wide variety of political positions there. For some, their lives in the village were essentially happy, and they left because personal problems developed for them during the 1970s. For others, life was miserable, either because their class status was officially defined as "bad" (e.g., they were the offspring of former landlords or rich peasants) or because they had run afoul of village political leaders. To check for and eliminate biases or prejudices in the points of view of our interviewees, my colleagues and I practiced to the best of our ability the kind of detective work developed by China scholars during more than twenty years of experience with emigrés. We carefully cross-checked various accounts, we sifted through individual accounts for inconsistencies, we tried to be sensitive to the ways different individuals might be biased by their various social statuses and political experiences. We also checked our data against the information compiled by other researchers on a wide range of villages and against the data provided in written documents published by the Chinese government. My two colleagues and I came away from our work convinced that the persons and events described in *Chen Village* were indeed "facts" that might have been noted by anyone in a position to see them.[7]

However, in my attempt to go beyond the describable "facts" of the history of Chen Village and the observable "certainties" of village life, I have tried to explicate underlying patterns of meaning and to link those patterns to broad cultural and political themes. For help in thinking through to these patterns of meaning, I am especially indebted to one of our interviewees, a woman named Ao Meihua. I met Ao in early 1975, a few months after she had arrived in Hong Kong. She became my research assistant, and over a period of about eight months I spent about 150 hours talking with her. My main contribution to the data base of *Chen Village* came from my notes of my conversations with her.

Ao Meihua came from what Chinese political authorities called a "free professional" background in Canton. Her father was a physician who

---

7. For a more detailed account of our methodology, see Chan, Madsen, and Unger, *Chen Village,* chap. 1.

had moved from Canton to Hong Kong in 1945, but who had returned to China out of a sense of patriotism in 1949, when the Communists assumed power. Because he was a physician, he was given the official class status of "free professional"—a status that placed him "among the people" but at a disadvantage with respect to the favored social classes of the new political order: workers, poor peasants, and revolutionary cadres.

Ao Meihua inherited from her father both his sense of patriotism and the political disadvantages that came from his official class status. By the time she was in the fifth grade of primary school, she had come to realize that her class background was markedly inferior to that of students from more politically "pure" backgrounds. A bright student with an independent character, a strong sense of youthful patriotism and, even at such a young age, keen ambitions, she began from that time to draw a clear line between herself and her parents. She spent most of her time after school helping her teachers perform chores around the school, talking to teachers and schoolmates about political matters, and in general striving to become a model Communist youth. She spent little time at home with her family. By the time she entered junior middle school, she had become known as one of the "Reddest" students in her class. In her second year in junior middle school, she entered the Young Communist League, almost immediately after turning fifteen years old, the minimum age for entry. In her classroom, only one other student had been able to join the Young Communist League so quickly. At this time, one's official class background, while still deemed important for determining political trustworthiness, was not considered as significant by the Chinese authorities as one's personal level of political consciousness and degree of revolutionary enthusiasm.

In 1963, when Ao was still in her second year of junior middle school, her school and indeed the whole Chinese Communist propaganda apparatus began a propaganda campaign to persuade young people from the cities to volunteer to live in the countryside.

Ao Meihua had originally planned to continue on to a senior middle school after her graduation from junior middle. She hoped to make great contributions to the cause of socialism in China by eventually becoming a writer of revolutionary propaganda literature. To make such a glorious contribution, she felt that she had to settle for nothing less than the best academic education. But when she took the examinations required to continue on to senior middle school, she failed to gain admittance to any of the foremost schools in Canton. Unwilling to settle for a second-rate school, she decided to volunteer to go to the countryside. Under the circumstances, she felt that this was the best way she could accomplish glorious deeds for socialism.

So, over the objections of her parents, Ao Meihua went to the countryside. She buried her disappointment at not getting into a prestigious senior middle school and plunged into her work with a fiery enthusiasm. She went to the countryside with a group of fifty young people, whose ages ranged from sixteen to twenty. Most of the members of this cohort shared personal ambitions and political liabilities similar to hers. From the Chinese Communist point of view, most of them had unfavorable official class backgrounds. Most of them wanted to compensate for those class backgrounds by enthusiastically responding to Communist propaganda appeals.

Led by Ao Meihua and the other Young Communist League members among them, this group of young people from Canton asked the authorities to send them to one of the most backward places in Guangdong Province—to a place where life would be the hardest and revolutionary struggle the most arduous, and thus a place where their contribution to socialism would be the most glorious. Although the authorities did not send them to the most remote and economically backward region of Guangdong, they did send them to a moderately poor region and to one of the poorest villages within that region. Even this turned out to be more than most of the Cantonese youth had bargained for.

Ao Meihua's cohort of young people from Canton arrived in their village—a place I will call Chen Village—in August 1964, just in time to witness the beginning of a tumultuous series of political events that would dramatically alter life there. In the chapters that follow, I will summarize those events and describe and analyze the relationship of Ao Meihua and her young urban comrades to them.

During their first several years in the village, Ao and her urban colleagues experienced their upward or downward political mobility as a matter of personal success or failure based on personal political zeal and skill. By the late 1960s, however, the Chinese government increasingly began to emphasize the importance of official class status as a determinant of an individual's political trustworthiness. When this happened, Ao Meihua, because of her poor class status, lost the position of prominence in village affairs that she had come to believe she had earned by her outstanding fervor and competence. Disillusioned by this experience, Ao began to lose her political commitment. She began to perceive the village not as a place where she could overcome the handicap of her bad class background by performing glorious deeds for socialism, but as a dumping ground for urban people with the wrong class backgrounds. Her commitment did not disappear overnight; her feelings of disillusionment took several years to crystallize. But by 1974, she had become convinced that she had no meaningful future in China. In March of 1974, she successfully undertook a dangerous and illegal swim to Hong Kong. About fifteen members of her urban youth cohort, also perceiving that their poor class backgrounds would keep them from ever playing a socially significant role within the village, also came to Hong Kong—some legally, some illegally—over a period of about three years, and many of them became the interviewees for our project on the history of Chen Village.

When I first began to interview her, Ao still habitually wore the dark pants and plain loose blouse that were typical of women's clothing in China but seemed so drab in fashion-conscious Hong Kong. And she still talked about her past in a vocabulary laden with Marxist terminology. I was introduced to her by friends who vouched for the legitimacy of my research interests in China. As time went on Ao developed a trust in me and believed my assurances that I would not use her information to harm her or the people of Chen Village. She liked to talk and seemed to enjoy playing the role of teacher about China to a somewhat ignorant but sympathetic foreigner. She had an extremely sharp memory and the eye of a novelist for significant detail. She also had a passionate enthusiasm for telling her story. She said that by participating in my research and by thus helping people outside China to better understand daily life there, she was making valuable use of her experience. She also said that by thinking through my questions she was coming to terms with her past and organizing her memories into a coherent whole.

In this process she not only provided me with raw data but helped me to think more profoundly about the ambiguities of Chinese moral discourse. The main form those ambiguities took was an inconsistency in the language used to judge the conduct of political leaders on the village scene. The first and most important kind of inconsistency was between the language of moral judgment and the conduct it was meant to portray. Thus, for example, Ao Meihua, the former zealous propagandist, typically used the terms of the Maoist political vision to justify the way she had lived. She had come to the village to serve the poor and lower-middle peasants of China; she and her fellow propagandists totally identified themselves with the poor and lower-middle peasants, loved and cared for them as Mao had commanded in his essay "Serve the People." Yet it was clear that she had never considered marrying any young, poor and lower-middle peasant from the village and that she looked with pity upon some of her female colleagues from Canton who had married village peasants and settled down to lives as ordinary peasant housewives. The idea of serving, loving, respecting, caring for, and identifying with the poor and lower-middle peasants clearly had its limits. It meant something like standing above the peasants and imparting to them the wisdom one had learned as a young, urban-educated Communist. As I questioned Ao

Meihua about such things, she also came to understand something about the essential arrogance of her stance toward the peasants. And yet that arrogance was not crass; it too had its ambiguities. From what she said (and others confirmed), she had clearly given generously of her time and energy to help many of the Chen Village peasants and had been inspired to do so by the teachings of Chairman Mao. Her arrogance was modified and perhaps in some way redeemed by a deeply idealistic spirit of generosity. Thus, I believe, my dialogue with her had a Socratic quality. The longer we talked, the more she came to "remember" dimensions of her moral commitments that she had not "known" before. And I too came to "remember" ideas about the intimate connections between self-sacrificing generosity and self-righteous arrogance that I had "learned" but never really understood from books and had experienced but never really admitted in my own life.[8]

Another ambiguity in Ao Meihua's language of moral discourse was an inconsistency in the terms she used to judge her own actions and those of others. She used the kind of Maoist rhetoric that one could constantly read in publications like the *People's Daily*: she spoke about having a correct class consciousness so that she could become aware of her historical mission to carry out class struggle and to selflessly serve the people, for example. But she also used a language deeply rooted in Chinese tradition. For instance, in describing a villager, she would often compare the person to a character in the *Dream of the Red Chamber* and would tend to judge the person by the moral frame of reference embedded in that Chinese classic. Out of inconsistencies like this I gradually began to "remember" themes that I had learned, but never fully understood, from Confucian philosophy as well as my own experiences in Taiwan and to sense how those themes might have become intermingled with Marxist-Leninist-Maoist ones within China. In short, from my long dialogues with Ao Meihua, I began to learn to think in a more subtle way than before about the ambiguities of revolutionary morality in general and Chinese revolutionary morality in particular. I developed a way of thinking and gained a pattern of intellectual sensitivities that enabled me to dig more deeply into the moral meanings buried in the texts provided by our other informants.

I am deeply grateful to Ao Meihua for helping me to muster many of the insights needed to construct this book. I have of course attempted to test the validity of those insights by confronting them with the empirical

8. These ideas about the "Socratic" nature of fieldwork have been stimulated by Paul Rabinow, "Masked I Go Forward: Observer and Observed in Anthropology," in *A Crack in the Mirror: Reflexive Perspectives in Anthropology,* ed. Jay Ruby (Philadelphia: University of Pennsylvania Press, 1982), 173–87; and his *Reflections on Fieldwork in Morocco* (Berkeley: University of California Press, 1977).

facts revealed by a systematic examination of the information produced by all of our interviewees together.

My explorations of the ambiguities of moral discourse in Chen Village have led me to this book, which marks my emergence from Daniel Bell's jungle, intellectually still alive, I think. My trophy from the adventure is an argument about the relationship between moral discourse, social predicament, and the development of moral character among grass-roots political activists in rural China.

I have already acknowledged some of the key people who helped me into and out of this intellectual adventure. I would also like to express my deep gratitude to Ezra Vogel, who advised and encouraged me at every step of the way. If my work has any scholarly merit, it is largely due to his qualities as a teacher and as a friend. I would also like to thank Theda Skocpol and Judith Strauch, who advised me on the Ph.D. dissertation that was this book's first incarnation, and William Parish, who made very useful suggestions for revising its next-to-final draft. Finally, I gratefully acknowledge my debt to Robert Bellah, Steven Tipton, Ann Swidler, and William Sullivan—four sociological colleagues with whom I now work to broaden and deepen the theoretical perspectives embodied here. Without the encouragement of Grant Barnes of the University of California Press, I might never have completed this book; without the superb editorial help of Jane Hedges, my prose would have been far clumsier than it is.

My share of the research on which this study was based was funded by National Defense Foreign Language Fellowships and a National Institute of Mental Health Comparative International Studies Training Grant. Funds for typing the final draft were made available by the Academic Senate of the University of California, San Diego. I would like to thank Nellie Miller and Julie Poteete for typing various versions of the manuscript.

Throughout the writing of this book, my wife, Judith Rosselli, provided a great abundance of encouragement and support. She also contributed immensely to the sensitivity to human issues that I have tried to weave into the fabric of the text. This book is gratefully dedicated to her.

1 Introduction
DISCOURSE, RITUAL, PREDICAMENTS AND CHARACTER

The Chinese Peasant as Moral Philosopher

What is a good society? What is a good person? How should a good person act in view of the fact that the society he lives in is inevitably imperfect? What should the representatives of society do in view of the fact that society's members are inevitably not all good? Questions like these have occupied the minds of great philosophers throughout history. They were key themes in the deliberations of Plato, Aristotle, and their successors in the history of Western thought as well as of Confucius, Mencius, and their heirs in the Chinese tradition. But they are not questions simply for scholars. Ordinary persons, in their own ways, ask them and deliberate about them as well; and as much as academicians, they are heirs of the great traditions of moral discourse that form the basis of their civilizations. In this book I will argue that ordinary peasants in China—even illiterate ones—ask such questions and sometimes argue and fight about them passionately.

They do not, of course, ask and argue in the systematic way of learned scholars. They do not think about moral issues in precisely defined abstract terms, and they do not make it a major priority to link such abstract terms together into logically consistent systems. They think about moral issues, as Clifford Geertz once put it, in "the half-formed, taken for granted, indifferently systematized notions that guide the normal activities of ordinary men in everyday life."[1] They "discuss" moral issues not just by speaking words but by performing dramatic gestures; they summarize their arguments not in essays but in aphorisms; they usually argue not by giving lectures but by uttering invectives; they evaluate each

---

1. Clifford Geertz, "Person, Time, and Conduct in Bali," in *The Interpretation of Cultures* (New York: Basic Books, 1973), 362.

other's arguments not in polite colloquia but in gossipy table talk, noisy altercations, and sometimes nowadays in raucous public meetings. In their discourse, they strive not for a theoretical consistency but for a felt integrity. Like professional philosophers, they often do not practice what they preach. But unlike professional philosophers (at least in the West), they constantly call each other to account for their actions as well as their words; thus their moral discourse involves a constant interplay between word and deed.

In this book, I wish to interpret the moral discourse engaged in by the residents of Chen Village—a small farming community with a present population of about eleven hundred in China's Guangdong Province—during a tumultuous two decades, from the early 1960s to the early 1980s, when the villagers faced a jarring series of crises. The villagers had plenty to argue about. Chen Village was (as is common in southeastern China) a single-lineage village: all the members of the village were surnamed Chen, and all the males and unmarried females were descended through their fathers from a common ancestor who had lived many generations in the past. The moral basis for such a social arrangement was a set of ideas about the fundamental importance of kinship ties and the specific responsibilities created by such ties. The socioeconomic basis was an amount of corporate property that supplied funds to carry on the work of the lineage ancestors and under certain circumstances to provide for the welfare of needy members of the lineage.[2] But after the Communist Liberation of China in 1949, the Chinese Communists moved quickly to destroy the socioeconomic basis for lineage solidarity. They distributed the lineage's corporate lands among the village's poor peasants. Moreover, they carried out a series of measures that directly attacked the moral basis of the lineage. They assigned each villager a particular social class designation—poor peasant, middle peasant, rich peasant, landlord, and so on—and they organized the poor peasants to attack, expropriate, and humiliate the rich peasants and landlords who were their kinsmen. The Communists thus made responsibilities to one's class more important than loyalties to one's kin. They also created a new village government controlled by locally recruited Communist Party members who were responsible to superiors at higher levels in the vast governmental bureaucracies that now enveloped the new China.

In the mid-1950s, the Chinese Communists collectivized village agriculture. Individual families were pressured to give up their privately owned land to "agricultural producers' co-ops." After a chaotic period of experimentation, the village ended up in the early 1960s with ten of these

2. For the classic anthropological study of lineage organization, see Maurice Freedman, *Lineage Organization in Southeastern China* (London: Athlone Press, 1958), especially 1–8.

co-ops, now called "production teams." Villagers' livelihoods now increasingly depended on how efficiently they worked together in these new teams, not on how faithfully they respected responsibilities to family members and kin.

Then in the mid-1960s, the Chinese Communist national leadership launched a drive explicitly to attack "feudalistic" moral conduct on the part of the villagers—especially among the village's leaders. Once again, villagers were mobilized en masse to attack fellow villagers, this time for failing to live up to the government's official standards of behavior. In the late 1960s, the Cultural Revolution occurred, and the events of that chaotic movement and its aftermath threw into doubt many of the moral standards that the Chinese government had so earnestly propagated a few years before.

Throughout all this, villagers had to make a long series of excruciating moral decisions. Was it right or wrong to attack brutally local landlords and rich peasants? Was it right or wrong to attack this or that person who was officially declared a political deviant? How should one balance one's responsibilities to one's social class, to the new production teams, and to the new national government? To what extent could one compromise what one believed to be morally right for what was politically expedient? What standards was one to use in making these decisions? How was one to develop and apply such standards?

Such questions came to a particularly pointed focus around the lives of the village's local political leaders. Political superiors in the Communist-led government evaluated them according to the canons of government ideology. Ordinary villagers judged them by the norms of local tradition. The local leaders were constantly having to justify themselves in terms that could make some sense to both superiors and constituents. And ordinary villagers and political superiors were constantly praising, criticizing, agreeing, and disagreeing with those justifications. This dynamic process created ever-moving whirlpools of moral argumentation around the characters of the local leaders. The currents of such whirlpools were continually shifting as argument and counterargument interacted with changing political situations to create new torrents of moral discourse.

I wish first of all to interpret those whirlpools of moral discourse swirling around the reputations of local political leaders. That is, I wish to distinguish between various claims and counterclaims about the goodness of particular village leaders. I wish to show how these claims and counterclaims formed separate themes—currents—that were characterized by different underlying assumptions about what constituted a good person and a good society and by different patterns of drawing moral conclusions from these basic assumptions. And I wish to explore the cultural dynamics that led certain themes to lose force and others to gain it and that caused some themes to flow together and others to flow apart.

But it was not only the fluid dynamics of moral argument and counter-argument that shaped the village's whirlpools of moral discourse. There was also the interaction between fluid ideas about moral "shoulds" and the hard structures of political "musts." To become successful political leaders, the local "cadres" (official office holders) and "activists" (officially recognized collaborators in local government) often had to adopt styles of action that clashed with at least some, perhaps many, and sometimes all of the currents of local moral thought. And to meet changing requirements for economic, social, and political well-being, ordinary villagers had to move in different directions than their moral rhetoric would have suggested. These tensions between "should" and "must" gave rise to new currents of moral discourse, and they also molded the moral characters of the villagers.

But I wish not just to learn *about* the moral philosophy of Chinese peasants but to learn *from* it. The peasant "philosophers" I will introduce in this book were what Aristotle would have called "practical" philosophers, interested not in knowing what good persons are like but in acting as good persons do. Their discourse about morality was part of the process through which they shaped their characters to reconcile their realistic life situations with their moral ideals. The ultimate aim of this study is also "practical science" in Aristotle's sense.[3] I wish to reflect on the leaders who emerged from the political and cultural matrices of Chen Village in order to make informed—although, of necessity, extremely tentative—judgments concerning whether their actions were morally good, not just in terms of traditional or modern Chinese cultural standards, but in terms that could be agreed upon by any civilized person. And by doing this I would like in some small way to stimulate enlightened moral reflection about the proper meaning and purpose of political action under the realistic conditions posed by the modern world.

The image presented here of the Chinese peasant as a practical philosopher is meant to both affirm the achievements and transcend the limitations of another image of the peasant currently popular in social scientific literature: that of the peasant as a shrewd calculator of self-interest. One of the best recent analyses of peasant society built around the latter image is Samuel Popkin's *The Rational Peasant*,[4] which is based on fieldwork

3. See Jonathan Barnes's introduction to *The Ethics of Aristotle,* trans. J. A. K. Thomson (London: Penguin Books, 1976), 17. For a defense of the position that modern social science ought to be a practical science in Aristotle's sense, see Robert N. Bellah, "The Ethical Aims of Social Inquiry," *Teachers College Record* 83, no. 1 (Fall 1981): 1–18.

4. Samuel L. Popkin, *The Rational Peasant: The Political Economy of Rural Society in Vietnam* (Berkeley and Los Angeles: University of California Press, 1979).

conducted in Vietnam. Popkin himself suggests that his study can be fruitfully applied to peasant communities in China.

In Popkin's account, a "rational" peasant is able systematically to calculate the best means of achieving long-term, individual self-interests and consistently to act on the basis of such calculations. "Assuming that peasants are self-interested," Professor Popkin writes, "I will analyze cooperation in peasant societies based on task-specific incentives and calculations." To be rational therefore means "that individuals evaluate the possible outcomes associated with their choices in accordance with their preferences and values. In doing this they discount the evaluation of each outcome in accordance with their subjective estimate of the likelihood of the outcome. Finally they make the choice which will maximize their expected utility."[5]

According to Professor Popkin, this does not mean that peasants are self-interested "in the narrow sense"—interested only in their own welfare as individuals. They do at different times care about families, friends, and villages. But it seems that they care about larger groups because their individual welfare is dependent upon them. Popkin assumes "that a peasant is primarily concerned with the welfare and security of self and family. Whatever his broad values and objectives, when the peasant takes into account the likelihood of receiving the preferred outcomes *on the basis of individual actions*, he usually will act in a self-interested manner."[6]

Popkin's insistence on the utilitarian individualistic rationality of peasants is intended as a critique of the explanations that "moral economists" provide for social change in peasant societies. The moral economists include such contemporary social scientists as James Scott, Eric Wolf, and Joel Migdal. Following the lead of earlier theorists such as Karl Polanyi, they argue that peasants the world over share a similar "traditional" morality that arises out of the social, political, and economic structures of "precapitalist corporate villages." This traditional moral order places extreme stress on intravillage harmony and leads villagers to become strongly committed to traditional norms and roles that "were successful in maintaining the steady state [of the village] in the past."[7] These norms discourage unlimited acquisitiveness and structure villages into a network of patron-client relations characterized by a "broad but imprecise spectrum of moral obligations consistent with the belief that the patron should display an almost paternal concern for and responsive-

5. Popkin, *Rational Peasant,* 31.
6. Popkin, *Rational Peasant,* 31.
7. Eric Wolf, "Types of Latin American Peasantry: A Preliminary Discussion," *American Anthropologist* 57, no. 3 (June 1955): 457; quoted in Popkin, *Rational Peasant,* 11.

ness to the needs of his client and that the latter should display almost filial loyalty to the patron."[8]

The moral economists view this traditional ethos as opposed to the moral basis of a modern market economy. This modern morality gives individuals freedom to pursue their own desires rather than be forced to conform to traditional community expectations. It places no restrictions on acquisitiveness, and it reduces all relationships to a narrow "cash nexus." Revolutionary social change arises out of the clash between traditional and modern morality. As traditional corporate villages become caught up in the impersonal, individualistic market relationships of the modern world, the villagers lose their sense of security. Poor peasants may then turn with fury against those who have profited from such market relationships, accusing them of having betrayed the norms of the traditional morality. Out of this confusion of moralities come peasant revolts.

Under certain circumstances, urban-educated intellectuals can turn incipient peasant revolt into revolutionary assaults against an old political order. Peasant rebellions become revolutions. But the rural peasants who form the backbone of the revolution have different hopes from the urban intellectuals who lead them. The peasants hope to return to an older, traditional form of life. But their urban-educated leaders want a rich, powerful nation state governed by detailed regulations and efficient bureaucracies. The peasants want a return to the past; their urban leaders want to move toward the future. After the revolution, then, the stage is set for a chronic conflict between national political officials and rural peasants. The peasants' reaction to all forms of modernization, whether capitalist or socialist, is thus ultimately hostile.

Popkin criticizes the moral economists—in my view correctly—for romanticizing traditional village life: for taking "too benign a view of villages and patron-client ties"[9] and too harsh a view of the modernization process. He shows how the self-interests of peasants make collective action extremely problematic for them—even collective action that promises to provide common benefits to all the individuals who participate in it. "There is a marked proclivity for individual-level adaptations to common problems whenever the only result of group action is 'common advantage for the entire group or for society.' As long as the only results of contributing to common goals are common advantages, the peasant may leave the contributions to others and expend his scarce resources in other ways."[10] One of the key deterents to such collective action is the risk

8. Carl Lande, "Networks and Groups in Southeast Asia," *American Political Science Review* 67, no. 1 (Mar. 1973): 105; quoted in Popkin, *Rational Peasant,* 13.

9. Popkin, *Rational Peasant,* 29.

10. Popkin, *Rational Peasant,* 252–53.

that the leaders will reap the benefits for themselves, leaving the rest of the participants no better off than before they started to cooperate.

My data support many of Popkin's arguments about the difficulties peasants have in carrying out collective action. For instance—to take an example from the story of Chen Village that is similar to examples Popkin cites from his Vietnam data—peasants are reluctant to pool their land into socialist agricultural co-ops, even though collective farming may be technically more efficient than individual family farming and therefore promises a better livelihood for all the members of the co-op. Their reluctance arises in large part from their fear of being cheated by the officials in charge of the co-op. If the gains in marginal productivity made possible through collective farming can be siphoned off by the leaders, then it of course makes no sense for peasants to engage in such collective action.

But in his attempt clearly to distinguish his approach from that of the moral economists, Popkin employs a conceptual framework that has difficulty accounting on its own terms for any kind of village solidarity, even the fragile kind that Popkin does admit exists. For if peasants are essentially interest-maximizing individuals, how can a peasant leader be expected to refrain from cheating, as long as he can get away with it? Popkin's argument implies that the kind of collective action that would help peasants solve common problems like the need to increase agricultural productivity can hardly ever be institutionalized by "rational peasants."

But Popkin acknowledges that large-scale collective action for the common good did in fact take place under various circumstances in Vietnam. Groups as different as various Buddhist sects, the Catholic Church, and the Communist Party were in various contexts able to "gain control of large sections of [Vietnam] and to channel significant peasant resources into creating new rural societies."[11] One major element of their success was their ability to provide credible leadership for collective action. But if people are in general interest-maximizing individuals, where can such trustworthy leadership be found? According to Popkin, the leaders were committed to moral codes stressing the importance of self-sacrifice, codes that were close enough to ordinary peasants' beliefs that peasants could understand them. Thus Popkin shows how collective action can and does occur among peasants when individualistic calculations of self-interest are embedded in compelling moral codes. But his conceptual framework, stressing the "investment logic" of self-interested action in a rural setting, provides little account of the origin of such moral codes and the reasons why leaders would be compelled by them.

In this study I provide much evidence of the ability of Chinese peasants shrewdly to calculate their self-interests, and of the ways in which

11. Popkin, *Rational Peasant,* 185.

their self-interested calculations make it extremely difficult for them to sustain coherent collective action on a scale larger than a family or close kin group. But I will also explore the processes of moral creativity that under certain circumstances have enabled them to make a commitment to common moral codes that could support collective political and economic endeavor.

My exploration starts with the observation that there is a tension between the moral ideals of the Chinese peasantry and the dictates of official Communist ideology, although I agree with Popkin that it is not helpful to make an extremely sharp contrast between a traditional morality, adhered to by peasants, and a modern one, adhered to by cosmopolitan economic developers and political revolutionaries. Traditional village morality consisted not of a tight system of norms that the peasants followed out of blind habit but of a tangle of notions that were handed down from the past, to be sure, but were constantly being woven by (inevitably self-interested) villagers to fit new situations in the present. This traditional morality permitted a range of interpretations that could lead not just to village harmony but to considerable conflict; not just to generous patronage by people of wealth and power but to crass selfishness; not just to loyal cooperation with patrons but to rebellious hostility towards them. Moreover, China's official socialist ideology also consists of a web of ideas that have again and again been woven into new patterns to fit new situations. Some of the patterns of this modern ideology can be woven so as to mesh with some possible patterns of traditional village thought. Villagers and outside government officials coming into the village were energetically trying to do such weaving and meshing, even as they bitterly argued about how it was to be done. The process of trying to interweave these traditional and modern themes is what I analyze under the rubrics of "moral discourse" and "ritual."

Moral Discourse and Ritual

By "moral discourse" I refer to an active social process of understanding, evaluating, and arguing about what is right or wrong in a given situation. The elements of discourse are symbols—"any object, act, event, quality, relation which serves as a vehicle for a conception."[12] When we think of "discourse," we usually think of a process carried out with words. But discourse can also involve complex combinations of both verbal and nonverbal symbols. For instance, political gestures can be thought of as a

---

12. Clifford Geertz, "Religion as a Cultural System," in *The Interpretation of Cultures,* 91. Geertz bases this definition on Suzanne Langer's in her *Philosophy in a New Key,* 4th ed. (Cambridge, Mass.: Harvard University Press, 1960).

contribution to the public moral discourse of Chinese peasants. I will be as concerned with complex symbolic statements like political gestures as with straightforward verbal ones, as concerned with the meanings implicit in certain styles of action as with those explicit in certain patterns of speech. In discoursing on morality, or on anything else for that matter, people try to combine the symbols available to them into new patterns of meaning to answer some kind of question. This is an intensely active process, a "running back and forth"—*discursus*—between available symbols, new experiences, new questions, answers to those questions, and judgments about the correctness of those answers. Moral discourse, then, attempts to understand the nature of moral responsibilities, to evaluate the conduct of oneself or of others in the light of such understandings, and to persuade others that one's understandings and evaluations are correct.

People make statements about their moral responsibilities to one another not only through discourse but also through rituals. A ritual is a set of "multivocal" symbolic actions that, taken together, express in a condensed, dramatic way the meaning of the shared values that bind a community together and, in the very act of expressing those shared values, deepen the community members' commitment to them.[13] Ritual does what the British critic Charles Morgan says theatrical drama also does: "The great impact [of the theater] is neither a persuasion of the intellect nor a beguiling of the senses. . . . It is the enveloping movement of the whole drama on the soul of man. We surrender and are changed."[14] Ritual is to discourse as harmony is to melody. Ritual brings many different levels of meaning together to form a resonant unity. Discourse moves from one statement to another. Ritual—when it works—unifies people around a complex of meaning. Discourse pursues the implications of one or another strand of meaning to make an argument. Thus the ritual of the Christian Eucharist expresses and brings into being the shared faith of the Christian community; but the arguments of theologians about the meaning of such a ritual can create controversies within the community.

Varieties of Moral Discourse

People who argue about moral issues often argue past one another. This is because there are different "paradigms" for moral discourse. People

13. This distinction between ritual and discourse owes much to Clifford Geertz, "Blurred Genres: The Refiguration of Social Thought," *The American Scholar* 49, no. 2 (1980): 165–79. The understanding of ritual is based on Victor Turner, *The Forest of Symbols: Aspects of Ndembu Ritual* (Ithaca, N.Y.: Cornell University Press, 1967), 19–20.

14. Quoted in Geertz, "Blurred Genres," 173.

have different basic assumptions about human nature, the relationship between self and society, and the nature of good action; in addition to such basic assumptions, they perceive different ways of proceeding from premises to conclusions, from basic assumptions to one's responsibilities in a concrete case. In a complex modern society, it is in fact likely that several different paradigms for moral discourse are available. This has indeed been the case in Chen Village.

The predominant paradigm for discourse about social morality in modern Western society is that of "utilitarian individualism."[15] This mode of moral reasoning starts with the assumption (first articulated in its modern form by Thomas Hobbes) that individual human beings always act in their own self-interest. As Hobbes put it: "Of the voluntary acts of every man, the object is some *good to himself.*"[16] Public moral conduct thus is and should be based on rational—in the sense of a "rational peasant"—calculations of individual self-interests.

For utilitarian individualism, then, the relationship between self and society is always one of at least potential conflict, because a person's self-interest clashes with the interests of the other individuals who make up the society. Individuals can be expected to restrain the pell-mell pursuit of their own immediate self-interests and to work for the public good only if they can see this as a means to the ultimate maximization of their

15. Robert N. Bellah, "New Religious Consciousness and the Crisis in Modernity," in *Interpretive Social Science: A Reader,* ed. Paul Rabinow and William M. Sullivan (Berkeley: University of California Press, 1979), 343–46. Bellah discusses the utilitarian individualist tradition more fully in *The Broken Covenant: American Civil Religion in Time of Trial* (New York: Seabury Press, 1975). According to Bellah, the utilitarian individualist tradition

> was rooted ultimately in the sophistic, skeptical, and hedonistic strands of ancient Greek philosophy but took its modern form initially in the theoretical writings of Thomas Hobbes. It became popular in America mainly through the somewhat softer and less consistent version of John Locke and his followers, a version deliberately designed to obscure the contrast with biblical religion. In its consistent original Hobbesian form, utilitarianism grew out of an effort to apply the methods of science to the understanding of man and was both atheistic and deterministic. While the commonsense Lockian version that has been the most pervasive current of American thought has not been fully conscious of these implications, the relation between utilitarianism and Anglo-American social science has been both close and continuous from Hobbes and Locke to the classical economists of the eighteenth and early nineteenth centuries to the social Darwinists of the late nineteenth century and finally to such influential present-day sociologists as George Homans. ("New Religious Consciousness," 343)

See also Steven Lukes, *Individualism* (Oxford: Oxford University Press, 1973), 79–109.

16. Thomas Hobbes, *Leviathan,* vol. 3 of *The English Works of Thomas Hobbes of Malmesbury* (1839; reprint, Aalen [Ger.]: Scientia, 1962), 120.

own self-interest. Thus, the focus of moral discourse is on the means by which individuals might cooperate to best achieve their self-interest. A good society is one in which the individuals who make up the society can each freely pursue their self-interests without undue fear of having those interests harmed. When discussing the public good, utilitarian individualists appeal not to common commitments to ultimate values—because they cannot assume that self-interested individuals will share such commitments—but to common perceptions of facts. When arguing with others over a given social arrangement, they try to show how certain agreed upon empirical facts will lead to consequences favorable to them all. Thus, for example, American politicians often try to argue that, given the "scientifically proven laws" of economics, a certain government regulation will stimulate the economy in ways ultimately beneficial to everyone in the society, and their opponents counter that other scientifically proven laws recommend other regulations.

Of course, even in America, public moral discourse is not exclusively utilitarian individualistic. American politicians and common citizens alike evoke shared conceptions of public decency, civic duty, and national purpose. Alexis de Tocqueville noted that although Americans "enjoy explaining almost every act of their lives on the principle of self-interest properly understood. . . . I think that in this way they do themselves less than justice, for sometimes in the United States, as elsewhere, one sees people carried away by the disinterested, spontaneous impulses natural to man."[17] And contemporary scholars like Robert Bellah, echoing the tradition of social thought that de Tocqueville contributed to, argue that utilitarian individualism by itself cannot provide the basis for a vital public life, either in the United States or anywhere else.[18] I agree with Professor Bellah, and this book tends to support his argument.

Unlike the Americans de Tocqueville described, the peasants of Chen Village did not use the utilitarian individualist paradigm of moral discourse to guide and justify their actions—they did not enjoy invoking the principle of self-interest rightly understood. (Thus, since self-interest calculations inevitably did play a major part in most of their decisions, they were, unlike de Tocqueville's Americans, often less moral than their moral discourse indicated.) Instead of a utilitarian individualistic paradigm for moral discourse, they tended to use one from the classic Confucian tradition.

I do not claim that villagers were self-consciously Confucian. Practically none of them had ever read the works of Confucius, and most of

17. Alexis de Tocqueville, *Democracy in America*, trans. George L. Lawrence (Garden City, N.Y.: Doubleday, 1964), 526.
18. Bellah argues this point most fully in *The Broken Covenant*.

them were not even clear about who Confucius was and when he lived. Yet I believe that the basic structure of their discourse about public morality fit the fundamental pattern used throughout the centuries by the moralists of China's venerable Confucian tradition. One way the villagers' commitment to the Confucian paradigm manifested itself was in their emphasis on the importance of good "human feeling" in political conduct. Often, for example, local political leaders would invoke "reasonable" regard for "human feelings" to give special favors to relatives and friends in return for gifts of money or food and for implicit promises of loyal support. Sometimes the leaders did this for generous reasons; often enough for very selfish reasons: they were trying to maximize their power and wealth. The point here is not whether they were being generous or selfish but that they and their constituents were using different terms to think about the relationship between public and private responsibilities than utilitarian individualists would use.

Utilitarians would expect officials, like everyone else, to be self-interested. But in their own self-interest they would demand that officials carry out their public duties in an impartial way to give all citizens an equal opportunity to pursue their self-interests. If officials were not going to be impartial, they would cover it up or try to rationalize it by marshalling a body of "facts" to "prove" that favoritism to a particular group would ultimately have good consequences for all. They would not appeal to a reasonable respect for good human feelings. Indeed, if leaders and ordinary citizens thought of their responsibilities toward public affairs in terms of a reasonable respect for good human feelings, they might create different patterns of cooperation and conflict than if they were "rational peasants."

If for instance villagers could expect that both leaders and their fellow villagers would consistently act to maximize their individual self-interests, they might indeed be able to cooperate together in a more consistent manner in socialist forms of collective agriculture than if they believed that some of them would and should act on the basis of a regard for good human feeling. If, to return to the example given earlier, they could increase their agricultural productivity by pooling their land and tilling it collectively, and if they could be sure that every worker would get a fair share of the increased productivity, they would see that it was in their interests to pool their land and to insist that strict procedures be followed to distribute the increased productivity fairly. They might indeed worry that the officials in charge of distributing collective income, being self-interested, would be tempted to cheat. But these worries might be satisfactorily alleviated if they could set up careful procedures for public review of the officials. Then most officials might be persuaded that it was not in their long-term self-interest to risk getting punished for a short-term gain.

But suppose that most officials and ordinary citizens tended to agree that a reasonable regard for human feelings should ultimately guide moral conduct, rather than a concern for individual interests, and that this meant that everyone should be especially partial to family members and certain close friends. They then might assume that their public officials would and under certain circumstances *should* play favorites. In such a case, no amount of technical procedures for public review of officials could work, and people who did not fall within the sphere of a leader's "good feeling" relationships would rightly worry that they would not share equally in any gain in productivity realized through collective agriculture. A cooperative venture would therefore not be worthwhile. This indeed was a problem the villagers sometimes encountered precisely because their moral discourse was not dominated by the kind of utilitarian moral logic supposedly characteristic of the "rational peasant."

The villagers' talk about good human feelings is an example of a form of moral discourse that does not make sense in the Western utilitarian moral tradition but does seem logical within the Confucian one. Unlike utilitarian individualism, the Confucian tradition starts with the notion that man is not by nature selfish.[19]

In Confucian thought, many people are indeed very selfish, but they do not have to be that way, and to be truly human is to be faithful to one's duties to society. The relationship between self and society is one of potential harmony. Individuals can achieve this harmony by becoming cognitively and affectively aware of the responsibilities that different social relationships place upon them. The most immediate, morally significant relationships are those within the family: father and son, older and younger brother, husband and wife. But these family ties are but the nearest connections in a web of human relationships extending to the ends of the earth. To order truly and well one's relationships with one's family, one

19. The literature on Confucianism is vast. For useful summaries of Confucian ideas on morality see Donald J. Munro, *The Concept of Man in Early China* (Stanford: Stanford University Press, 1969) and "The Concept of 'Interest' in Chinese Thought" (Paper presented at the Workshop on the Pursuit of Political Interest in the People's Republic of China, Ann Arbor, Michigan, August 1977). For a provocative argument about compatibility between Confucian ideas and societal modernization, see Thomas Metzger, *Escape from Predicament* (New York: Columbia University Press, 1977). For a splendid account of how a famous twentieth-century Chinese intellectual tried to use the Confucian tradition to think through the problems of rural China, see Guy S. Alitto, *The Last Confucian: Liang Shu-ming and the Chinese Dilemma of Modernity* (Berkeley: University of California Press, 1979).

must see one's family in the widest possible context—the context of one's lineage, one's village, one's province, one's empire.

Thus, to do what is right or wrong in a given situation, one cannot mechanically invoke fixed norms governing the relationships to one's father, son, or other relatives; instead one must gain both an understanding of and a feel for one's total situation. One cannot simply assume that one should favor one's relatives over wider groups. To be truly faithful to one's duties towards one's family, for instance, one might under appropriate circumstances be obligated to endanger the welfare of one's family for the good of one's village, or one's province, or one's empire. All of this may involve complex moral reasoning, but it is a different kind of reasoning than Professor Popkin speaks of in *The Rational Peasant*. It is not an instrumental logic that would calculate the best means to advance the long-term interests of oneself or one's family. It is rather an intuitively intelligent exploration of the basic principles that define the total context of responsibilities within which one stands. Using this type of moral reasoning, one might argue with another not over whether such a course of action would be good for both but over whether the other person is able to see his responsibilities in the proper broad context.

As we shall see, this kind of moral argumentation was indeed used under certain circumstances both by leaders and ordinary citizens within the village. It can produce extremely bitter controversy because there are no hard and fast rules defining just when persons should sacrifice the welfare of their narrow social circle for the good of a wider group. Thus arguments over whether a person is doing right or wrong tend to center around a general imprecise standard of reasonable behavior and a common intuitive appreciation for the nature of a situation. For instance, to demand that villagers look to the good of their community as a whole rather than just to the good of their own families, an appeal can be made to a sense that the whole village is in danger. But in the absence of a very clear and present danger, such arguments are usually controversial. And they may become very ad hominem, because if someone disagrees with one's moral appraisal, it means that his or her basic moral faculties are deficient: you have erred not because you have had a lapse of judgment or yielded to a particular temptation but because you are basically a bad person, unable to understand and to fulfill your proper responsibilities. We shall see a lot of this kind of impassioned, ad hominem moral argument in the story of Chen Village.

But moral argumentation within the village was not solely conducted within the Confucian paradigm; it was complicated by the introduction of new paradigms vigorously propagated by the Communist government. One of these government-sponsored paradigms was the Maoist one.[20] This was the style of moral thinking advocated by Mao Zedong during the 1930s and 1940s in such writings as "Serve the People," "In Memory of Norman Bethune," and "The Foolish Old Man Who Moved the Mountains." In the early 1960s, such Maoist dicta were given the status of sacred scriptures and were elaborated by a flood of official commentaries into a comprehensive guide to moral life in China. In the mid-1960s, the government made a major effort to instill this mode of moral thinking into the consciousness of rural peasants. According to the particular interpretation of Marxism-Leninism that Mao and his associates were advocating in the 1960s, people were not by nature selfish. Selfishness and greed came from the structure of feudal and capitalistic societies; they were the normal characteristics of the exploiting classes in such societies. People from the good classes, the former exploited classes, were also often selfish and greedy. Their moral thought could and should be reformed. Reform would come from assiduously studying the thought of Chairman Mao. The highest good was to devote one's life selflessly to "serving the people"; this was the categorical imperative proclaimed by Chairman Mao. To "serve the people" meant having a spirit of "utter devotion to others, without any thought of self." The people one was to serve consisted of all the inhabitants of China, with the exception of class enemies, and by extension all the oppressed peoples of the world. To *serve* the people was to lead them in the struggle against class enemies. One could know who the class enemies were and in the last analysis how one should struggle against them by studying the thought of Chairman Mao. One could therefore know what was good in a particular case by applying the words of Maoist authority in a kind of casuistry to the situation at hand. Casuistry from authoritative teaching to concrete

20. The *loci classici* for Mao Zedong's prescriptions about ideal political virtue are "Combat Liberalism" in the *Selected Works of Mao Tse-tung*, 4 vols. (Beijing: Foreign Languages Press, 1961–65), 2:31–35; "In Memory of Norman Bethune," *Selected Works*, 2:337–39; "On Correcting Mistaken Ideas in the Party," *Selected Works*, 1:105–17; "Rectify the Party's Style of Work," *Selected Works*, 3:35–53; "Get Organized!" *Selected Works*, 3:153–63; "Serve the People," *Selected Works*, 3:177–79; "The Foolish Old Man Who Moved the Mountains," *Selected Works*, 3:271–74; "On Practice," *Selected Works*, 1:295–310; "On Policy," *Selected Works*, 2:441–50; "Reform our Study," *Selected Works*, 3:17–26. The literature on Maoism in Western languages is probably about equal in quantity, if not in quality, to that on Confucianism. Some of the most useful works on the moral dimensions of Mao's Thought are: Stuart Schram, *The Political Thought of Mao Tse-tung* (New York: Praeger, 1969); Frederic Wakeman, Jr., *History and Will: Philosophical Perspectives of Mao Tse-tung's Thought* (Berkeley: University of California Press, 1973); Benjamin Schwartz, *Communism and China: Ideology in Flux* (Cambridge, Mass.: Harvard University Press, 1968), especially 162–242; and John Bryan Starr, *Continuing the Revolution: The Political Thought of Mao* (Princeton: Princeton University Press, 1979).

situations involves complex processes of discursive reasoning. But it is a different kind of reasoning from that employed by the Confucian or the utilitarian paradigms.

The Maoist paradigm for moral discourse can lead to coherent moral discussion only if all members of a group are intimately familiar with the details of the authoritative teaching. Such a system, then, works best among people who are literate and have the time to study the authoritative writings thoroughly. The way is then open for such people to claim that they form a moral aristocracy within communities of illiterates. Thus in Chen Village during the mid-1960s, the main carriers of the Maoist paradigm for moral discourse were members of an outside "work team" and a band of urban youths who settled in the village. To lead to coherent moral discussion, the authoritative mode of moral discourse also requires that the voice of authority be clear. If the words of the teaching are not clear, an infallible authority is needed to evaluate canonical interpretations of the teachings. In the mid-1960s, the highest officials of the central government were supposed to provide such authority. But when the Cultural Revolution began in 1966, the moral authority of the central government was demolished, and it suddenly became possible for different groups to advance their own interpretation of Mao's writings, causing tremendous political and moral chaos. Much of the moral tension among Chen Villagers in the second half of the 1960s came from the interaction between the Maoist moral paradigm, imported from outside, and the villagers' Confucian paradigm.

But moral discourse in the village was further complicated by the fact that Mao Zedong's version of Marxism-Leninism was not the only version. By the 1960s, Mao's rivals, Liu Shaoqi and Deng Xiaoping and their followers were adopting approaches to Marxism that were in sharp contrast to Mao's own.[21] By the mid-1960s, the Communist propaganda the villagers heard was almost purely Maoist. In the 1970s, though, villagers began to hear propaganda containing a paradigm for moral discourse akin to that implied by the ideology of Liu and Deng. Since Mao's death and the fall of the Gang of Four in 1976, that Liuist paradigm has become dominant. The Liuist paradigm has an essentially utilitarian individualist deep structure. Human beings are basically self-interested. They will restrain the pursuit of their self-interests and cooperate with one another if they calculate that this will be for their own good in the long run. In a society in which production is carried out with advanced technology and

21. The contrast between Liu Shaoqi's moral philosophy and that of the followers of Mao is succinctly summarized in Lowell Dittmer, "The Radical Critique of Political Interest: 1966–1978," *Modern China* 6, no. 4 (October 1980):363–96. See also Lowell Dittmer, *Liu Shao-ch'i and the Chinese Cultural Revolution: The Politics of Mass Criticism* (Berkeley: University of California Press, 1974).

a complex division of labor, it can be proven "scientifically" (by applying technical reason to empirical data) that intense cooperation in publicly owned industries is in the best interest of the greatest number of people. However, in an agrarian economy that relies on labor-intensive technology and a rudimentary division of labor, it is not necessarily in the best interest of most individuals to work closely together in socialist collectives. Thus the peasants in a farming village should not be asked to live as intense a collective life as Mao suggested. In any case, the goodness or badness of public policy in a farming village should be judged by how it contributes to the individual welfare of the majority of the villagers.[22]

People who argue within such a paradigm would dispute each other's facts and each other's technical rationality. Leaders would justify a controversial course of action by trying to prove that the results would benefit at least a majority of their followers. A good leader would be considered someone who was intelligent, competent, and capable. We shall see how a new generation of village leaders in the 1970s used this utilitarian form of Marxist-Leninist morality to justify their conduct and how ordinary villagers themselves came increasingly to adopt it. The adoption of this paradigm made special sense as a way out of the deep moral confusion caused by the clash between a traditional Confucianism and a disintegrating Maoism.[23]

22. Dittmer, "Radical Critique," 368 – 69.

23. In analyzing the contrasting logic of the three paradigms for moral discourse presented here, I have made use of a schema of four styles of moral reasoning developed by Ralph Potter and recently applied to American religious movements by Steven Tipton. See Steven Tipton, *Getting Saved from the Sixties* (Berkeley: University of California Press, 1981).

The four styles are: (1) revelational-authoritative; (2) regular; (3) situational-expressive; and (4) consequential.

The revelational-authoritative style seeks to understand the difference between right and wrong by looking to an authority known by faith. Disagreements over a moral issue are resolved by exegeting authoritative dogma. In my analysis, the Maoist ethic is an essentially revelational-authoritative style.

The regular style looks to rules or principles known by reason. Moral disagreement is resolved through appeals to the rational consistency of such principles.

The situational-expressive style looks to the quality of personal feelings and to an intuitive grasp of a whole situation. Disagreement is resolved by appealing to a sense of the general context. In my analysis, the Confucian ethic employs a combination of regular and situational-expressive styles.

The consequential style looks to the consequences of an act known by empirical calculation. This style judges acts solely in terms of their effectiveness as means to an end without attributing any intrinsic value to them. Disagreement is resolved by reviewing the pertinent empirical evidence. The Liuist paradigm contains a consequential style of ethical evaluation.

This typology of styles of ethical evaluation is highly abstract and by itself tells us nothing about the *content* of any moral evaluation. The potential content of any

Thus, when the leaders of Chen Village tried to justify their conduct to the villagers, and when ordinary villagers sought to criticize their leaders, they had available to them variations on the Confucian, Maoist, and Liuist paradigms for moral discourse outlined above. Different villagers used different paradigms at different times. To explain why they did so, we cannot simply assume that they acted out of a disinterested love for a particular kind of moral discourse. When the village leaders adopted a particular moral stance, political considerations were certainly involved: this was what political superiors wanted; this was what the ordinary citizens would respond to; this is how one needed to act if one was going to get and keep some political power. When the ordinary villagers criticized their leaders, similar political considerations were very important. But that does not mean that moral arguments in the village were simply a mask for political interests and a weapon in political struggles. Let me briefly explain my understanding of the relationship between moral argument and political calculation.

Political Capital, Political Structure, and Moral Predicament

As some of our interviewees put it, people in China have different kinds of "political capital," different personal resources that can be translated into power. Among these are different abilities to make various sorts of impassioned moral arguments and to shape one's life in accordance with them. Sometimes, it has been very useful to one's political career to be exceptionally able to quote chapter and verse from Mao's writings, to apply these quotations creatively to every facet of daily life, and to live the kind of earnest, ascetic life-style the quotes demanded. This could be especially important if the main way to get a leadership position was to win the approval of superiors in a Maoist-dominated bureaucracy. At

---

person's or group's moral convictions depends on what ideas are available in their cultural traditions about such issues as: what (if any) principles of moral order can reason uncover; what (if anything) can be agreed upon about the overall quality of a situation; what are the facts (if they are knowable at all) pertinent to calculating the consequences of an action? The actual content of any group's moral evaluations depends on the particular ideas shared by that group about any of the above issues; the content of any individual's evaluations also hinges on his or her own idiosyncratic beliefs, interpretations, and perceptions. This typology of evaluative styles is useful, however, for making us sensitive to the way people might proceed to moral conclusions if they start from revealed commandments, rationally discovered principles, and so forth. It offers a kind of grammar for moral discourse, although not a vocabulary.

other times it has been more important to demonstrate the proper sensitivity to good human feelings in a specific situation. This could be especially important if the main way to get ahead was to be good at speaking to the hopes and sensibilities of ordinary peasants at the village level. At other times it has been useful to be able to speak the language of utilitarian efficiency. This became especially important in the 1970s. All of these abilities at moral discourse were potential forms of political capital. But which ability offered effective political capital in the village at a given time depended on the precise political situation: how aggressively the government was committed to changing the village, how cautiously the government was trying to gain the villagers' goodwill, what local faction within the village had gained the upper hand, and so on. The political situation in the village never remained stable for very long. This meant that some forms of political capital were always becoming obsolete while others were gaining new value. Chinese politics has been extraordinarily mercurial in recent years.

One can explain why certain leaders adopted certain moral stands at certain times by showing how that gave them the political capital they needed to get or keep their jobs. And one can explain why certain ordinary villagers supported or criticized their leaders by showing how those ordinary citizens also hoped to gain political capital, not necessarily to become village leaders themselves, but to gain special favors from the leadership. This explanation is especially useful in accounting for the stance new political generations adopted as they tried to establish themselves in power. But once one has adopted a particular moral position, one is stuck with it to an important degree. For example, if one learns to talk passionately like a Maoist true believer at a time when that is politically expedient, various psychological and sociological factors may force one to keep on talking in that way even when it is no longer expedient: to abruptly give up talking like a true believer could lead to a great deal of personal psychological confusion or earn one the scorn of being perceived a hypocrite. Thus we will meet leaders in Chen Village who developed a certain style of moral discourse probably at least partly for reasons of political expediency but who continued to use that style even when it no longer constituted good political capital, indeed, even when it may have hurt them politically.

A disjunction between a political leader's moral stance—his or her commitment to a particular mode of moral discourse—and the requirements for getting and keeping political power in the village is a moral predicament. Villagers were constantly faced with such predicaments, and they found them extremely painful. To escape from their predicaments, they needed to expand their repertoire of moral discourse to include forms of moral rhetoric that could provide good current political capital. How and to what extent could this be done? The answer to that question provides interesting insights into the ways in which patterns of moral meaning in China have changed under fluid political conditions: villagers attempted to escape from their predicaments by mixing paradigms of moral discourse together to form a new syncretic synthesis that would give them both current political capital and new ways of understanding and justifying their position in the world.

This finding yields a particular perspective on the relationship between cultural traditions and modernity in contemporary China. I suggest neither that Chinese traditional values have yielded directly to modern ones; nor that modern Chinese values are simply traditional forms of culture in disguise; nor that contemporary Chinese culture has ever been a neat fusion of traditional and modern ideas. Instead I suggest that people in rural communities like Chen Village play down certain themes in their traditional culture and emphasize others that fit their contemporary social situation and that they do the same for the modern themes of the official ideology. And then, I suggest, they mix traditional and modern themes into a synthesis composed of partially integrated, partially contradictory parts. Thus, when they try to understand and justify the moral quality of their lives, they often use a complex of not altogether consistent arguments. Local political leaders are perhaps especially prone to manifest such contradictions because they are so directly caught between the demands of superiors above and different factions of villagers below. But the fact that one's culture is composed of inconsistent elements does not necessarily make it absurd. Probably all complex, vital cultures contain unreconciled contradictions. Perhaps Chinese peasants have needed to create such a syncretic culture to make adequate moral sense of their complex political situation. And just because a Chinese peasant political leader seems to justify his life by a set of not totally consistent moral principles does not mean that he is a moral schizophrenic or a moral fraud. As I will suggest, the character of a good politician is a living synthesis of partially contradictory elements. Those who organize their work around a single principle tend to become either power-hungry fanatics or power-hungry opportunists.

But how and under what circumstances do villagers create the confluence of partially integrated, partially contradictory themes needed to form the basis of a vital political culture? Which social processes further this confluence and which break it down? How does the content of a culture's disparate ideas shape this integrative process? The confluence of disparate cultural themes, I suggest, occurs through village rituals, so it behooves us to analyze such rituals.

Ceremonies of Innocence and Rituals of Struggle

In the rituals described in this study, the ritual participants pour a rich variety of emotions into the performance of a series of stylized actions that are held to represent some phase of the fundamental meaning of their life together. The main symbols making up the rituals are actions rather than words. In some cases these emotionally resonant symbols express a richer meaning than can be put into any discursive verbal argument. This emotional resonance and fertile noetic ambiguity is what gives rituals everywhere their integrative power. The participants in a ritual become a community of feeling and sharers in a common experience that is drenched with meaning but cannot be expressed by any single set of discursive ideas.[24] They often experience the ritual as expressing a common primordial understanding that is the font of subsequent discursive understandings.[25] This does not mean that one can discursively interpret a ritual in any way one wishes. There is usually a range of orthodox interpretations of a ritual and some clear ideas about which interpretations would be unorthodox. But often the range of orthodox interpretations is fairly wide, so that a ritual can unite a broad group of people with different approaches toward life. Thus regular participants in certain rituals can within limits argue about their common moral re-

24. My conceptualization here owes much to Victor Turner's studies of ritual. See especially his *The Forest of Symbols*, 1–58. See also his *The Ritual Process* (Ithaca, N.Y.: Cornell University Press, 1977). An analysis of political ritual parallel to mine (but one that I did not become aware of until after I had finished this chapter) is W. Lance Bennett, "Imitation, Ambiguity and Drama in Political Life: Civil Religion and the Dilemmas of Public Morality," *Journal of Politics* 41, no. 1 (February 1979):106–33.

25. This distinction between "primordial understanding" and "discursive understanding" is inspired by the philosophy of Martin Heidegger. For a good explication of Heidegger's concept of "primordial understanding" and an interesting argument about the need for social scientists to take Heidegger's idea into account in their work, see Hubert Dreyfus, "Holism and Hermeneutics," *Review of Metaphysics* 34, no. 1 (September 1980):3–23.

Practical understanding [what Heidegger calls primordial understanding] is holistic in an entirely different way from theoretical understanding. Although practical understanding—everyday coping with things and people—involves explicit beliefs and hypotheses, these can only be meaningful in specific contexts and against a background of shared practices. And just as we can learn to swim without consciously acquiring a theory of swimming, we acquire our social practices by being trained in them, not by forming beliefs and following rules. . . . Such skills embody a whole cultural interpretation of what it means to be a human being and what counts as real. (p. 7)

sponsibilities to their community and yet recognize that they are united by a shared moral understanding that transcends their words. Rituals that can integrate a wide range of different points of view I call (borrowing from Yeats) "ceremonies of innocence."

But some rituals do not unite people with diverse points of view. They celebrate one narrow set of ideas and turn those who hold them against everyone who does not. I call these "rituals of struggle." Is there anything in the form rather than in the consequences of rituals of struggle that distinguishes them from ceremonies of innocence? One important difference, I would suggest, concerns the interplay of action and words within the ritual. In most rituals, dramatic gestures are accompanied by words that comment on them, interpret, or explain them: a child is plunged into a pool of water and words are spoken linking the event to the passage of the Israelites through the Red Sea, the passage of Christ from death into life, and the passage of the individual from outside to inside the Christian community. When the discursive, verbal part of the ritual serves essentially as a commentary on the nonverbal, dramatic part, it is often possible to attach a wide variety of other meanings to the dramatic action: for some Christians, baptism not only symbolizes the crossing of the Red Sea but the washing away of sins (and thus sin is thought of as a kind of pollution rather than as a separation from God). This wide range of possible interpretations makes the ritual a ceremony of innocence. In some rituals, however, the primary ritual action *is* the stylized recitation of sacred doctrine. Thus, in the Protestant sects of the Reformation, the main rituals were Bible readings and long sermons. This identification of ritual action with doctrinal preaching is, I suggest, characteristic of sectarian rituals of struggle. Ritual becomes the expression of sharply focused sacred doctrine, rather than the doctrine becoming an expression of the primordial experience expressed in the ritual gesture. Thus participants in the ritual see themselves as united around a clearly defined common doctrine that separates them from the rest of the world.[26]

In lineage communities like Chen Village, traditional village rituals punctuated the cycles of the year—New Year, Qing Ming, and so on—and the events of a person's life—birth, marriage, death—and linked those cycles and events to the passage of ancestral generations that defined one's place in the present. In my terminology, these were ceremonies of innocence. They evoked a sense of unity between the villagers

26. This analysis is consistent with that of Mary Douglas, *Natural Symbols* (New York: Vintage, 1973). Douglas's work helps to make understandable the paradox that revolts (such as that of the Maoists) against "magical" or "superstitious" rituals are usually deeply ritualistic themselves and often involve the celebration of a ritual that pits a small group of righteous believers against a mass of evil nonbelievers.

on the basis of their common past, but they did not freeze the villagers into commitment to a set of rigidly defined rules specifying in precise detail their moral responsibilities in the village. One was to honor one's ancestors, respect one's elders, obey one's father, but there was an important degree of flexibility in the precise meaning one could attach to these norms.[27] We shall see how some people could claim that respect for their heritage demanded that they place the welfare of their immediate families over the welfare of the village as a whole, while others could claim that it demanded the reverse. We shall see how villagers could argue quite fiercely about such matters while continuing to communicate with one another and perhaps under most circumstances affirming a basic respect for one another that transcended their disagreements.

And we shall also see how the Communist government concocted its own rituals to make the villagers into good socialist citizens. In the 1960s, these Communist rituals were celebrations of Mao's Words, which had been exalted to the status of sacred teachings. Because of this focus on Mao's teachings, these became rituals of struggle. They divided villagers into sharply composed camps: those who accepted the teachings, and those who did not. Yet the Maoist rituals of struggle were tempered by their own ceremonies of innocence, at the heart of which were powerful gestures of respect for the person of Mao rather than for his teachings. This focus on Mao's person enabled villagers to interpret the teachings in flexible ways and to fuse those teachings with strands of their traditional discourse about their responsibilities in the world. As far as it went, this fusion made an important cultural contribution to the village: it helped villagers to maintain their moral roots in the past while giving them the cultural resources to participate positively in the construction of a modern, national polity.

The Maoist cultural synthesis, however, was fatally flawed. The culturally disintegrative effects of the rituals of struggle, centered around Mao's apotheosized teachings, could not ultimately be separated from the integrative effects of the ceremonies of innocence, centered around reverence for Mao's person. In the Cultural Revolution, the Maoist rituals

27. For a fascinating analysis, based on Taiwan fieldwork, of the way in which the symbols used by Chinese peasants in their ritual life allow for a wide range of interpretations, allowing peasants to express their rivalries toward one another even while they reaffirm their common traditions, see Arthur P. Wolf, "Gods, Ghosts, and Ancestors," in *Religion and Ritual in Chinese Society,* ed. Arthur P. Wolf (Stanford: Stanford University Press, 1974). In Taiwan at least, whenever peasants think of the supernatural, they do so in terms of three classes of spirits: gods, ghosts, and ancestors. But a peasant's understanding of the nature of these beings depends on his or her social perspectives. Thus, one person's fearsome ghosts are another person's revered ancestors.

became purely rituals of struggle, and they forced villagers to emphasize one particular strand of contemporary China's complex tangled culture to the exclusion of all else. These Maoist rituals of struggle destroyed the lived synthesis of different cultural themes that was so important in enabling the villagers to come to terms with their predicaments. The result was an explosion of pure moral zeal that ironically led to the demoralization of the village and to the degradation of the moral character of some village leaders. But how can I presume to judge the moral character of village leaders? Let me conclude this section of this chapter with a rationale for my presumptuousness.

Moral Character and the Vocation of Politics

In analyzing how villagers may argue about the goodness or badness of their leaders, I shall show how their conceptions of political morality are relative. For example, a leader who would be considered corrupt according to orthodox Maoist moral logic may be merely showing sensitivity to fundamentally important responsibilities toward family members according to Confucian moral logic. But I wish to go beyond this relativism and to make normative judgments, albeit tentative ones, about the value of certain character types found among the leaders of Chen Village.

To do this I make certain basic assumptions about the politician's vocation. I assume that a politician has to have some concern for the overall welfare of the people whom he leads. I expect that there will be controversy over what that welfare is and how it can be attained. I recognize that politicians are concerned not only with enhancing the general welfare but with building up their own power, wealth, and prestige. If a politician is solely concerned with his own aggrandisement to the exclusion of any concern for the people's welfare, then he or she is an immoral politician in a sense that could be agreed to by any civilized person. In the latter stages of the Cultural Revolution in Chen Village, several of the village's prominent political leaders were becoming immoral in this sense.

Like most polities, Chen Village's government had certain structural arrangements which assured that village leaders had to show some concern for the overall welfare of the political community in order to get and keep their jobs. During the Cultural Revolution, these structural arrangements broke down. But that is not sufficient to explain political immorality. As important as social structural constraints are in restraining political immorality, the ideas of good and evil that form the moral culture of a people are even more important. What I am especially concerned with in this study is the way in which a breakdown of this moral framework led to a breakdown of moral character.

The moral framework broke down when the rituals of struggle destroyed the ceremonies of innocence. The ceremonies of innocence fused several different moral paradigms into a tentative synthesis. No single moral paradigm was sufficient to provide adequate guidance in meeting the moral challenges posed by the village's situation. People might be more committed to one paradigm or another, but to make adequate sense out of their lives, they needed to affirm some of the others also. They had to bring them together into a lived synthesis.

This was especially true of the political leaders. The Cultural Revolution, with its rituals of struggle, promoted various kinds of moral purism. Leadership styles became dominated by various moral principles. This led to fanaticism as different leaders tried forcefully to impose their particular principles on everyone else. Fanaticism led to an utter disregard of the sensibilities of anyone who did not also fanatically hold one's purist principles. Having no respect for those who did not share their principles, the minority of single-minded leaders who won the struggle for power felt no moral constraints on how they handled the losers. They tended to pursue power without regard for the general interests of the people they dominated. The losers in the struggle for power, on the other hand, became cynical about the political process and sought to make the best of a bad situation by pursuing their individual interests. Local politics became demoralized, and the character of local politicians, by almost anyone's standards, became debased.

All of this suggests that in a complex society the character of a good politician has to be complex: a tension-filled blend of different commitments pulled together in a lived synthesis appropriate to the situation at hand. This is perhaps what Aristotle meant when he discussed the virtues that make up the character of a good person. There are different basic virtues pulling in different directions: courage, leading one to push past all obstacles; justice, leading one to respect the principles of equity as one courageously pushes oneself forward; temperance, leading one to pursue all things, even courage and justice, with moderation appropriate to the realistic circumstances at hand; and prudence, the highest of virtues, defined by Aristotle not as cautious timidity but as practical wisdom enabling one to fashion just the right mix of courage, justice, and temperance for any specific human situation. Without the dynamic wisdom called prudence, a politician cannot know how to be virtuous.[28] The

28. Aristotle, *Nicomachean Ethics*, especially Book VI. See also Hans-Georg Gadamer, "The Problem of Historical Consciousness," in *Interpretive Social Science: A Reader*, ed. Paul Rabinow and William M. Sullivan (Berkeley: University of California Press, 1979), 135–45; and Ralph Potter, "Justice and Beyond in Moral Education" (Address at the Regional Conference on Moral Development of Youth, Wayzata, Minnesota, June 1977).

rituals of struggle in Chen Village destroyed the cultural guidelines by which village leaders could learn to be prudent and thus to be moral.

Theory and History

Up until now, I have presented a logically ordered array of abstract ideas: a series of questions to be asked and concepts to be used in seeking answers to these questions. But the purpose of this theoretical apparatus is to interpret a portion of the messy flow of concrete events that was the recent history of Chen Village. Different phases of village history were characterized by distinct configurations of moral paradigms, predicaments, and rituals, and these configurations had different consequences for the development of the moral character of the village's political leaders. Thus, I will discuss paradigms, predicaments, rituals, and character in four successive phases of village history.

In the first phase (Chapters 2 and 3) moral discourse arising from a Confucian paradigm collided with a Maoist critique. As this phase began, the basic mode of moral discourse used by the village's leading local cadres was Confucian. In Chapter 2, I will discuss the ways in which Chen Village's two most powerful cadres justified their styles of action and the ways in which various groups of ordinary villagers criticized those justifications. The discourse swirling around these justifications and critiques was essentially Confucian. The Confucian paradigm gave rise to two distinct visions of how village leaders should exercise their authority and, implicitly, two views on how the village should be organized. These two visions were connected with different forms of political capital in the village.

This moral situation was complicated when a work team of outside Communist cadres entered the village in 1965 to carry out the Socialist Education Movement (Chapter 3). Launched by the highest echelons of Party leadership, this campaign was supposed to "teach the peasants philosophy," to teach them to understand and practice moral values appropriate to China's new socialist society. The mode of discourse the work team tried to teach was Maoist. It did this by conducting violently emotional rituals of struggle. In these rituals almost all of the village cadres were called to account for not living up to Maoist moral norms and dragged before emotion-charged "struggle sessions" where the assembled villagers passionately cursed them for their moral failures. All this placed both village leaders and ordinary citizens in deep predicaments: if they wanted political success and security, they had to affirm alien moral ideas that they did not fully understand. I suggest, however, that the Communist government's handling of the Socialist Education Movement left a way out of such predicaments. The government-commanded rituals of struggle were quickly followed by government-sponsored cere-monies of innocence. The work team reaffirmed the honor of most of the condemned village cadres, even though if one believed what the work team had said during the struggle sessions, these local leaders should never have been rehabilitated. These revolutionary actions made it possi-ble for villagers to fuse certain themes from their Confucian discourse with other themes from the official Maoist discourse into a fragile but workable synthesis. I will examine how this synthesis affected the moral character of leading village cadres.

In the second phase of our story (Chapters 4 and 5), the state-spon-sored Maoist morality began to undergo a kind of Confucian transforma-tion within the village. To deepen the synthesis between Mao's moral teaching and the villagers' traditional moral discourse, the government inaugurated a campaign to venerate Mao and his teachings. Centered around respect for Mao as a person, these government-sponsored cere-monies of innocence drew the villagers' attention away from the details of his teachings while allowing the villagers to mingle their own moral sensibilities with some of the most general perspectives of Mao's Thought. But these ceremonies of innocence were fundamentally flawed.

Mao was supposed to be venerated precisely because of the literal cor-rectness of his teachings. But those teachings were untenable if taken literally. As long as the villagers were not forced to pay attention to the details of the teaching, they could venerate Mao as a great person and let themselves be influenced by some of his more lofty ideals. But when forced to confront the absurdity of his teaching, they were not able to take Mao seriously.

To demonstrate the moral problems created by taking Mao's teaching literally, I discuss the "sent-down" city youth who came to live in Chen Village in late 1964 (Chapter 4). For a while many of these young people made a heroic effort to live like good Maoists, but their attempt led them into unresolvable predicaments. The logic of Mao's teachings inevitably contributed to these predicaments. In Chapter 5, I examine the structure of the village ceremonies to honor Mao, show how those ceremonies be-gan to create a synthesis between Maoist and Confucian moral discourse and how that synthesis was undermined by the scandalous spectacle of the moral predicaments of the sent-down youth.

In the third phase of our story, an irreparable breakdown occurred in the moral synthesis created by the campaign to venerate Mao. The break-down came about because of the dynamics of the Cultural Revolution (Chapter 6) and its immediate aftermath, the Cleansing of the Class Ranks campaign (Chapter 7). The main events of this historical phase were rituals of struggle. I will explain how those rituals came into being and how, utterly shattering the synthesis of moral discourse fashioned by mid-1966, they made it impossible for villagers to argue about matters of public morality in a constructive way. This breakdown in the basis for moral communication led to a pervasive cynicism about morality, and this in turn tended to bring out the most vicious aspects of the village's leading cadres and activists.

In the fourth phase of our story (Chapter 8), a new moral order began to emerge in the village, an order increasingly dominated by a utilitarian individualistic paradigm and associated with the thought of Mao's enemy during the Cultural Revolution, Liu Shaoqi. This new ethos began to emerge in the early 1970s and became more pronounced as the decade wore on. It was most pronounced in the new generation of village cadres appointed after the Cultural Revolution, but it also influenced older cadres. To explicate the logic of this utilitarian mode of moral discourse, I will focus especially on the ways in which the new generation of cadres tried to justify their styles of life and work. This new mode of discourse became prominent partly because Chinese government policies made it an important part of the political capital of an aspiring local cadre. But the utilitarian mode of moral discourse was also needed to fill a moral vacuum created by the destructive cultural chaos of the Cultural Revolution. The new utilitarian ethos has, in turn, given rise to new predicaments that have not yet been resolved.

In the final chapter I depart from the flow of history to summarize what I have learned by this application of theory to history. There, I delineate four different ideal types of local-level political leaders and distinguish between them on the basis of distinctive styles of political action, forms of political capital, modes of morally justifying styles of action, types of moral predicaments, and strengths or weaknesses in moral character.

The Particularity of the Universal

In developing my general arguments about the moral basis of political conduct in China, I am not as concerned with what makes the residents of Chen Village themselves "typical" of all other people in China as with what makes them particular and individually unique. I am concerned, that is, with examining in detail how people in a particular place have experienced the typical moral dilemmas faced throughout China. The people of Chen Village shared a cultural heritage common to all contemporary Chinese, and they had to face up to moral issues that people throughout rural China have had to confront: how can traditional Chinese values and modern Communist ideology be reconciled? How can private and public responsibilities be balanced? How can pragmatic and principled politics be made to complement one another? But a general cultural heritage exists only in specific individuals in specific situations. And general moral dilemmas only come about when particular persons try to reconcile certain moral beliefs in the light of specific social realities. Thus one can understand in a very abstract way the general themes that underlie a cultural heritage and the tensions that make up prevalent moral dilemmas, but such an understanding does not tell one much; it is crude and superficial. A subtle understanding depends on being able to show how general themes and common tensions are understood and acted upon by specific persons in specific contexts. Thus it is the very specificity of person and place described here that deepens our understanding of the general issues of moral discourse, predicament, ritual, and character with which we have begun this book. And having deepened our own understanding, we can then venture to suggest how scholars might think more subtly about discourse, predicament, ritual, and character in other contexts.[29]

This book, then, is about particular individuals creating their own unique moral character in a process that can be partially diagnosed in general terms. In China's official Communist parlance, the process of creating a good socialist character is called *duanlian*. The word means to "temper" or to "forge," as a piece of steel. But it also refers to the exercise an athlete must undergo to ready his body for competition. The word *duanlian* thus has a semantic range similar to that of the Western concept of asceticism, a word derived from the Greek *askesis*, denoting the physical exercises of an athlete and extended by Christian monks to denote the arduous spiritual exercises needed to develop a committed Christian character.

One of our interviewees used to say that to be a local political cadre or activist in China was to be like a piece of metal being hammered on a blacksmith's anvil: exposed to fire and caught between political hammering from above and the hard, unyielding resistance of the ordinary citizens below. This metaphor recalls the primary meaning of *duanlian*—to temper or to forge. I will try to plot the angle of the political blows and the direction of the moral fire that impinged upon different village activists as they went through the *duanlian* that sometimes shaped and sometimes shattered their characters.

But the image of *duanlian* as tempering or forging does not exhaust the reality of the arduous process of shaping moral character in China. *Duanlian* is also asceticism—spiritual exercise consciously and deliberately

29. For this conception of the relationship between detailed case studies and broader interpretations and analyses, I am indebted to Clifford Geertz, "Thick Description: Toward an Interpretive Theory of Culture," in *The Interpretation of Cultures*, 20–22.

undertaken. For me the most satisfying part of my research has come from seeing the ways in which the activists of Chen Village were *not* like inert pieces of metal being shaped by impersonal forces; they were also conscious human agents who, while being shaped, twisted, bent, and sometimes broken by forces beyond their control, still struggled morally to comprehend their situation and to improve their world—so that they made history while making themselves.

PART ONE

THE CONFUCIAN
TRADITION AND ITS
MAOIST CRITIQUE

2 Tensions Within a Moral Tradition

Chen Longyong was one of two men whom the Chen villagers called "local emperor." The other was Longyong's old nemesis Chen Qingfa.[1] People did not call Longyong and Qingfa "local emperor" to their faces. The term was used carefully by rather bold people in political gossip at times when the authority of these men had been weakened by the impact of political campaigns. When people called Longyong or Qingfa "local emperor," they were not referring to the benevolent majesty sometimes associated with emperorhood but rather to its fearsome power. Both Longyong and Qingfa were exceedingly powerful men by virtue of their physical prowess, personal drive, social status, and political position. Their power was fearsome, not necessarily because it was perceived as malevolent, but because it was raw, explosive, sometimes unchecked, and always very close at hand. Rather than being malevolent, the power of both Longyong and Qingfa had produced considerable benefits for Chen Village. Most of the villagers acknowledged these benefits and were, if not enthusiastically grateful, at least grudgingly appreciative. People also respected Longyong—albeit sometimes grudgingly and not without reservations—for his courage, honesty, and fairness. Public opinion of Qingfa, however, was somewhat more complex: everyone acknowledged his contributions, but some people—especially those who had not been favored by him—had contempt for his corrupt style of living and working.

1. The characters Qingfa and Longyong are also introduced in chapter 1 of Anita Chan, Richard Madsen, and Jonathan Unger, *Chen Village: The Recent History of a Peasant Community in Mao's China* (Berkeley: University of California Press, 1984); their careers are described throughout that book. See also Richard P. Madsen, "The Maoist Ethic and the Moral Basis of Political Activism in Rural China," in *Moral Behavior in Chinese Society*, ed. Richard W. Wilson, Sidney L. Greenblatt, and Amy Auerbacker Wilson (New York: Praeger, 1981).

In 1964, Qingfa was Chen Village's local emperor, but Longyong was threatening his authority. A year later, Qingfa met his downfall, and Longyong gradually rose to become the village strong man. But Qingfa continued to struggle and eventually regained a measure of his former power. The moral climate of life in Chen Village over the past two decades has been considerably influenced by the personal political struggles between these two men, because each was committed to a distinctly different concept of local moral order.

Longyong

By the standards of South China, Chen Longyong was an enormously big and strong man. He was about six feet tall—one of the tallest people in Chen Village. In 1964, he was thirty-two years old, in the prime of his life, and he could match any person in the village in physical strength. The men of Chen Village greatly valued physical strength. After the harvest was completed, the young men would gather around the scales used to weigh the winnowed rice and would compete to see who could lift the heaviest sack of grain. The strongest could lift a sack weighing about 250 pounds to their shoulders. Longyong was as strong as any of them. But first-rate labor power in a farming village does not merely consist of brute strength. It also involves endurance—the stamina to work steadily for long periods of time—and the ability to work fast, efficiently, and skillfully. By all these criteria, Longyong was one of the best workers in the village. The combination of physical strength and practical skill required of a first-rate farm laborer was almost indispensable for the attainment of social prestige in Chen Village. And without such prestige, one would not be accepted as a leader. Every cadre of any stature in Chen Village could be classified as a first-rate laborer. Individuals who were weak and clumsy were simply not accepted as leaders. Longyong's physical strength and farming skill were important ingredients of his authority.

Longyong had no formal education and was almost completely illiterate. He could barely sign his name. But he was almost universally regarded as extremely intelligent. In this study, the reader will find ample evidence of his astuteness, especially in the ways of handling power. In 1964, his lack of education was not a serious handicap. Very few people in the village were educated at that time, and most of the few who were educated were in no position to assume a leadership role. The village's few landlords and rich peasants had been educated, but they were ostracized socially, constantly harassed politically, and in no position to wield any direct influence over village life. A few local youths were beginning middle school, but they were too young to play any role in the village yet. A few adult men of poor and lower-middle peasant background were semiliterate, but they were not nearly as clever intellectually or as dynamic personally as Longyong. At any rate, in 1964, the skills imparted by a formal education were of little relevance to social, political, or economic life in the village. A formal education was of little use in carrying out the traditional agricultural tasks around which the village's economic life was organized. Moreover, the ability required to get ahead socially and politically was not the knowledge that came from reading books but the understanding that came from shrewd perceptions of the feelings and hopes of those people with whom one had constant close contact. As new technologies were introduced into the village and as the Chinese state emphasized the need for political study, Longyong's lack of education eventually became something of a handicap. But these changes were still a few years away.

For the Chinese, much more than for us, physiognomy has traditionally been a very important indicator of a person's character and fate. When Chen villagers considered Longyong's moral worth and social importance, they often thought in terms of the impression made by his facial appearance. He was an ugly man; his face was marked with smallpox scars. He was nicknamed "Old Pockmark"—a nickname no one used to his face. His eyes were constantly squinting; his face, said one interviewee, "was always like a dark cloud." His visage corresponded to and symbolized the uncompromising fierceness of his personality.

Longyong was a man of immense determination. If he decided that he wanted to get something done, he would proceed toward his goal with all of his strength. He could be quite ruthless in pushing anyone opposing him aside. Longyong dominated public meetings and private encounters. He had a powerful temper that he seems to have controlled to maximum effect. If someone confronted him in a meeting, for example, he could fly into a rage, shouting and cursing and pounding a table. His passion thoroughly intimidated most people, and only very few dared to argue with him. Yet, when he was in a situation in which a naked display of passion could be counterproductive—for instance if he could be accused of vindictively bullying someone who had the sympathy of the Chen Village public—then he could restrain himself and work against such a person from behind the scenes. Some people said that he had the "cow spirit," which means approximately the same as our "bullheaded." He was stubborn and became more rigid the more people opposed him. As one person put it:

> If the brigade had a meeting to solve a problem, Longyong certainly had to give the nod for it to be passed. If he didn't say anything, that indicated that he didn't agree. If he didn't agree, the matter couldn't be pushed through. Because, if you were going to do something, it wouldn't necessarily be successful. It could fail. There could be mistakes and deficiencies. If he didn't

agree with something and it failed, he would grasp the mistakes and fierce-ly attack them. So people were very afraid of him. In order to avoid respon-sibility for a mistake, most people let him give the nod. If he himself made a mistake, there would be no problem, because he had a lot of prestige. If he made a small mistake, no one would dare talk about it. But if other people made a mistake, he was very fierce towards them.

Although Longyong's fierce determination inspired fear and not a lit-tle resentment, it also inspired considerable respect, for he directed most of his enormous energy to the public good. He projected an image of being "unselfishly devoted to the public welfare" (*da gong wu si*). His un-selfishness, as we shall see, was not necessarily the result of any radical generosity of personal intention. Indeed, there is ample evidence to sug-gest that his surface unselfishness was closely intertwined with a most profound (and dangerous) form of selfishness, the hunger for power. Longyong was not a saint but a politician; his righteousness was as much a weapon as a virtue. Let us now analyze what his selflessness meant to the villagers and examine how and with what consequences he could use it as a weapon in his personal quest for power.

First and foremost, Longyong's selflessness meant an intense dedica-tion to giving Chen Village collective power and prestige above the other communities in its commune. To understand the origins and the force of this commitment, one must appreciate the relative poverty of Chen Vil-lage and the feelings the villagers shared about that poverty. Chen Vil-lage had been the victim of collective downward mobility. In the 1920s and 1930s the village seems to have enjoyed a modest degree of prosper-ity, but in the turmoil of the last few years of the 1930s and the 1940s, it seems to have lost ground to its neighbors. The villagers used to say that when they went to the commune or county seat, Chen villagers stood out from others because they were "thin as joss sticks," ragged, and uncouth. When cadres from Longyong's generation went to meetings at the com-mune or county levels they were embarrassed by the fact that while their peers from other villages could take notes, they themselves were unable to read or write. The women of the village half-jokingly used to say that they must have made some mistake in the process of reincarnation, to be fated to end up in such an unfavorable place. There was a good deal of tension between Chen Village and its neighboring communities. When women from neighboring Song Village would pass by, Chen Village men sometimes heckled them with comments like: "Hey, wouldn't you like to get married into our village?" (Because their village was so poor in the 1950s and 1960s, Chen Village men often had trouble finding brides from other villages.) The people from Song Village sometimes put broken glass on the path leading from Chen Village to the commune seat to puncture the tires of Chen Village bicycles. Villagers respected Longyong because he was committed to bringing their community power and glory over its neighbors.

This incident remembered by one of our interviewees gives a good feel for the impression of collective dedication that Longyong could make.

> On the day after we arrived in the village, we saw him for the first time. When we saw him, we were afraid of him, afraid to look at him. He was so big, so ugly, and seemed so harsh. But then, on our third day there, a big flood hit the village. I can still remember going outside with the rain driving down and the water pouring in from the overflowing river and seeing this man wielding a huge pick hacking away dirt to build up a dam for the river. An extremely impressive sight. Such a tremendous amount of energy, conviction, authority. It is an image that has stuck with me up to the present day.

An image of dynamic energy poured into the collective affairs of the village was one that Longyong pursued with all of his heart. One component of that image was a powerful devotion to both physical labor and mental effort on behalf of the village. While some of the brigade cadres used to find ways to shirk physical labor (according to government guidelines they were supposed to participate in 100 days of labor a year), Longyong revelled in his ability to do hard physical work on behalf of the collective. People felt a mixture of fear and pride at being assigned to work with him in the village's collective fields, because he worked like a fanatic, pushing his companions along. During the agricultural slack season, he would lead handpicked groups of the strongest young men of the village to take part in public works projects (mostly road and river-dike building) organized by the commune. He would lead them to work furiously hard, accomplishing in four hours what contingents from other villages took eight hours to do. The authorities at the commune headquarters recognized Chen Village's public works contributions as the best in the commune, and thus Longyong helped to bring a great deal of glory to Chen Village and, in the process, to himself. When he was not doing physical labor, he worked tirelessly in planning capital improvements for the village, such as improved irrigation systems and the construction of small-scale industries.

Besides being passionately dedicated to the collective welfare of the village, Longyong was fiercely protective of those interests. Authorities at the commune seat often found him difficult to deal with. Once when the authority of the commune level of government was relatively weak, a cadre from the commune came to the village and criticized Longyong for his handling of some matter: Longyong threw him out of the village. Usually, Longyong was a faithful supporter of policies that higher levels of authority were determined to implement. He made sure, for instance, that Chen villagers faithfully delivered their assigned grain quotas to the state. He was shrewd enough to know that to fail in such a serious matter could create much trouble for him and for the village. But in areas where it appeared that he might successfully defy commune wishes for the sake of the collective interests of the village, he was not afraid to do so. For instance, in the mid-1970s, he tried to build a dike to prevent trouble-some flooding in the river that bordered the village, even though build-ing the dike might have created a flooding problem for a neighboring village. This attempt provoked a fight with the commune cadres, a fight that he lost. But the incident illustrates the way his dedication to the vil-lage often took precedence over his loyalty to the commune or to other higher levels of state authority.

Longyong's image of passionate dedication to the collective welfare of Chen Village commanded local respect as is evidenced by the attitudes of both those interviewees who had for a while at least been his faithful followers and genuine admirers and those who had chafed under his rule. Those who had been loyal to him tended to speak of him as sincerely devoted to the common good of the village, thus justifying their loyalty. Those who had never been especially loyal to him or who had suffered from his actions had to admit in the end that compared with other cadres he was relatively unselfish and relatively devoted to the collective; but they kept trying to deflate his image, kept looking for and finding flaws in his dedication to the collective, and kept trying to suggest how his labors for the village's collective glory could really be seen as a means of aug-menting his personal glory. The tenacity with which such people tried to undermine Longyong's image of dedication to the collective was a func-tion of their need to escape the burden of respect that this image imposed.

Another component of Longyong's persona that earned the respect of the peasants was his strictness not only with others but also with him-self. He lived in one of the poorer houses of the village, and his diet was relatively sparse. Although his work-point income was one of the high-est in the village, his total personal income was rather low. (As a brigade cadre he received work points equal to a first-rate farm laborer; more-over, he received work points every day, whereas ordinary farmers re-ceived points only for those days on which they actually worked. The value of his work points was equal to the average value of the work points of the village's three most productive production teams.) At least one-third of total household income in Chen Village is earned not through collective work points but through the private sector of the village, through each household's private "sidelines," centered around each household's private plots. Longyong spent so much time working at his public duties that his private plots were neglected. For Chen villagers one of the most important indicators of a family's income is the type of food it eats. Even in the early 1970s when many families in Chen Village began to eat very well—having meat, fish, or poultry with their meals several times a week—Longyong's family still ate meat only rarely. He and his family flavored their rice only with small amounts of a strong-tasting pickled bean curd, small salted fish, and a small amount of vegetables. This austere style of life commanded the villagers' respect.

Moreover, while other cadres augmented their income with personal "gifts" received from peasants in return for favors, Longyong was almost rigidly incorrupt. In a celebrated case when one hapless peasant offered a fish to Longyong's family, Longyong "cursed him out like a beggar." The gift was a rather trifling kind of present that practically no other cadre in Chen Village would have hesitated to accept, and the giver offered it not as an outright bribe but as a minor attempt to ingratiate himself with Longyong. Longyong's histrionic reaction was seen as something extraordinary, as a case of overly rigid righteousness, but it enhanced his image as a person who could not be bought and thus as someone who commanded respect. The respect demanded by Longyong's incorruptibility gave him a license to condemn petty corruption among cadres throughout the village and thus gave him moral leverage over them.

Although he condemned corruption among cadres within the village, Longyong was quite willing to engage in such activity with cadres outside of the village in order to secure hard-to-get supplies like lumber and nails for the village. As brigade chief it was his responsibility to obtain such supplies. The only effective way to get scarce supplies was to offer small (and sometimes not so small) bribes to cadres at the commune or county seats. Thus, Longyong would go off on his purchasing errands loaded down with peanut oil, food-ration coupons, and sugar with which to win the good graces of cadres responsible for allocating supplies to production brigades. His abhorrence of corruption stopped at the boundaries of the village.

A final component of Longyong's moral image was a consistency toward villagers high and low, near to and far from him. He did not, as the Chinese saying puts it, "flatter the high and insult the lowly." He acted in the same fierce way toward everyone.

He was even harsh toward his own family. He had been married twice. He was particularly hard on his first wife, always yelling at her. This wife died while still in her twenties, leaving him two sons. Although she died of an illness, gossips said that it was really because of her husband's harsh treatment. With his first wife dead, he desperately needed a second wife to take care of his house and his children. Through a marriage broker, he found a second wife from a village about ten miles away. This woman was a young widow, who had had an affair with a man in her in-law's village after her husband's death and had become pregnant. Her in-laws, still the ones who controlled her destiny according to custom, were eager to cover up the affair by quickly marrying her off to someone, par-ticularly a rising young cadre, even if he had something of a reputation as a wife-killer. Longyong, for his part, could not be too fastidious. Realiz-ing more keenly now the value of a good wife, he was somewhat kinder toward his second wife, though still severe. This woman was an obedient spouse and a hard worker, well respected in the village. She was thus an important political asset to Longyong. Several cadres in Chen Village had unruly wives who were always meddling in other people's affairs and disrupting social order in the village. This ruined the credibility of their cadre husbands, because villagers believe that a leader should not pre-sume to tell them what to do if he cannot even control his own wife.

The way Longyong treated his family did not endear him to the vil-lagers, but it did help to command their respect. It showed them that his harshness was a genuine part of his character, not a tactic to be applied to keep people in line who bore no personal relationship to him. It also proved him to be someone who could effectively keep people under con-trol. There are a few cadres in the village who are easy going, "nice guys" (*shan liang*); but just because they are easy going, no one listens to them, and no one respects them as leaders. Longyong's harshness did not make him widely liked, but it helped to make him widely respected and even more widely obeyed.

Longyong's persona, the public image he projected of himself, was an important part of his political capital, a resource to be translated into power. His fierceness inspired fear; his dynamism, awe; his public spirit-edness, admiration; his austerity and his honesty, respect. Longyong shrewdly used these personal characteristics to extend his influence over Chen Village. He used them by appealing to a certain vision of moral order and social expectation shared in different degrees by most mem-bers of the village. He was, as I have said, not a saint but a politician. The self-sacrificing public-spiritedness and honesty that were such an impor-tant part of his political persona were not straightforward emanations of his personality, as those interviewees who (often for good reason) hated him were fond of pointing out. For one thing, he was most scrupulous about not using his political office to obtain material advantages during the late 1960s, when an image of incorruptibility was his most important asset in striving for power. Moreover, his unwillingness to accept bribes did not coexist with a willingness to treat every person with strict justice and fairness: he was in many ways a very unfair person, helpful to those who followed his orders, but sometimes ruthlessly cruel to those who defied his authority. Finally, as we shall see in more detail later, some of his efforts on behalf of the village as a whole brought considerable suffering to many residents of the village, even as they gave Longyong greater power and glory.

All the same, Longyong could not be called a hypocrite, in the common use of that term. There was not a radical disjunction between his private and public behavior. The head of a large bureaucracy, helped by an efficient public relations or propaganda apparatus, can sometimes have the luxury of presenting for public consumption an official image fundamentally different from his private one. In a small village where everyone knows everyone else's business, this is not possible. Thus Longyong tailored his private life so closely to his public performance that the distinction between the two was difficult to discern. I do not presume to judge where the "real" Longyong began and the public image ended. I merely want to show how the social and historical context in which he lived and worked presented a particular set of opportunities to a man who could create his kind of persona and thus led him to have a particularly profound influence on the moral tenor and tone of life in his community. To understand how, why, and with what consequences Longyong created his political persona, let us examine the social and political context within which he lived and worked.

The Chinese Communist government officially assigned Longyong the class status of poor peasant. Like all members of his generation, Longyong was given his official class status by Communist work teams in the initial stages of land reform in Chen Village in the early 1950s. Poor peasant status was given to those adults whose families had owned no land, at least not since 1946. To be classified as a poor peasant was to be given a uniquely privileged position in the new political order established by the Communists. Poor peasants received first priority on the land and property redistributed from the landlords and rich peasants. More importantly, poor peasants were given a preeminent position of political trust. Whenever possible, the government was to rely on poor and lower-middle peasants to be the cadres and backbone elements of the new political order.[2] The Communist government did not rely on poor peasants to an equal degree in all stages of socialist transformation and construction. In many localities in the early 1960s, for instance, when the Chinese economy was in a shambles following the problems created by the Great Leap Forward, the government tended to give important leadership roles to middle and upper-middle peasants, who were more skilled at traditional farming techniques and more adept at organizing their community members to work along traditional lines than many

2. For the most comprehensive available account of Chinese Communist use of class labels, see Richard Curt Kraus, *Class Conflict in Chinese Socialism* (New York: Columbia University Press, 1981).

poor peasants. In Chen Village, however, since the overwhelming majority of the population consisted of poor peasants and since the ranks of the poor peasants had produced a number of persons who had farming skills and organizational abilities equal to almost any of the village's middle, upper-middle, and rich peasants, control of the village remained firmly in the hands of poor or lower-middle peasants, even during the "hard years" from 1960 to 1963.

Almost all of the village's cadres of any importance came from poor or lower-middle peasant backgrounds. When middle or upper-middle peasants, with the approval of Communist Party authorities, did attain positions of authority, they found it rather difficult to exercise that authority because of a lack of support not from the central government but from their fellow peasants. The poor and lower-middle peasants of Chen Village were very conscious of their privileged position in the new society, and they were adept at using that privilege to their own advantage. For example, when an upper-middle peasant was put in charge of a production team, he could not push the poor and lower-middle peasants as hard as he might wish or as his role demanded because his upper-middle peasant status made him vulnerable to political criticism from the poor and lower-middle peasants and he did not dare offend them. This situation intensified in the latter half of the 1960s as the government increased its emphasis on the "class line." Thus, Longyong's official poor peasant status was a sine qua non for his political ascendancy.

Not all poor and lower-middle peasants in Chen Village were really poor, however. Some had relatives living overseas who sent them remittances that enabled them to live comfortably. Others were blessed with favorable circumstances—exceptional skill or good luck in farming; strong, healthy sons; absence of sickness in the family; and so forth—that enabled them to accumulate considerably more than average wealth. Others belonged to networks of kin within the village that cooperated easily in political and economic matters and thus gained relatively large shares of wealth and power. Such relatively fortunate poor peasants often tended to be more committed to the status quo and less "revolutionary" than poor peasants who were genuinely poor. In Chen Village, the poor and lower-middle peasants (politically defined) who were genuinely poor tended to be found in the western part of the village. Longyong lived in this part of the village. To understand the social relations that helped shape Longyong's commitments and focus his political efforts, we must understand the following features of the social geography of Chen Village.

Chen Village, as I have noted, was a lineage village; almost all the villagers claimed descent from a single ancestor. The lineage was divided into five branches or sublineages whose members were bound together by common descent from sons or grandsons of the original ancestor. Members of each branch tended to be grouped in different sections of the village. The branch that occupied the geographical center of the village was called the "Lotus" branch and was the richest branch of the lineage. The richest of the two landlords of Chen Village, as well as two of its three rich peasants, came from this branch. Social relationships in the middle of the village, where most members of the Lotus branch lived, tended to be, as some interviewees put it, "more complicated"[3] than relationships in other parts of the village. The word *complicated* in Chinese usage carries vaguely sinister connotations when applied to human relationships. It refers to particularistic loyalties that lead certain people to cooperate for their mutual benefit, often at the expense of people outside the boundaries of the special relationship. "Complicated relationships" come into being in rural China when loyalties based on kinship and friendship are invoked to secure special access to public resources that should be equally available to all according to official principles.

Traditional Confucian social ethics placed a sacred value on loyalties generated by kinship and friendship. This ethos coincided nicely with the interests of China's rural gentry. Wealthy people in rural China could afford to have more children than the humbler members of their communities. Having more children, they tended to have more relatives. Their wealth also gave them the time and material resources to cultivate extensive networks of friends. They could then very effectively use the loyalties generated by those relationships to extend their influence over their communities. In a lineage village, a landlord's closest kin would be those from the lineage branch to which he belonged; many of his most loyal friends would probably also be found within that branch. His influence would extend from the lineage branch throughout the rest of the village.[4] Such seems to have been the case in Chen Village before Liberation. The village's richest landlord seems to have used a circle of supporters recruited largely from among relatives and friends belonging to the Lotus branch of the lineage to extend his influence over the rest of the village.

After Liberation, the village's landlords and rich peasants were totally stripped of their power. They lost their property during land reform. They were classified as members of the Four Bad Types, kept under con-

3. For a brief but useful discussion of the Chinese term *fuza,* here translated as "complicated," see Martin King Whyte, *Small Groups and Political Rituals in China* (Berkeley: University of California Press, 1974), 85.

4. See Maurice Freedman, *Lineage Organization in Southeastern China* (London: Athlone Press, 1958); Hugh D. R. Baker, *A Chinese Lineage Village: Sheung Shui* (New York: Columbia University Press, 1968); and Baker, *Chinese Family and Kinship* (New York: Columbia University Press, 1979).

stant surveillance, excluded from all political activities, struggled against during most political campaigns, and in general shunned in public by all members of the community except their immediate families and in private by all except their closest kin. The particularistic loyalties the landlords used to extend their influence throughout the village were officially condemned as "reactionary" and "feudal."

Yet the networks of kin that once surrounded Chen Village's landlords still existed. The government could forbid its citizens to place any importance on the loyalties traditionally generated by such networks, but it could not obliterate the objective fact that certain groups of people shared more kinship relations than others. The densest networks of kin within Chen Village were to be found in the middle of the village; they were the remnant of the old Lotus branch of the lineage. Although most of the participants in these networks were officially classified as poor and lower-middle peasants, they seemed to be somewhat better off, on the average, than poor and lower-middle peasants from other parts of the village. Many of the benefits enjoyed by the members of the old Lotus branch of the lineage were quite legitimately gained. They had, for instance, more relatives in Hong Kong than peasants from other parts of the village, and they quite legitimately benefitted from money sent by these relatives. Moreover, they cooperated effectively in collective labor. But to some extent the relative wealth enjoyed by this part of the village also seemed due to the fact that many of the members of the old Lotus branch, in the early 1960s at least, were able to use particularistic loyalties traditionally imputed to kinship relationships to wrest what in the new Communist dispensation were considered illegitimate favors from some of the village's leading cadres. Peasants from other parts of the village could seize on this fact to justify their jealousy of the residents of the middle of the village, especially the members of the old Lotus branch of the lineage.

The "Pine" and "Bamboo" branches of the Chen lineage had once been grouped in the eastern part of the village but most of their members were now scattered throughout the community and manifested little sense of corporate identity. In general, residents of the eastern sector of the village were considerably poorer than residents of the central sector. No landlords or rich peasants came from this part of the community. The kinship networks of the eastern part of the village were not nearly as richly ramifying as those Lotus branch relationships that dominated the center of the village. The lives of farmers in the eastern village were considerably more precarious than those of peasants in the center of the village, although peasants in the eastern part of the village seemed to possess a stability, albeit a precarious one, that was denied to many of the inhabitants of the western part of the village before Liberation. The northeastern part of the village contained rather large clusters of middle peasants; the poor peasants from both northeastern and northwestern parts of the village farmed land that they had rented for a long period of time. The relative self-sufficiency of the families in this part of the village may have led them to relate to one another like the French peasants described in Marx's *Eighteenth Brumaire:* a mass of people formed by the simple addition of homologous magnitudes, "much as potatoes in a sack form a sack of potatoes."[5] In any case, to this day, the peasants of the eastern village mind their own business and attend to their private affairs. Recruiting cadres to lead the production teams located in this part of the village has been very difficult, and the eastern sector of the village has produced no important brigade cadres either. The productivity of the collective farming in the eastern village was the lowest in Chen Village, but the quality of the private sidelines farmed by peasants from that sector was the highest.

The western part of the village was the poorest of all. Small ancestral halls of the "Fidelity" and "Loyalty" branches of the lineage were located here, but members of these branches had long been dispersed throughout the community. Before Liberation, many of the peasants in the western part of the village were not even tenant farmers but simply hired farm laborers. When in the late 1960s, "speak bitterness" rituals were held in the village, it was the western village that provided the most horrifying tales of the misery of life before Liberation. There was the story, for instance, of the resident of the western village who had left the village to become a beggar; he starved to death and his body was mutilated by wild dogs. Another man, nicknamed "Cow Dung," came from such a poor family, it was said, that his relatives could not even afford a coffin for him—the most minimal ritual expression of filial piety—when he died. Not a few of the men in this part of the village were too poor to get married. The number of surviving children among those who did get married must certainly have been low. Few networks of kinship relations bound families from this part of the village together. The poor and lower-middle peasants from the western sector of the village were thus truly poor: poor financially and poor in social relations. Four of the five men from Chen Village who joined Communist guerrilla bands or cooperated closely with such groups before 1949 had come from this part of the village. The western part of Chen Village remained the staunchest supporter of the Chinese revolution in its community. Sixty percent of the village cadres came from this sector. The members of the western village engaged in collective production more vigorously than the rest of the village. Long-

5. Karl Marx, "The Eighteenth Brumaire of Louis Bonaparte," in *Karl Marx and Frederick Engels: Selected Works* (New York: International Press, 1968), 172.

yong's style of behavior, I will argue, was deeply influenced by his origins in the western part of the village.

Longyong's father had been a hired laborer who worked outside the village. Longyong was the oldest of two sons. Both sons followed in their father's footsteps until Liberation. The father died shortly after Liberation. Longyong's mother is still alive and lives in Longyong's household. She is a doughty old woman who still has a fierce mouth and is one of the sharpest tongued gossipers in the village. Longyong, perhaps inheriting some of her fierceness, was quickly recognized as a potential leader by the work teams that came to Chen Village to carry out land reform in 1951. He was an important backbone element during land reform in Chen Village and later travelled with a work team to a nearby village that, being largely composed of rich peasants, was proving very difficult to crack. He played an important part in making land reform a success there. Several years later, when the movement to form agricultural producer cooperatives started, he was put to work getting together a nucleus of poor peasants to set up the first cooperative in the village. Because of his proven leadership ability in this movement, he became a member of the Communist Party around 1957. During the Great Leap Forward (1958), Longyong was a leader of the village's Youth Shock Brigade, a group that tackled particularly difficult labor tasks because of its strength and vigor. At this time, Qingfa was Chen Village's Party branch secretary, Longyong's political superior. After the Great Leap Forward, around 1961, Longyong became the chief of the Chen Village brigade. He was still formally Qingfa's subordinate, but he was in a position to exercise a great deal of influence over the village and to challenge Qingfa for leadership. As brigade chief, Longyong was formally responsible for the day-to-day supervision of the brigade management committee. The management committee (consisting of a chief, deputy chief, economic management cadre, deputy economic management cadre, public security officer, militia chief, and a man who jointly held the posts of cashier and secretarial clerk) was in charge of supervising and coordinating the affairs of Chen Village brigade's ten production teams, of carrying out propaganda and public security work, and of directing the brigade's militia company. Parallel to the brigade management committee was a seven-member Party branch committee (consisting of a secretary; deputy secretary; a man who combined the posts of political, study, and propaganda committee person; an organizational committee person; youth committee person; women's committee person; and a secretarial clerk). Membership on these committees changed over time, but as a rule, all but one or two persons on the management committee were invariably also members of the Party branch committee. When wearing the hat of Party branch committee member, the leaders of the brigade made all major decisions regarding general policy for the brigade. While wearing the hat of brigade management committee member, they carried out the day-to-day administration of the brigade. Ultimate (formal) authority within the brigade fell to the Party branch committee, and the Party branch secretary was ultimately held responsible for everything that happened within the brigade.

Qingfa, as Party branch secretary, was formally Longyong's superior. But the extent of a person's real power within the brigade did not necessarily depend on his position in the formal chain of command. Longyong has never been Party branch secretary, but his skill, his personality, and the loyalty of many people, especially from the western part of Chen Village, eventually combined to make him the local emperor of Chen Village—but only after Qingfa had fallen. In 1964, Qingfa, formally head of the village and a superbly effective leader in his own right, was the village's strong man, its local emperor, and Longyong was only a troublesome contender.

Qingfa

Qingfa and Longyong had much in common: both had strong bodies, quick minds, and fierce personalities; they belonged to the same generation. In 1964, they were both about thirty-two years old. When they were young, they were quite close. As the people of Chen Village put it, "they wore the same pants." However, the fact that they shared so many qualities helped to throw their personal differences into sharper relief, and these same qualities made them both natural leaders. Their differences led them to seek power along somewhat dissimilar routes. In their struggles for power, they tended to emphasize those aspects of their characters that appealed to different conceptions of what a good leader's life and work should be. Thus their personal struggles both reflected and focused two visions of life within Chen Village and two sets of possibilities for its future development.

Like Longyong, Qingfa was a first-rate farm laborer. Though about five inches shorter than Longyong, he was almost as strong. To his physical strength was added an enormous amount of stamina and dexterity. He was the third or fourth best farm worker in the village. Like Longyong, he had no formal education and was almost completely illiterate; also like Longyong, he had an extremely keen mind by all accounts. Our interviewees were deeply impressed by the way both he and Longyong could give long, coherent, and detailed reports about what transpired at higher level cadre meetings without having taken any notes. Of the two, Qingfa was considered somewhat more articulate than Longyong, "a really smooth talker." Qingfa's career, like Longyong's, demonstrates his shrewd perception of personal strengths and weaknesses among the Chen villagers and a considerable talent for both planning and plotting.

Qingfa's nickname was "Hot Sauce." The nickname pointed to the intensity of his personality. Like Longyong he had a volatile temper ready to explode at appropriate moments into controlled but fearsome rage. Unlike Longyong, however, he was willing on occasion to add physical assault to his cursing and blustering. On several occasions, he is reported to have slapped and punched people whom he felt had stepped out of line.

While Longyong's fierce personality inspired respect—albeit a sometimes resentful respect—along with fear, Qingfa's fierce personality provoked a bitter scorn because his severity toward others was not matched by a similar sternness towards himself. Here was one of the fundamental differences between the two men. Longyong's fierceness was an encompassing force that shaped both his public and his private life: he was hard on the villagers, he was hard on his family, he was hard on himself; whatever he did, he did with a ferocious single-mindedness. But Qingfa, as certain interviewees put it, was somewhat "complex."

Longyong scared away would-be friends. Qingfa had many friendly relationships: he very much enjoyed getting together with a large circle of friends for meals and relaxed talk. Longyong lived in a small, run-down house and ate meager food. Qingfa liked comfort. His house was spacious and relatively well furnished; he ate plenty of chicken, duck, and pork. If for whatever reason, Longyong did not work for a day, he was scrupulous about not accepting work points for that day even though, because of his position, no one would deny him work points if he wanted them. Qingfa had no such scruples, so that his work-point totals were always higher than Longyong's. He tended his private plot more carefully than Longyong. Unlike Longyong, he had a substantial source of income from relatives in Hong Kong. Furthermore, he seems to have supplemented his income with "gifts" from friends in the village in return for favors.

People felt that Qingfa was better "able to handle human relations" (*hui zuo ren*) than Longyong: that is, he was more willing and able to engage in the exchanges of favors, accompanied by appropriate expressions of gratitude and graciousness, that have traditionally formed such an important part of the fabric of personal relations in China. Those who had benefitted—or might potentially benefit—from such relationships with Qingfa, felt something reassuringly familiar in the character of the man. Those who felt only his harshness found plenty to resent.

Like Longyong, Qingfa had a wife who was a political asset rather than a liability. She was a rather homely woman of good class background from a village located within the traditional marketing region of

Chen Village whose older brother was a cadre in her home village. Qingfa's wife was a diligent worker who devoted more time than most women to collective labor. She was not fond of gossip and maintained correct, if somewhat distant, relationships with other women in the village. Her relationship with her husband was smooth and cooperative. An older sister of hers also married into the village, and her husband was the head of Qingfa's production team in 1964.

Like Longyong, Qingfa's official class status was that of poor peasant. Qingfa's social background, however, was significantly different from Longyong's. Qingfa came from the middle part of the village and was a member of the rich Lotus branch of the Chen lineage. His grandfather was a well-to-do landlord who had two sons. The oldest son became one of the two landlords of Chen Village and was now one of the politically stigmatized Four Bad Types. The other son, Qingfa's father, might also have been one of Chen Village's landlords, except for personal misfortune. By the early 1940s he had wasted all of his resources on opium and gambling; both he and his wife died an early death. Qingfa, the only son, was barely a teenager when his parents died, but he failed to obtain any significant help from his landlord uncle. He had to beg for food and shelter and was finally able to make a meager living by hiring himself out to tend his landlord uncle's water buffalo. By the late 1940s, he was so bitter at his fate and so desperate that he joined a band of Communist guerrillas operating in the hills behind Chen Village. But after only a few months, he left the guerrillas (his detractors said it was because he found the life too arduous) and returned to Chen Village, though continuing to maintain contact with them. During land reform, he was classified as a poor peasant and worked enthusiastically and capably with the Communists. He became a member of the Young Communist League and in 1953 became a Communist Party member and the Young Communist League branch secretary. In the Great Leap Forward, he became Party branch secretary.

Unlike Longyong, then, Qingfa belonged to a complicated network of close relatives that included the richest members of Chen Village prior to 1949. He seems to have been sufficiently bitter about the lack of help afforded his family by his rich kin to have been willing to struggle against his kin during land reform and to have supported the harsh political controls that made landlords and rich peasants permanent outcasts in their home village. But in the early 1960s he found it convenient to make use of the network of kin to which he belonged to fashion a web of loyal supporters and, incidentally, to acquire some benefits for himself.

In the retrenchment following the Great Leap Forward, Chen Village brigade was divided into ten production teams. Each team consisted of about twenty-five neighboring households (about 125 people in all). The teams were the basic units of collective ownership and management in the Chinese countryside. Each team owned its own land and major farming tools. Each team's management committee decided which team members were to do which type of work and coordinated the labor of the team's workers. Each team member received work points according to his or her contribution to the team's collective production. After each team paid its taxes, sold its quota of grain to the state for an artificially low price set by the state, and reinvested a portion of its product, the team's net profit was divided among the team members in accordance with the number of work points they had earned. The better the land a team owned and the more efficiently organized it was, the higher the value of its work points.

When the production teams were formed (around 1961), each team was supposed to be given the same amount and the same quality of land. But Qingfa, in charge of the distribution process, cheated in favor of the members of the Lotus branch of the lineage. The village's land was divided into a number of different grades, ranging from fertile paddy land near the village to only marginally arable land located in mountain valleys up to three hours walk from the village. Each grade of land was divided into ten roughly equal portions. Because of the complexity of the village's topography, however, it was not possible to make every portion exactly equal to the others. So a lottery was set up to determine which portions of land each team would receive. Qingfa rigged the lottery so that team no. 6 got most of the best portions of land. Team no. 6 was located in the middle of the village; most of its members belonged to the Lotus branch of the lineage.

Qingfa's trickery did not constitute a major swindle. It enabled team no. 6 to come out only slightly ahead in the land allocation. But it was a gesture of loyalty toward his kinfolk, a gesture that made perfectly good sense in terms of a traditional ethos that stressed the importance of kinship ties. Members of team no. 6—especially Qingfa's relatives, but also those team members who were not directly related to him—could be expected to reciprocate by being especially helpful to Qingfa. The most important kind of help they could give him was political.

They could help Qingfa do his job well and hence look good to his political superiors. As the person in charge of the affairs of a production brigade in the early 1960s, Qingfa had a problem: although he was responsible to superiors at the commune and county seats for maintaining law and order in his brigade, for assuring that production quotas were met, and for laying the foundations for brigadewide development, he had only meager resources for carrying out his responsibilities. Each production team was economically self-sufficient, and each production team's leadership controlled the management of its collective labor and the distribution of its collective wealth. The brigade administration was funded by a small tax levied on each of the teams and had barely enough money to pay the salaries of its cadres. The brigade administration had no economic leverage to enforce compliance with its policies. As a cadre in another part of southern China is reported to have complained at this time: "If there is not rice in your hands, even the chickens will not come to you."[6] Since Qingfa could not exert any regular economic leverage over the village, it was very useful to him to have the loyalty of a corps of kin and friends whom he had helped, when given the opportunity, with small favors. He could count on the members of production team no. 6 to back him up if he proposed a mildly controversial program for village economic development. Here were people who might support him if he had to call a meeting to criticize political offenders in the brigade. Here were people from among whose ranks he could recruit new Party members who would be loyal to him.

Moreover, once Qingfa had discreetly established an example of patronage politics by aiding his kinsmen and neighbors in team no. 6, he in effect served notice that he was open to extending some patronage to other segments of the village. He helped some production team heads by overlooking instances when they gave friends or relatives in their teams special favors, such as favorable work assignments, in return for small gifts or for loyal cooperation. Qingfa thus brought some moral leverage to bear on team cadres in various parts of the village and compensated even more for his lack of economic leverage. He seems to have done this especially with respect to team cadres from the eastern part of the village. Starting from his relatives in production team no. 6, Qingfa thus judiciously used patronage politics to build up a network of influence that enabled him to meet his official responsibilities.

Besides using patronage to increase his effective power over the brigade, Qingfa could also not resist the temptation to use it to increase his wealth. In the early 1960s, he accepted money on at least one occasion from a family to allow it to leave for Hong Kong illegally. And he ate many tasty meals offered by various peasants in return for small favors.

Qingfa thus won the loyalty of a substantial following in the village by favoring it with sympathetic understanding and modest largess. Toward those persons in Chen Village who were not a part of this following—especially toward many residents of the western part of the village—he displayed considerable intimidating bluster. Outside this circle of his friends and relatives there were plenty of enemies ready to condemn the moral principles implicit in his style of leadership.

6. *Nanfang Ri Bao* (South China Daily), April 2 and 8, 1962, quoted in John Wilson Lewis, "The Leadership Doctrine of the Chinese Communist Party: The Lesson of the People's Commune," *Asian Survey* 3, no. 10 (October 1963):17.

Qingfa, Longyong, and Chinese Communist Ideology

Both Qingfa and Longyong were generally committed to "following the socialist road." In 1964 at least, their differences did not involve a conflict over whether or not to faithfully carry out the general policy line formulated by the Party Central. The policy line of the early 1960s was a relatively liberal one, allowing for the reintroduction of private plots, private sideline production, and free markets in the countryside and making the small production team the basic unit of economic ownership, management, and distribution. These liberal policies were pushed to extremes in the area around Chen Village in the early 1960s, when they were so interpreted as to give groups of two or three households virtual control over a piece of land and freedom to manage production on that land to their mutual profit in any way they chose as long as they could produce the quota to be handed over to the team and eventually to the state. While greatly fostering individual initiative, this system increased economic inequalities in the countryside and stimulated the rise of private rather than collective thinking.[7] By 1964, however, Chen Village, under the direction of county authorities, was moving away from this extremely decentralized system to one that placed principal managerial responsibility in the hands of production team leaders and rewarded laborers according to a piece-rate system. Longyong and Qingfa both seem to have acquiesced to whatever policies were formulated by their political superiors. They did not differ at that time on how much "free enterprise" was to be allowed in Chen Village. The difference between the two men was not a difference between one "taking the capitalist road" and one "taking the socialist road."

Both men, indeed, were similar in their relative lack of preoccupation with policies formulated by the central government. They did not oppose those policies; in fact, they basically supported them. But the implementation of these policies was not what occupied most of their time and most of their mental and physical energy. Rather, they were both primarily concerned with increasing the power, wealth, and prestige of Chen Village. Chen Village, scorned, exploited, almost destroyed by more powerful lineage villages in its neighborhood before 1949, was to be made into a new socialist village. The socialism of Chen Village was to be a means for making it *new*—strong, respectable, and rich. Qingfa in 1964 was hard at work developing plans for the electrification of the village to be accomplished in 1965. Longyong spent much of his time going to the

7. For a discussion of how this policy line was implemented in rural Guangdong, see Ezra F. Vogel, *Canton under Communism: Programs and Politics in a Provincial Capital, 1949–1968* (Cambridge, Mass.: Harvard University Press, 1969), 275–87.

commune and county seats making friends and securing "connections"—exactly the type of corruption that he righteously abhorred
within his village—in order to get priority for the village in the allocation
of scarce building resources: cement for new grain-drying yards, lumber
and nails for new buildings. Marxist-Leninist doctrine was abstract and
complicated, especially for an illiterate peasant. The central government
was rather distant, and in the early 1960s it was not intruding itself very
deeply into local affairs. What was vivid for both Longyong and Qingfa
were the people of Chen Village, sharers of common memories, interests, resentments, hopes.

An intense concern for central government policy or a fervent desire
to understand the subtleties of Marxism-Leninism-Mao Zedong
Thought could bring few rewards to Qingfa and Longyong. If they had
harbored realistic ambitions of climbing higher into the state bureaucracy, such preoccupations might have offered potential rewards. But, especially because of their lack of education, the highest position they
could aspire to was that of local emperor of Chen Village. The economic
rewards of such a status depended on their success in transforming the
village into a flourishing community and on the villagers' recognition of
their contribution. The effective power they could exercise was to a large
degree contingent upon the amount of loyalty they could inspire among
the villagers. The political position, emotional attachments, and cogni-
tive horizons of both men closely linked them to their village and committed them before all else to the fulfillment of its collective hopes.

Those collective hopes were complicated, ambiguous, and usually
submerged in a welter of petty, private, conflicting hopes and interests.
Day-to-day life in the village seemed to involve constant squabbling over
who was to get how many work points, who was to be assigned to which
job, who would be allowed what small privilege, and so on. Villagers did
not often pay much explicit attention to the larger concerns of the village,
much less to the affairs of the Chinese nation. But beneath all of these
petty squabbles were some fundamental, shared commitments to advancing the collective wealth and pride of the village community and
some basic conflicts about how the benefits of that collective wealth and
pride should be distributed.

In the 1960s and early 1970s at least, the villagers accepted socialism.
Our interviews suggest that most poor and lower-middle peasants accepted it with some enthusiasm, grateful for the way their lot in life had
improved since the Communist takeover. Most of the rest were at least
reconciled to it; there was no realistic hope for a return to a completely
private economy. In a socialist village, individual material well-being was
closely linked to the prosperity of one's production team and of the brigade as a whole. Moreover, villagers' sense of self-worth was linked to

the glory of the village as a whole, to its prestige among its neighbors. The villagers were willing to work together for a prosperous and proud Chen Village brigade.

But who would pay the costs of such development and who would benefit from it? That depended on the basic structure of village society. Chen villagers did not hold formal debates on this issue. But, I contend, they did argue passionately about it, not by debating abstract ideas, but by criticizing concrete, vivid personalities. They debated the relative goodness and evilness of the political morality exemplified by leaders like Longyong and Qingfa.

Implicit in the contrasting moral stances taken by Longyong and Qingfa were two different visions of social reality and possibility in Chen Village. One was a vision of the village community as a hierarchically structured federation of families bound together by a common residence and a common ancestry and managed through the giving of patronage and the receiving of loyalty by a few relatively privileged families. The other was a vision of the village community as one big family composed of more or less equal members and managed with stern but righteous authority by a powerful head. The conflict between these two visions was not completely congruent with the struggles between various ideological lines taking place among the Marxist-Leninists at the head of the Chinese state, yet it was by no means irrelevant to them. Qingfa, because of the path he had taken to personal power, came to symbolize the first of these visions; Longyong, the second.

Qingfa, Longyong, and the moral discourse of Chen Villagers

In the Confucian tradition, morality was particularistic. One's moral obligations to others were defined by their positions within one's network of personal affiliations. In Confucian moral discourse, the configuration of Chinese society was, as the great Chinese anthropologist Fei Xiaotong expressed it, "like the rings of successive ripples that are propelled outward on the surface when you throw a stone into water. Each individual is the center of the rings emanating from his social influence. Wherever the ripples reach, affiliations occur. The rings used by each person at any given time or place are not necessarily the same."[8] Fei illustrated the par-

8. Fei Xiaotong, "Chinese Social Structure and its Values," in *Changing China: Readings in the History of China From the Opium War to the Present*, ed. J. Mason Gentzler (New York: Praeger, 1977), 211. Originally published as *Xiangtu Zhongguo* (Rural China) (Shanghai, 1948). I am indebted to Professor Gentzler for pointing this article out to me.

ticularistic nature of this system by showing how it applied to kin-ship relations:

> The most important kinship relations in our society have the characteristics of these ripples of concentric circles formed by throwing a stone. Kinship relations are social relationships based on the facts of birth and marriage. The network formed by birth and marriage can emanate outward to include an infinite number of persons, past, present, and future. . . . This network, like a spider's web, has a center, which is oneself. Every one of us has such a web of kinship relations, but no web covers the same people as another. The people [in a society of this kind] can use the same system to identify their kin relations, but they share only this system. A system is an abstract configuration, a conceptual category. When we apply this system to iden-tify actual relatives, those recognized by each person are different. . . . It is impossible for any two people in the world to have the exact same relatives. Brothers of course have the same parents, but each has his own wife and children. Consequently, the network of social relations formed by the af-filiations of kinship relations is particularistic. Every network has a "self" as center, and the center of each and every network is different.[9]

In such a particularistic configuration, the nature of one's moral obli-gations to another depended on the precise nature of one's relationship to the other: for instance, a son's obligations to his father were different from a father's obligations to his son. And the intensity of one's obliga-tions depended on the closeness of the relations. As Fei described it, the further the ripples of one's social relations were propelled, the fainter they became.[10] Thus, one's obligations to immediate family members were more intense than obligations to distant kin.

Yet the network of personal relations that defined the sphere of one's closest loyalties was, as Fei said, highly "elastic." Thus, for example, the range of people whom one could consider as belonging to one's family could vary enormously. As Fei observed, if a friend in England or Amer-ica wrote a letter saying that he was going to "bring his family" to visit, the recipient knows very well who will be coming with him. But "in China, although we frequently see the phrase 'Your entire family is in-vited,' very few people could say exactly which persons really should be included under 'family.'"[11] A wealthy, powerful person may include in his family anyone who is related in any way. But with a reversal of for-tune, one's family could shrink to a very small group. At the extreme, said Fei, "it can be like Su Qin (an impoverished itinerant scholar of the War-ring States period) returning home a failure: 'His wife did not consider

9. Fei, "Chinese Social Structure," 211–12.
10. Fei, "Chinese Social Structure," 213.
11. Fei, "Chinese Social Structure," 211.

him her husband and his elder brother's wife did not consider him her brother-in-law.'"[12]

Relations to kin were the most morally significant of the relationships celebrated in the Confucian tradition, but they were by no means the only significant relationships. Relations to neighbors, to friends, to teachers, and to political authorities were also considered important. But the particularistic ties of kinship provided the dominant metaphor through which the character of other morally significant relationships was conceived: thus, for instance, an imperial magistrate was supposed to be like a "father and mother" to his subjects. Like family ties, these other morally significant relationships were seen as a kind of elastic sphere that could expand and contract according to circumstances. Thus, for example, the size of the neighborhood to which one owed close loyalties could vary greatly. As Fei wrote: "The neighborhood of an influential family can extend throughout the entire village, while the neighborhood of a poor family is only two or three next-door neighbors."[13]

In traditional Chinese ethics, then, the size of the social sphere toward which one owed loyalty and from which one could expect cooperation depended in part on the amount of power and influence at the sphere's center. But the nature of the threats impinging on the sphere from the outside also played a role. Thus, for example, if a lineage village were under attack from outside neighbors, the whole village might unite in firm solidarity around its leaders, and the leaders might selflessly devote themselves to the welfare of the village as a whole, rather than simply to a small segment of it. Under such circumstances the nature of a leader's claims on his community members might also change from what it was in times of peace. In peaceful circumstances, a village leader's power—his ability to bring into being and secure the cooperation of a wide circle of influence—would probably be determined by his wealth, which could produce the resources to cement affiliations through patronage. In times of threat, a leader's power might derive from his ability effectively to mobilize people to meet the threat.[14]

A Confucian mode of moral reasoning, then, could indeed lead people to conclude that they ought to sacrifice the narrow, "private" interests of their immediate families and closest neighbors for the good of a larger public group. But it could also be used to rationalize sacrifice of the larger group to the smaller.

12. Fei, "Chinese Social Structure," 212.
13. Fei, "Chinese Social Structure," 212.
14. See Frederic Wakeman, Jr., *Strangers at the Gate: Social Disorder in South China, 1839–1861* (Berkeley: University of California Press, 1966), 106–16.

> Sacrificing the family for oneself, sacrificing one's lineage for one's family—this formula is an actual fact. Under such a formula what would someone say if you called him self-centered? He would not be able to see it that way, because when he sacrificed his clan, he might have done it for his family, and the way he looks at it, his family is the common interest. When he sacrificed the nation for the benefit of his small group in the struggle for power, he was also doing it for the common interest—for the common interest of his small group. . . . Common interest [*gong,* also translatable as "public interest"] and selfishness [*si,* also translatable as "private interest"] are relative terms; anything within the circle in which one is standing can be called common."[15]

In contrast to Confucian morality, Western moral discourse is universalistic. One's moral obligations toward another are defined by general norms equally applicable to all persons of a particular category.

> In some ways Western society bears a resemblance to the way we bundle kindling wood in the fields. A few rice stalks are bound together to make a handful, several handfuls are bound together to make a small bundle, several small bundles are bound together to make a larger bundle, and several larger bundles are bound together to make a stack to carry on a pole. Every single stalk in the entire stack belongs to one specific large bundle, one specific small bundle, and one specific handful. Similar stalks are assembled together, clearly classified, and then bound together. In a society these units are groups. . . . The group has a definite demarcation line. . . . Members of the group are partners, all sharing the same relation to the group. If there are subdivisions or ranks within the group, these are stipulated in advance.[16]

In such a universalistic group configuration, the nature of one's moral obligations to another is determined by what specific common groups one belongs to and by what norms govern the conduct of everyone in such groups. Thus, for example, one belongs to a family, which is conceived of as a specific, clearly bounded group whose members share certain common obligations, and one belongs to a nation and shares certain clearly defined rights and duties with other citizens of the nation. Sometimes one's private duties to one's family conflict with one's public duties towards one's nation, but for the most part, family duties and civic duties are of a different sort. Accordingly, for example, a public official is expected to abide by the provisions of his country's constitution, not by the norms defining his duties to his family.

15. Fei, "Chinese Social Structure," 213.
16. Fei, "Chinese Social Structure," 211.

Like Western morality, official Chinese Communist morality—in both its Maoist and Liuist versions—is universalistic. General norms define the responsibilities incumbent on Chinese citizens, Party members, commune members, members of a production brigade or production team. Such public responsibilities are fundamentally different from one's responsibilities to private groups, such as one's family. One should not allow responsibilities to such private groups to interfere with one's disciplined commitment to public duties.

Official Communist universalistic morality has not, however, totally replaced traditional Chinese particularistic morality. Both Qingfa and Longyong guided and justified their public action according to the logic of a particularistic morality rooted in the Confucian moral tradition. But each of them represented a different style of particularism, with different implications for the regulation of social life within Chen Village.

We can gain an appreciation for the way in which the moral stances of Qingfa and Longyong differed from each other and from official Communist morality, and for the social implications of those differences, by reflecting on the language Chen villagers use when addressing one another. Like people throughout rural China, the villagers commonly called each other by their given names plus an appropriate kinship term: "Uncle," "Big Brother," or "Little Brother" for men and "Big Sister," "Little Sister," or "Grandmother" for women. Thus Qingfa was customarily called (by people outside of his immediate family) "Uncle Qingfa." But besides referring to one another by appropriate kinship terms, the Chen villagers called each other by a host of colorful nicknames. Some of these nicknames were bestowed playfully and referred to physical or psychological traits that were the object of friendly jesting: one person, for example, was nicknamed "The Crab" because he walked with a peculiar sideways gait; another was called "The Big Bowl" because he was short and squat; one of the more vocal women of the village was dubbed "The Gong" because of her loud mouth. Longyong was "Old Pockmark" and Qingfa, "Hot Sauce."

To address people as if they were kinfolk, when they are at best only very distantly related, is to do them the courtesy of suggesting that you would treat them like close relatives. But a moral imagination shaped by such an idiom will tend to differentiate carefully between obligations to closer and to more distant "relatives." If the morality of village leaders were shaped by such an idiom of kinship, it would tend to create a stratified community in which wealth and power were distributed according to the position of villagers in the personal networks of the village's leaders.

But the village is not simply an intricate web of kinship relations. It is a community of individuals who through constant interaction and mutual evaluation develop a shared tradition and a common set of mutual understandings. The way villagers give and receive nicknames substantiates this. Nicknaming points to the fact that villagers view each other not just in terms of their occupation or status in an extended kinship system but in terms of familiar knowledge of each other achieved through constant face-to-face interaction. Nicknaming apprehends each person in his or her uniqueness and evaluates him or her in terms of a particular style of behavior. Nicknames change over time as personalities develop and communal histories unfold. Nicknaming springs from a process of social discourse by which villagers recognize that they all occupy a common zone of familiarity with shared traditions, interests, and hopes.

That common zone of familiarity could, as we have suggested, also become the focus of a Confucian moral imagination. One could—and sometimes should—care for one's whole community as if it were one's close family. If everyone in the village thought and acted in this way, the result would be a relatively egalitarian community united in a tightly disciplined way to achieve its interests.

But when should one treat one's whole village—or for that matter one's whole nation—as a kind of metaphorical extension of one's close family, and when should one treat it as a differentiated network of close and distant kin? When should one pay as much attention to the needs of one's distant neighbors as to those of one's close neighbors? As we have noted, there were no clear-cut rules defining these boundaries. In theory, a person who properly cultivated his moral sensibilities should intuitively know such things. But in practice, the wealthy and powerful members of Chinese society tended to interpret the demands of Confucian ethics to justify their social positions.

Traditionally, especially in times of relative stability and conditions of relative prosperity, lineage villages like Chen Village in South China were organized for offense, defense, and mutual welfare through the structure of loyalties imposed upon people by their positions in the kinship networks of the community. Through their connections with national elites, wealthy, well-educated members of the community—the "gentry"—were able to secure for the lineage what benefits were available from the state and at the same time to protect the lineage from the demands of predatory government officials. Within the lineage community, the gentry, by virtue of their power and skills, controlled the management of the lineage's common property and tended to appropriate many of the advantages of that property. The gentry used their power to provide minimal benefits for the humbler members of the lineage; but most of the benefits to be obtained from their wealth and power were channeled through their closer relatives. The closer the relatives, the more call they had on the gentry's largess.

In return for the assistance provided by their richer relatives, the poorer kinfolk were expected—indeed morally obliged—to give deference and loyal cooperation. Since an especially sacred mystique was attached to kinship ties—particularly to close kinship ties—the gentry were expected to conduct their political and economic business with their kin in a warmly ceremonious rather than in a crassly utilitarian way: they cemented their relationships with their closest associates by "wasting time" with them, enjoying relaxed meals and conversation with them, exchanging gifts of concern and expressions of gratitude. The gentry did not necessarily confine their helpfulness to kin. They might well develop affiliations with unrelated people who had shared similar education, with neighbors who shared similar interests, and so forth. They often clothed these affiliations with a ceremoniousness which suggested that they were like kinship relations. But a less genteel visage might be displayed toward unruly members of the community who were not closely related by blood or alliance: the circle of associates of a man of wealth and power often included a few thugs who could apply naked force to the recalcitrant poor of the community. The leader of such a community was like a powerful uncle who did not normally interfere in the household affairs of his relatives but who solidified obligations of loyalty from the families close to him by providing them with largess. In many respects, this is the role Qingfa came to play in the early 1960s.

Based on the interpretation of the Confucian ethos the gentry had used to extend their influence, Qingfa's political morality, if pushed to extremes and left unchecked, could lead to the type of stratified social order once dominated by the old gentry. There is no indication that most villagers wanted a complete return to such an order, and even if they had, the Chinese Communist government would not have permitted it. But many villagers did favor procedures and practices that made Chen Village a little more like a gentry-dominated lineage community than official Communist policy allowed.

Most of the formal trappings of the lineage structure of Chen Village have been eliminated by the Communists. The lineage ancestral hall has been turned into a school (which, interestingly enough, is what such buildings were often used for in pre-Liberation China when they were not being used for actual worship); the tables of the ancestors were destroyed during the Cultural Revolution; younger people barely remember the names of the lineage branches to which they belong.

Villagers do not seem overly concerned about the loss of the ancestor cult and other ritual trappings of lineage organization. A few old people, especially old women, still privately offer incense to the spirits of their ancestors, using incenselike mosquito-repellent coils; some people still ritually clean the graves of their ancestors on the Qing Ming festival. But I was impressed by how little evidence there was of such activity. In Chen Village, at least, most people seem to take the loss of the old customs rather lightly.[17]

But important remnants of the moral culture that supported the old gentry-dominated lineage still exist. Although Chen villagers do not want to revive their lineage in its past form, they do want their social life to be characterized by what they refer to as "humanity" (*ren dao*) expressed in relationships involving "the flavor of human feeling" (*ren qing wei*). The concern for "humanity" involves a regard for a dimension of life that cuts across the tasks of working hard to fulfill and overfulfill state production quotas, carrying out class struggle, creating more efficient forms of work organization, or developing social structures for a more egalitarian distribution of wealth. To have "humanity" means to be aware of one's roots in the past and to hope that one's life will be carried on in future generations of progeny. It means to respect, cherish, and be faithful to the ties that bind one to one's contemporaries by virtue of a common ancestry; to have sympathy for one's friends (who in a rural context often consist of one's relatives), show kindness and courtesy toward them, exchange favors with them; to be able to relax and enjoy good food and comfortable lodging if one can and share such goods on occasion with one's humbler relatives and friends in return for favors in accordance with their means. Such convictions about the importance of "humanity" and "the flavor of human feelings" remain deeply rooted in the minds of Chen villagers, even in the minds of the most politically committed among them. Once, Ao Meihua, my research assistant, had just given an especially impassioned propaganda lecture on Dazhai, the model production brigade in Shanxi Province, where people, it was said, worked fifteen hours a day, seven days a week, without any vacations, to make spectacular contributions to the state.[18] But Ao's roommate, a peasant girl who was one of Chen Village's model workers, said to her in the

17. In this respect, Chen Village seems somewhat more "secular" than many villages in Guangdong. According to William Parish and Martin Whyte, traditional religious rituals surrounding the events of the family life cycle are still frequently practiced in many villages in Guangdong. The traditional rituals celebrating lineage solidarity are almost never practiced, however. William L. Parish and Martin King Whyte, *Village and Family in Contemporary China* (Chicago: University of Chicago Press, 1978), 248–97.

18. Beginning in the early 1960s the Dazhai production brigade in Shanxi province came to be heralded as a model for all of China. Under Maoist sponsorship its Party branch secretary, Chen Yongguei, eventually rose to national political prominence as a member of the Chinese Politburo. Since the late 1970s, however, with the defeat of the Maoists by forces led by Deng Xiaoping, the official press has claimed that the success of Dazhai was illusory, and Chen Yongguei has been denounced as a fraud.

privacy of their home: "How can you really believe that stuff about Dazhai; that way of life just isn't human!"

In the cultural context of Chen Village, to desire to be "human" means to respect the particularistic relationships that the gentry manipulated in order to extend their influence over the village; to accept the right of a powerful person to bestow patronage, especially along kinship lines; and to acknowledge the need of recipients of such patronage to maintain loyalty to him. Being "human" also involves respecting the right of someone who has gained, through skill or good fortune, a little extra wealth or power to enjoy a modicum of good food and comfortable living as privileges of that good fortune, so long as one has not gained those privileges through the obvious exploitation of someone else and so long as one does not flaunt such privileges in an arrogant way. Those villagers who welcome the idea of a socialist economy, but who are nevertheless concerned about the preservation of "humanity" within such an economy, wish to see the wealth of the village more equally distributed than in the past and to have leadership in the village more genuinely exercised for the common good than in the past. But they also want to maintain a continuity with their past, with benevolent forms of nepotism and the giving and receiving of favors, even if these expressions of "humanity" weaken a little the egalitarianism of the village and slightly slow its economic development.

Those villagers who come from the middle section of the village with its rich networks of kin had, of course, the most to gain from an arrangement in which human feelings played an important part in politically significant relationships. Thus they supported it more firmly than people from other parts of the village, especially those from the western section of the village, who, bereft of extensive networks of kin, had the most to lose from an excessive emphasis on "humanity." But almost everyone shared this concern with "humanity" to some extent. And even the people who were most concerned about preserving this "humanity" were ambivalent about it and aware of its dangers. We shall see indications of this in the way many of Qingfa's supporters treated him during the crises that affected Chen Village in the latter part of the 1960s.

But the same moral logic that could lead one to favor a personal network of relatives and friends within a village community could also lead one to stand in solidarity with all members of that community against the outside world. Longyong encouraged this kind of moral logic.

When asked to enumerate Longyong's good qualities, several interviewees spontaneously said that one of his greatest virtues was that he "treated the village like his big family."[19] That is not an approved phrase

19. Although according to our interviewees this phrase does not seem to have been officially approved in the 1960s and 1970s, in the early phases of the estab-

in socialist China, and its free use could get one into political trouble. Longyong, and those who approved of him, would have said in orthodox Communist terminology that he was "working selflessly for the collective." But that phrase, "treating the village like one's big family," almost a slip of the tongue, captures, I think, an important element of Longyong's moral stance—an element that distinguishes it from orthodox Communist "devotion to the collective." Longyong acted toward the village like the patriarch of a big family, a stern and authoritarian patriarch who could guide a threatened family to achieve its interests over against the world.[20]

If consistently followed through to its logical conclusion, Longyong's moral stance would have led to a relatively egalitarian village united around a common task, in which status would be achieved through one's ability to contribute to that common task. It would have been the type of village community that once would have struggled against hostile enemies in clan wars. Perhaps it would also have been like the kind of community that angry men sometimes formed when they left their homes in times of social upheaval to form rebel bands of sworn brothers. The vision implicit in Longyong's moral stance is one that appealed to people who shared both a familiar knowledge of one another and common hopes and who felt a pressing need for dedicated solidarity to advance those hopes.[21]

This was a vision of social reality and possibility with special appeal to those villagers who felt an urgent need to respond to the new dangers and opportunities posed by a changing political environment and who felt that these circumstances demanded a renunciation of the gracious ideals represented by the "flavor of human feeling." People from the

---

lishment of agricultural co-ops, at least some official propaganda seems to have explicitly stressed the idea that one should think of one's collective unit as one's own family. Thus according to Judith Stacey, "In promotional literature on agricultural co-ops a team leader might be praised because 'He takes care of the whole team like a father.' And peasants were enticed to work together 'as a brotherly collective'" (Judith Stacey, "Toward a Theory of Women, the Family and Revolution: An Historical and Theoretical Analysis of the Chinese Case" [Ph.D. dissertation, Brandeis University, 1979], 209). In reference to this point, Stacey cites Jack Chen, *New Earth: How the Peasants in One Chinese County Solved the Problem of Poverty* (Beijing: New World Press, 1957), 76, 127. See also Judith Stacey, *Patriarchy and Socialist Revolution in China* (Berkeley: University of California Press, 1983).

20. For a vivid description and a sensitive analysis of the values governing the relationships between members of a traditional Chinese family, see Margery Wolf, *The House of Lim: A Study of a Chinese Farm Family* (New York: Appleton-Century-Crofts, 1968).

21. See Freedman, *Lineage Organization,* 114–25; and Wakeman, *Strangers at the Gate,* 117–25.

western part of the village were especially receptive to this vision. Traditionally cut off from the networks of kinship and friendship through which the landlords of the middle village had channeled their patronage, the people from the western village tended to see in the opportunities presented by the new Communist regime a chance to create a new political order in which they could play a powerful part. They were thus especially prone to rally behind a leader who appealed to everyone in the village to work together on an equal footing for the good of the whole community. But people from other parts of the village could also be enthusiastic about the vision of a tightly unified village order implied by the public morality of a Longyong—especially during times of political crisis.

For both the Maoist and Liuist versions of Chinese Communist theory, the idea of the village as a federation of households linked by exchanges of favor along the lines of kinship networks is too "soft" an idea of the nature of a socialist community. It deflects the course of the class struggle, subverts the achievement of equality, and undermines the consistent commitment to exact procedures necessary for efficiently regulating large and complex economic endeavors. But the idea of the village as a unified big family is too "hard" for official Communist ideology. For one thing, it suggests an authoritarian role for the leaders of the family that tends to subvert the orthodox ideas of collective decision making, participatory democracy, the "mass line." More importantly, the intensity of the solidarity implicit in the idea of the village community as a big family tends to set that community apart from and in opposition to the "national family" (*guojia*), the state. It fosters the deviation of "localism." To the degree that it must be based on a sense of crisis, it cannot lead to a steady commitment to the village as a whole. Insofar as Qingfa adopted a moral stance that fostered the image of the village as a federation of kinship-connected families, and Longyong a position that encouraged the idea of the village as a big family, *both* were wrong from the Communist point of view. But, under certain circumstances as we shall see, Qingfa's ethos might be made to resonate with the Liuist version of Chinese communism, and Longyong's with the Maoist.

Personal rivalry, political capital, and the ideological polarization of Chen Village

At the end of the Cultural Revolution, when Qingfa was being condemned and struggled against, his attackers used a little jingle to propagate a theory about the origin of the ideas that had guided his conduct: "The stem of the plant determines the fruit; the class of a man determines his thought." Since Qingfa's ancestral roots were in the landlord class, his ideas and behavior were allegedly marked by the ideas of that class. It may be true that Qingfa's public morality and the vision of social and political order it implied were partly shaped by his childhood experiences in a fairly well-off family. But that family had disintegrated through the failings of its head, and Qingfa had been refused any significant amount of assistance by his wealthy relatives. In the late 1940s, Qingfa seems to have been a genuinely bitter young man, eager to work with the revolutionaries. His background would hardly make him ineluctably sympathetic to a vision of social order traditionally congenial to China's rural upper classes. A more important cause of Qingfa's public moral stance was his assessment of the best way of fulfilling his private ambitions for power in view of his personal resources and of bringing order and prosperity to the village in the process.

Qingfa's political capital was in most important respects remarkably similar to Longyong's. Both men possessed a set of extraordinary personal qualities that Chen villagers considered prerequisites for a would-be leader: the physical strength, stamina, and skill of a first-rate farm worker; decisive, aggressive personalities; and extraordinary ability to conceive, articulate, and carry out systematic plans. Furthermore, each possessed an excellent official class status: poor peasant. The main difference between the political capital of the two men was the quality of their social relations. Qingfa possessed a network of relatives and old friends within the village: people who, having received a little largess, were predisposed to help him maintain order within the community and to cooperate with him in carrying out village development projects— people who could help him be an effective brigade leader. Longyong lacked such ties. But the absence of kinship connections and close friends could, under the right circumstances, itself become a political asset: Longyong could claim to be a politically "pure" leader.

The political situation prevalent in the early 1960s made it very easy for Qingfa to use his networks of kin and friends to build and consolidate his influence. He was the formal head of a production brigade at a time when the brigade level of administration controlled few of the village's economic resources and thus could bring little economic leverage to bear on its constituent production teams. It made good sense for him to bolster his influence by extending patronage along the kinship and friendship networks so handy to him. The villagers, tired of the collective tumult created by the failed Great Leap Forward, were perhaps generally inclined to see in his leadership style a welcome return to a "human" ethos.

Longyong, on the other hand, was eager to move past his political superior Qingfa and was ready to get whatever mileage he could out of his relative lack of compromising connections. In late 1964 a political campaign was on its way to the village that would eventually enable Longyong to use his political purity to gain the advantage over Qingfa.

The Socialist Education Movement, a political movement led by the Chinese central government to clean up cadre corruption in the country-side, brought Chen Village into contact with what the Communists called the "struggle between two lines" within their Party, a struggle between the different ideological positions and political policies that eventually became identified with Mao Zedong and Liu Shaoqi. An outside work team was about to link the contrasting moral stances taken by Longyong and Qingfa to the struggle between two lines within Chinese commu-nism. The fit was not perfect. But there was enough of a fit to initiate a process that would engulf Longyong, Qingfa, and their close supporters in a great deal of passion and pain. It was an affair of high drama—strong men having their personal struggles caught up and magnified by pow-erful social, economic, and political movements over which they had little control.

3 Making Moral Revolution

THE SOCIALIST EDUCATION MOVEMENT

Around the end of January 1965, a work team composed of thirteen "comrades" entered Chen Village. The villagers called all state cadres who did not belong to the village "comrades." It was a term used respectfully to acknowledge their power and to indicate their separation from the zone of familiarity that was the village. The work team had been organized in the Guangdong Province "special district" (an administrative unit encompassing several counties) to which Chen Village belonged and was part of a larger team that had established headquarters in the commune seat and sent branches into all of the production brigades of the commune.

Within a few days after the comrades arrived, they convened a mass meeting at which they officially announced their purpose in coming. The announcement went something like this:

> Chairman Mao has said: "Whatever you do, never forget the class struggle!" Having been liberated for so many years, you might have come to think that there is no longer any need for class struggle. After all, you might think, landlords and rich peasants don't have their property any more, and counterrevolutionaries are kept under tight political control. Thus your consciousness might have been deadened. But these bad classes and their thought are still around. The most concrete manifestation of this is the behavior of your cadres. Capitalist ideology still exists in cadres' minds, without their knowing it. Cadres are afraid of hard work. They are greedy. They desire pleasure. They have a bad attitude toward peasants. They don't work for the public good. They won't listen to the ideas of peasants. They take revenge against people if criticized. They advocate getting special privileges for themselves. They don't take part in manual labor. They eat the public's food and take the public's money!
>
> If your cadres change like this, this dictatorship of the proletariat will also change. Things will become like in the old days. Peasants will be swindled

and will suffer. Production will be poor. People will eat poorly, dress poorly, and constantly be swindled.

Really! Cadres are beating people, cursing people, arbitrarily cheating people. They're doing all sorts of vicious things. This is not democratic behavior. It's feudal behavior!

So we're going to have a campaign now to teach the cadres, to correct the cadres and straighten them out. We will make them follow the revolutionary line of Mao Zedong and be proper leaders of the people. We will have them make self-confessions. If they have done anything bad, the masses should make it known.

Ordinary peasants were uneasy; the cadres were filled with fear. A political tornado was about to hit the village and things would never be quite the same again. But what sense could anyone make out of the inflammatory message of the work team? A continuing class struggle, consciousness deadened, remnants of capitalist ideology, cadre corruption—what could those words and ideas *mean*? The rhetoric of these comrades implied a vision of social reality and moral obligation which was different from that customarily used by the villagers to make sense out of their world. The comrades in the work team were going to make many changes in the village, but the most important one they were going to attempt was the transformation of the symbol system through which the villagers thought about the nature of the world and the requirements of morality. They were going to try to teach the peasants a new language for moral discourse. In this chapter, I will try to explicate the structure of that language; describe the process through which it was taught; and show how that teaching tried, tested, and shaped the character of the village's political activists, especially Qingfa and Longyong.[1]

Mao Zedong and the Socialist Education Movement

The project to teach a new moral language to China's peasants had sprung from the concerns of Chairman Mao. In September 1962, at the Tenth Plenum of the Chinese Communist Party's Central Committee, Mao Zedong had made an impassioned plea: "Whatever you do, never forget the class struggle!"[2] In response to this plea, the Socialist Educa-

1. The course of the Socialist Education Movement is also described in chapters 1 and 2 of Anita Chan, Richard Madsen, and Jonathan Unger, *Chen Village: The Recent History of a Peasant Community in Mao's China* (Berkeley: University of California Press, 1984). The political dimensions of the campaign are described in more detail in that book, and a fuller account is given of the techniques the work team and villagers used to manipulate the power struggles occasioned by the campaign.

2. Quoted in Richard Baum, *Prelude to Revolution: Mao, the Party and the Peasant Question, 1962–1966* (New York: Columbia University Press, 1975), 2. My descrip-

tion Movement was launched. The work team came to Chen Village to bring this campaign to its inhabitants.

Mao's purposes in launching the Socialist Education Movement were political, economic, organizational, and ideological. Mao was worried about the emergency economic reforms and political retreats that had taken the rural heartland of China away from the path toward communism in the early 1960s. Carried out in response to the economic setbacks created by the Great Leap Forward, these reforms and retreats included the introduction of private plots and private sideline production, the decentralization of economic and political decision making to the level of the small production team, and the use of individual material incentives to raise the "productive enthusiasm" of China's peasants. Mao wanted this slide toward private economic enterprise stopped, and he wanted more emphasis given to collective production and political discipline. He was also concerned that the Communist Party and government were developing into rigid bureaucracies and were losing touch with the hopes and aspirations of ordinary people. Party and state officials were beginning to "indulge in idleness and hate work, eat too much and own too much, strive for status, act like [old-style, arrogant] officials, put on bureaucratic airs, pay no heed to the plight of the people, and care nothing about the interests of the state."[3] Mao wanted more flexible forms of political organization that would be both more responsive to the wishes of central authority and in better communication with the Chinese masses.[4]

But beyond these political, economic, and organizational concerns was an ideological one—an uneasiness about the way the Chinese people were coming to understand and appreciate the meaning and purpose of life in a socialist society. Mao's concerns for the purity of China's revolutionary ideology seem to have been provoked by what he considered erroneous thinking manifested in the discourse and conduct of some of the highest officials in the Communist Party and government. For Mao, authentic revolutionary virtue was acquired through self-sacrificing participation in class struggle. But officials like Liu Shaoqi and Deng Xiaoping seemed to believe that the time for such class struggle was over. The old ruling classes, such thinking went, had been vanquished. The Chinese economy had been collectivized for the most part. Chinese political life was dominated by proletarians and poor and lower-middle peasants.

---

tion of the political background of the Socialist Education Movement is based largely on the account given in Professor Baum's book.

3. *Hongqi* (Red Flag), no. 13–14 (July 1963):11. Quoted in Baum, *Prelude to Revolution,* 3.

4. See Baum, *Prelude to Revolution,* 3.

Massive political struggles were thus no longer needed to propel China further down the path toward economic and political development. Under China's firmly established socialist economic and political framework, the routine pursuit of self-interest by China's citizens would slowly but surely propel China toward the realization of the Communist utopia.[5]

But Mao seems to have been suspicious of such a vision. The class struggle, he tended to think, did not simply end with the collectivization of the economy and the establishment of a powerful state apparatus directed by a strong Party organization. The old ruling classes still retained enough influence to undermine the progress of the revolution. And a new class of complacent, self-interested bureaucrats who might slow or even stop the advancement of the revolution might be developing. The new class struggle was not simply a clash between owners and nonowners of the means of production. It was a clash between those elements in society that manifested a way of *thinking* and *acting* characteristic of the ruling elites of the old society on the one hand, and those elements that wholeheartedly believed in the values of a new socialist society on the other hand. Even more than the old class struggle that had brought the Communists to power, the new class struggle was a conflict not between economic interests but between moral visions.

In 1962, Mao seems to have believed that the most important area for launching this new class struggle was the countryside. In the countryside, Mao seemed to think, the "contradiction" between correct and incorrect moral visions manifested itself in the conduct of the leadership of rural production brigades and teams. Mao was concerned that the rural cadres who had taken charge in the years after the Great Leap Forward were manifesting ways of thinking and acting incompatible with his hopes for a new socialist society.[6]

It was not just a matter of some officials being corrupt, stealing public funds, taking bribes, disregarding official regulations. If it were simply a problem of some officials deliberately transgressing the generally accepted rules that defined their responsibilities, the solution would be relatively simple: dismiss the corrupt officials, punish them, and install new ones in their place. But the problem went deeper than that. Many officials were becoming corrupt (by Mao's standards) without even *knowing* that they were corrupt, without even feeling that they had done anything wrong. And ordinary peasants were not clearly aware that what their

5. See Lowell Dittmer, "The Radical Critique of Political Interest: 1966–1978," *Modern China* 6, no. 4 (October 1980):364–70.

6. For an overview of the problems of corruption developing among rural cadres, see Baum, *Prelude to Revolution,* 11–41.

officials were doing was wrong. Neither officials nor ordinary peasants fully realized that the class struggle was still continuing and that its main form was now *moral*: a conflict between those whose class consciousness and class stance were correct and those whose were not. Thus, there was the need for a Socialist Education Movement, to teach the peasants about the existence of this morally laden class conflict and to mobilize them to participate in it.

The Socialist Education Movement was launched by a document called "The First Ten Points," issued under Mao's direct supervision in early 1963. According to this document, the basic issue posed by the rise of corruption, sabotage by the Four Bad Types, and "spontaneous tendencies toward capitalism" in the Chinese countryside was an apocalyptic one: "Who will win in the struggle between socialism and capitalism . . . between Marxism-Leninism and revisionism?" Since the major obstacle to grasping class struggle in China's rural villages was poor cadre leadership, all village-level cadres would be required to "wash their hands and bodies" and become "clean of hand and foot" as a precondition to launching the struggle against class enemies in the countryside.[7] For this purpose, the first phase of the Socialist Education Movement would have to be the Four Cleanups campaign designed to purify cadres by exposing and correcting corruption and mismanagement in four areas: economic accounting, allocation and use of state and collective properties, management of collective granaries and warehouses, and assessment of work points in communes and rural production brigades. The major guarantee for ensuring conscientious implementation of the Four Cleanups was to be the active participation of the rural peasants in the cleansing process.[8]

For many Chinese officials, all this spelled great potential trouble. The apocalyptic ring to Mao's directives suggested that the campaign ought to have an extremely wide scope and be carried out with zealous ferocity. The call for mass participation indicated that attempts would be made to whip up the peasant masses to heights of emotional fury as had been done during land reform; as was sometimes the case in land reform, that fury could easily get out of control. Also, the idea that the class enemy might now manifest itself in the immorality of persons who came from objectively good class backgrounds gave the campaign an ominously uncertain trajectory. Practically anyone could be accused of having morally failed in some way or other. Exactly how was one going to draw the line between the guilty and the innocent? Thus, from the highest to the low-

7. "The First Ten Points," Article 10. Quoted in Baum, *Prelude to Revolution,* 22.
8. Baum, *Prelude to Revolution,* 24.

est levels of the Party and state bureaucracies, officials furiously maneuvered to control the interpretation and implementation of the campaign to avoid changing their favored policies and damaging their careers. The way the campaign was finally conducted in Chen Village, two years after the promulgation of The First Ten Points, was not necessarily the way Mao had originally intended. Richard Baum in his book *Prelude to Revolution* has analyzed the high-level political infighting among people like Liu Shaoqi, Deng Xiaoping, and Mao that shaped the actual course of the campaign. My colleagues and I have detailed the complex political processes that generated the ebb and flow of the campaign in Chen Village.[9] But for all the vast amount of politics that determined who was helped and who hurt by the campaign, the Socialist Education Movement continued to be an *educational* campaign, and the content of that education was essentially Maoist. Peasants were made to listen to Mao's ideas about the continuing conflict between good and evil in socialist China, and those ideas challenged and transformed their way of thinking about what was right and wrong.

Political Rhetoric and Peasant Discourse: A Confusion of Tongues

When the work team announced to the people of Chen Village the meaning and purpose of the Socialist Education Movement, what could that rhetoric have meant to the villagers? What sense could the villagers have made out of the idea that the campaign would help decide "who will win in the struggle between Marxism-Leninism and revisionism"? Practically none of them, not even the cadres, had ever read any of the works of Marx, Lenin, or even Mao. There was as yet no electricity in the village, and few people at that time had battery-operated radios. So (even if they had wanted to) the villagers could not even have listened to official Communist propaganda on a regular basis. "The struggle between Marxism-Leninism and revisionism" was an abstraction without content. "The struggle between socialism and capitalism" had perhaps a little more meaning. Socialism was collective agricultural production, carried out in production teams; capitalism was private production on one's private plots, or in one's sideline enterprises. The campaign would probably have something to do with restricting private production in favor of the collective. But how was this to be related to an ongoing class struggle? What, after all, was "class," and why should classes continue to struggle?

As noted in the previous chapter, the villagers were quite familiar with the term *social class*. It played a most important role in their lives;

9. Chan, Madsen, and Unger, *Chen Village*, chap. 2.

everyone in the village belonged to a class. There were poor peasants, lower-middle peasants (these two categories were for all practical purposes collapsed into one), upper-middle peasants, and the Four Bad Types: rich peasants, landlords, counterrevolutionaries, and "bad elements." These class labels had been given to adults during land reform, and children had inherited them from their fathers. One's class label was a major determinant of one's chances in life and affected whether one could enter the Communist Party or advance to a cadre position and whether one normally had to fear punishment for even relatively minor political mistakes. One's official class status even determined whether one had access to the best available medical care, whether one's children could take advantage of the best available opportunities for education, and whether they would have available to them a wide range of possible marriage partners. Social class was a familiar and important item in the villagers' vocabulary.

But an idea takes its meaning from its position in a complex universe of discourse. And when the villagers talked about class, they placed the term in a different universe of discourse than that represented by the government's official ideology. To put it another way, the villagers' ideas about class were part of a vision of reality and society different from the government's official view.

In the official ideology adopted by the members of the work team, class struggle was the key to understanding the sweep of human history. The dominant metaphor for social life was that of a titanic military struggle. The opponents in this struggle were classes. Classes were like great, modern armies. Like a modern army, a class army was knit together like a huge machine composed of masses of individual parts working together in a complex division of labor toward common ends. An individual's ultimate worth was measured by his contribution to the goals of his class. Thus Lei Feng, the humble People's Liberation Army soldier who in the mid-1960s was lionized as a revolutionary saint, had written that all he wanted was to perform well his task of being a small screw in the great locomotive of the revolution.[10]

People became members of opposing classes because of their interests and ideals. Before Liberation their interests and ideals had been shaped by their relationship to China's system of production, so that owners of the means of production had interests and ideals significantly different from those of nonowners. But with collectivization, the system of pro-

10. For an account of the campaign to emulate Lei Feng, see Mary Sheridan, "The Emulation of Heroes," *The China Quarterly*, no. 33 (1968):47–72. The quote about being a screw in the locomotive of the revolution is found in *Excerpts from Lei Feng's Diary* (Beijing, 1964).

duction became mostly socialized, and the differences between owners and nonowners diminished. Now there were just individuals who because of their past histories would tend to have different interests and ideals and could thus be presumed to enlist on one side or the other in the great war between the classes. Final victory would be a long time in coming, but it would ultimately belong to the union of proletarians and poor and lower-middle peasants. The reason for this was that the good classes possessed virtue the other classes lacked. Workers and poor and lower-middle peasants were ready selflessly to sacrifice themselves to their cause. People in the bad classes were motivated only by selfish interests and therefore could never create the kind of fighting machine capable of ultimate victory.

Just because someone's historical background gave him a good class label, did not mean, however, that he would automatically possess the moral virtue needed to be a good fighter for his class. People who came from proletarian or poor peasant backgrounds could be seduced by the "sugar-coated bullets" of the class enemy. Their minds could be clouded by the desire for personal well-being, and they could retard or even betray the historical progress of their class. They might even secretly work for the interests of the enemy class. One could tell if a person who purported to be fighting for the true interests of workers and peasants was really doing so by observing his behavior. Mao had laid down standards of conduct in essays like "Serve the People," "In Memory of Norman Bethune," and "The Foolish Old Man Who Moved the Mountains." These essays authoritatively defined a code of absolute, disciplined, persevering self-sacrifice for the good of the revolution. Authoritative commentaries on Mao's Thought operationalized such lofty ideals into norms governing the conduct of persons performing specific functions in the great task of class struggle. Thus cadres were supposed to work hard at their tasks, be impartial, refuse to use their public posts to pursue private purposes, be intimately in touch with the ordinary "masses," and so forth. A person's worth, like that of a good soldier, was determined by how effectively he contributed to the historical mission of the proletarian and poor and lower-middle peasant classes—how good a screw he was in the great locomotive of the revolution.[11]

11. This summary of Mao's ideas on class warfare is based on such analyses as: Stuart Schram, *The Political Thought of Mao Tse-tung* (New York: Praeger, 1969); Benjamin Schwartz, "Modernization and the Maoist Vision: Some Reflections on Chinese Communist Goals," *The China Quarterly*, no. 21 (1965):3–19; and Schwartz, "The Reign of Virtue: Some Broad Perspectives on Leader and Party in the Cultural Revolution," *The China Quarterly*, no. 35 (1968):1–17; Maurice Meisner, "Utopian Goals and Ascetic Values in Chinese Communist Ideology," *Journal of Asian Studies* 28 (1968):101–10; Frederic Wakeman, Jr., *History and Will:*

This vision of social history was different from that held by the residents of Chen Village. For one thing, the official Communist vision was much broader in scope; it encompassed the full sweep of Chinese history and indeed of world history. Chen villagers knew and seemingly cared little about the outside world and thought in terms of the past and future of their own community. Moreover, in the official Communist vision, the fundamental units of society were smaller than in the local vision: they were individual human beings. Each individual had certain ideals and interests. These may have been shaped by his position in the productive relationships of the old society; however, since production had been socialized, they were no longer being supported by ongoing social relations but by the individual's own moral character. Depending on their personal characteristics, individuals fought either for or against the historical mission of the worker and poor peasant classes.

For the villagers, however, the main units of society were ensembles of familiar relationships. Each villager was the center of a complex network of affiliations linking him to family members, neighbors, and friends, and he defined who he was and what he was supposed to do in terms of his position in those networks. As I have suggested, there were different ways of perceiving the obligations imposed upon one by those networks of relationships, but local moral discourse assumed that personal identity and moral responsibility were primarily defined in terms of a set of familiar relationships located at the level of the village. [12]

Thus, when villagers talked about how they belonged to various social classes, they did not think of themselves as participating on various sides of vast struggles that would change the shape of Chinese and indeed world history. For them, class designations were labels that outside government officials had pinned onto them and that gave each of them particular assets and liabilities in their quest to live satisfying lives within the village. Having a good class label was like having an extra supply of money in the old society. One could use it to extend one's influence within the community, to provide security and honor for one's family,

---

Philosophical Perspectives of Mao Tse-tung's Thought (Berkeley: University of California Press, 1973); and John Bryan Starr, *Continuing the Revolution: The Political Thought of Mao* (Princeton: Princeton University Press, 1979). It should be emphasized that Mao's Thought was a continuously evolving set of ideas; what I call "Maoism" in this book was Mao's Thought as officially promulgated in the 1960s.

12. In a study of the conduct of Hunan peasants, Vivienne Shue has drawn a similar contrast between peasant thinking, organized around personal relationship categories, and official Party thinking, organized around class categories. She has analyzed the consequences of these differences for peasant politics during land reform. Vivienne Shue, *Peasant China in Transition: The Dynamics of Development Toward Socialism, 1949–1956* (Berkeley: University of California Press, 1980).

and perhaps to help one's whole community to prosper and thus ensure that one's heritage would be gloriously remembered for generations to come. Class was a resource to be used in developing one's identity within the context of one's local community, but it was not the ultimate definer of identity.

With these ideas in mind, we can make sense out of the differences in outlook between the work team and the villagers about the moral failings of the local cadres. The work team said that good cadres were supposed to totally forget self-interests and dedicate themselves to the collective good. They were to identify with the collective interests of the poor and lower-middle peasants, eschew all special privileges, refuse to use their posts for personal profit, be humble, modest, and open to criticism from the masses. But, the work team contended, cadres had become selfish and greedy, accepted bribes in exchange for doing favors, and embezzled public funds. They had, moreover, become lazy and afraid of hard work and had assumed an insufficiently democratic style of work, refusing to listen to the masses' ideas and seeking revenge against critics. They were, in sum, more concerned with their selfish interests than with the public good. Thus, the cadres had to be "cleaned up" economically, organizationally, politically, and—most important—ideologically.

But villagers, using a Confucian style of moral discourse, tended to judge the character of their cadres in a somewhat different fashion. Take, for example, the matter of economic corruption. They expected cadres to profit financially from their posts by taking small gifts for doing modest favors, by using their official positions to gain access to scarce goods like building materials for one's house, and even by juggling account books to appropriate some public funds. As one of our peasant interviewees said: *Of course* cadres will use their positions to gain some material advantages; if they couldn't do so, what would be the point in becoming a cadre? This idea, that peasant cadres would certainly want to profit from their posts, was not simply a recognition of human weakness. There was a sense that it was natural for cadres to consider such matters, indeed, that within limits, they ought to. Ordinary peasants, after all, pursued narrowly defined personal or familial interests with unashamed gusto. They were constantly bickering with their neighbors over tiny matters, over whether so and so had cheated one out of a few cents here or insulted one in a tiny matter there. (Indeed, our interviewees who had been sent from Canton to the village were often in turn amused and disgusted by what they considered the crass, unreasonable selfishness of the peasants.) If ordinary peasants were so intensely concerned about their own and their families' welfare, how could they expect their local cadres to be fundamentally different?

Villagers certainly did not give cadres carte blanche to pursue private interests at public expense. Peasant interviewees were quite bitter about the ways in which some cadres had belonged to the "King Snake Party"—that is, were unredeemably lazy—and the "Big Eating Party"— that is, enjoyed the luxury of good meals at public expense. Interviewees bitterly told stories about cadres who had taken large amounts of public money and even used their power to extort sexual favors from village women. But most of these stories involved cadres whom they had heard about in other villages. Some Chen Village cadres were like that, but the most prominent cadres in the village seemed to be relatively good, even though they might not have measured up to the Socialist Education Movement work team's exacting standards of proper behavior. What this testimony points to is a different way of looking at economic irregularities than that of the official government ideology advocated by the work team.

For the work team the matter was relatively simple. A rural cadre was a leader of the poor and lower-middle peasant masses in their struggle against the class enemy. The entire value of his work was determined by how well he performed this public task and how closely he followed certain rules that specified how he was to handle public money. To see how good or bad he was, all one had to do was count the number of his deviations and weigh their gravity using these rules. But for the villagers, a cadre's goodness or evilness could be determined by more subtle, less easily quantifiable judgments.

As we suggested in the last chapter, for the peasants, a person's moral character was judged not by how well one adhered to certain hard and fast rules but by how one conducted oneself within a complex context of fluid human relationships. Thus, a cadre had certain responsibilities toward his family and other responsibilities for the public welfare of his production team or his production brigade. But there was no rigid line separating his responsibilities toward the public from those toward his family. In taking up a public post, a cadre ought not forget the welfare of his family. If he were willing to take on the extra work and anxiety that such a post entailed, then he ought to take advantage of that opportunity to help out his family's finances. He should not be so greedy as seriously to harm his production team or village, but he should not scruple at taking a little more from the public coffers than the impersonal government rules would entitle him. How much he should take would depend partly on how much effort he was exerting for his production team or brigade and how seriously his taking public funds would hurt other villagers. Moreover, a cadre had special responsibilities for the welfare of the members of his extended kinship group and of the people in his home neighborhood, and he should give particular help to such groups if he acquired a cadre post. Again, how much special consideration a cadre should give these groups would depend on how much special help they needed and how much giving such help would hurt the wider public. All these were matters for complex, intuitive moral judgments that had to be constantly revised in the light of specific historical circumstances. For example, in times of danger to the whole production brigade or to a whole production team, a cadre might have to subordinate the interests of smaller groups to those of the collective to a greater extent than he would during times of peace.

Being complex and intuitive, such judgments could be very controversial. Furthermore, as I argued in the last chapter, there was a strand of village thought that tended to hold that a really good cadre should be much more concerned about the village as a whole than about his own small family, that he indeed ought to treat the whole village as his big family. So villagers could have many different opinions about the morality of different cadres. However, their moral judgments were not simply based on adherence to a set of clearly fixed rules but on the quality of a cadre's conduct within the total context of his village's life.

The villagers' way of thinking about the morality of cadres' political and organizational conduct also differed from that of the work team. The work team said that cadres should work wholeheartedly for the interests of all poor and lower-middle peasants. This meant that cadres should, first of all, favor the poor and lower-middle peasants over other villagers. In any allocation of scarce goods, these peasants were to have precedence, and the other classes—especially the Four Bad Types—were to be systematically slighted. Moreover, within each class, each person was to be treated with total impartiality. Cadres should not play favorites. But the same principles of village thinking about economic morality applied to their thinking about more general issues of impartiality in politics. Cadres were expected to play favorites with people who were close to them because of the affiliations of kinship, friendship, or residential propinquity. Exactly how much the cadres should play favorites would depend on the complex configuration of a specific social context.

With regard to political attitude, the work team said that the cadres should be "democratic." This did not mean, of course, that cadres should simply do what the majority wanted but rather that they should follow "mass-line" principles of leadership.[13] They should be intimately in touch with the hopes and aspirations of the masses and formulate policies reflecting their true interests while at the same time fulfilling the

13. For a detailed definition of the "mass line" and a discussion of the use of the concept in Chinese Communist theory and practice, see Mark Selden, *The Yenan Way in Revolutionary China* (Cambridge, Mass.: Harvard University Press, 1971), 208–76.

spirit of higher-level directives. The key to accomplishing this was a proper attitude on the part of the cadres. The cadres had to prove to the masses that they were willing to listen to them. They should do this by encouraging mass discussion of the issues. If an ordinary poor and lower-middle peasant said something that a cadre did not like, the cadre should accept the remark with good grace. If ordinary poor and lower-middle peasants disagreed with a cadre, the cadre should win the peasant over with persuasion not threaten him with coercion.

But as one interviewee put it: "Cadres never speak to you softly, say, 'Do you mind doing this today?' . . . They always yell at you: 'You do this, you do that!'" In the eyes of the work team, this harshly authoritarian style of leadership was wrong. It went against the idea that a cadre was, above all, a representative of the real interests of the poor and lower-middle peasants of China. But the fact that practically all local cadres—at least all effective local cadres—adopted a no nonsense, authoritarian leadership style pointed to a traditional way of thinking about authority that differed from that of the Maoist ideology.

As I suggested in the last chapter, villagers did not see their leaders as simply representing the interests of combined masses of poor and lower-middle peasants. They saw them as maintaining the orderly pattern of social relations that made their community viable. At the heart of any viable community, according to traditional Chinese thought, is a set of authority relations, asymmetrical bonds between fathers and sons, husbands and wives, leaders and subjects. Those in authority have to insist upon their right and duty to command or the whole order of society might collapse. For the Chen villagers, a good village leader was not a democratic but a patriarchal figure. Like a good Chinese father who makes his family into a disciplined unit by establishing his authority, the good village leader shapes his collectivity into a flourishing community by maintaining a healthy respect for his right to command. Villagers thought it wrong for a cadre to be without empathy for his people. An interviewee, for example, spoke bitterly of a certain production team cadre who showed "no feeling" toward his team members by ordering them to do some unnecessary work during a driving rainstorm. And interviewees clearly disapproved of brutal behavior, for example, Qingfa's slapping some youngsters who irritated him. A cadre could clearly be too harsh, although one's judgment of *too* harsh depended on the circumstances. But it was considered natural for cadres to be authoritarian rather than democratic in their basic approach to the people.

Thus, in terms of the Maoist vision of social reality and moral order, the cadres of Chen Village indeed had an "ideological problem" rooted in the culture of the whole village. And this problem was the difference between not simply two static sets of ideas but two dynamic ways of thinking about the world—indeed, two distinctive visions of the world. The clash between the work team's rhetoric and the village's discourse created a confusion of tongues. How was the work team going to teach the villagers to understand and eventually to accept its new language for social analysis and moral discourse?

In traditional Chinese pedagogy (a type of pedagogy that continues in the schools and colleges of contemporary China), a student is first expected to memorize an important text and only after that to begin the lengthy process of trying to understand it. Similarly, the first stage of the political pedagogy of the Socialist Education Movement was to burn a dramatic social "text" into the memory of the villagers and then slowly to help them understand it.

Preaching the Word Through Dramatic Deed

The dramatic text for the villagers to ponder took the form of the Four Cleanups rectification campaign—a violent ritual of political struggle in which the villagers were led to condemn living symbols of the wrong ideology and to embrace symbols of the right one. In a rectification campaign, a corps of righteous leaders exposes political turpitude and brings the evildoers before the assembled masses of poor and lower-middle peasants. Then a series of "denunciation sessions" and "struggle sessions" begins.

Both denunciation and struggle sessions are intense political rituals in which members of a political unit condemn the behavior of a fellow member. Denunciation sessions are for minor failings: moral lapses that involve a "contradiction among the people," not a contradiction between an enemy of the people and the people. In a denunciation session, a person acting as a "master of ceremonies" goes in front of an assembly and announces that the purpose of the meeting is to criticize so and so, who by certain misdeeds has seriously transgressed the revolutionary line. Then the guilty person stands up and confesses that he has done wrong and that his misdeeds betray a lack of political awareness. The confession is very important. It builds the impression that there is indeed a clear-cut code of orthodox conduct that any rational person, even the wrongdoer, sees and accepts; that the wrongdoer deviated from this code simply because of a defect in his character, not because of any defect in the code; and that by an act of repentance and the support of the community, the wrongdoer can correct his character defect and become a good Communist. After his confession, the wrongdoer sits down in a front row of the assembly. He remains "among the people." Then members of the assembly "spontaneously" arise to criticize the wrongdoing and show how it goes against correct socialist ideology. (In fact the criticism is usually led by carefully prepared enthusiasts, but no overt cues are given to these people during the performance of the session. The form of this ritual is that of a spontaneous outburst of criticism.) At the end of the session, the guilty person faces the people again, humbly admits again that he has done wrong, thanks the assembly for pointing out his faults, and promises that he will never commit them again. (In fact, of course, it is quite possible that the wrongdoer feels no compunction at all and is simply making the best of a bad situation by going through some necessary motions. But the carefully constructed *form* of the ritual is that of a humbly repentant sinner returning to the path of righteousness.) Then the repentant wrongdoer sits down again among the people and the "master of ceremonies" summarizes the proceedings and dismisses the assembly. It is a terribly humiliating experience for the guilty person (all objects of such sessions are presumed guilty), but not as totally devastating as the struggle session.

In a struggle session, the guilty person is defined as an enemy of the people. His wrongdoing is so evil that he must be totally vilified, his reputation utterly destroyed. To open the session, the "master of ceremonies" whips the crowd into an emotional frenzy by portraying the person's crimes in as lurid a light as possible. From the crowd, carefully prepared activists scream out cursing cries of rage. Others get caught up in the enthusiasm and start yelling out as well. Then the accused is led out by the local armed militia; he does not come out under his own volition but is *brought* before the enraged people by representatives of its public order. He is often made to wear a heavy placard branding him a traitor, class enemy, and so on. He cannot look at the people but must bow his head in abject shame. (If he does not bow deeply enough, his militia guardians will push his head lower.) He makes a self-confession. No matter what he says, prepared activists yell out: "Insincere!" As an enemy of the people, he must be presumed so corrupt that he cannot reform himself by a simple act of will. He knows enough to be aware that he has done wrong: his (by official definition) half-hearted attempt at confession is clear evidence of the fact that even he is aware of the transcendent rightness of the code he has transgressed. But the fundamental rottenness at the core of his personality makes it correct and necessary for the masses to vent their indignation against him. People from the crowd "spontaneously" bring forth evidence that amplifies his misdeeds and shows that these are part of a whole despicable pattern of wrongdoing. Shouted curses fill the air. Sometimes strong young militiamen rise from their seats and beat the enemy of the people. This is not officially permitted, but depending on the purposes of the session it is sometimes informally encouraged and tacitly condoned. The guilty person stands facing the people during this whole ordeal (which can last several hours); he is an object of struggle by the people, not one of the people. When the session is over, he is dragged away in total disgrace. He has been symbolically destroyed.

Denunciation and struggle sessions have many political uses. They are helpful for punishing crimes, deterring deviance, doing away with enemies, and exacting revenge. Different factions in the Chen Village power structure tried to use the Four Cleanups for all of these purposes. But denunciation and struggle sessions, and the processes of investigation, mass mobilization, and explanation that accompany them, are not just instruments to be used for political purposes. They are rituals. As ritual, the Four Cleanups campaign was a phase in a process of socialist education aimed at teaching villagers to know and to love the vision of life and virtue promulgated by Chairman Mao.

To appreciate the importance of the various procedures the work team used to construct its public rituals, we must consider what had happened in Chen Village just before the work team arrived. In late 1964 an earlier phase of the Four Cleanups had taken place in Chen Village, a phase known as the "small Four Cleanups."[14] There was no work team to direct this earlier phase. Qingfa, the village Party branch secretary, had been in charge of it. In Qingfa's hands, the small Four Cleanups had been all too obviously a political tool, and because of this, its efficacy as ritual was diminished. Qingfa had orders to clean up bad economic, organizational, political, and ideological habits among Chen Village's cadres. He had to find a certain amount of wrongdoing and attack it or incur the displeasure of his superiors in the commune and county Party apparatuses. But he did not want to hurt any of the cadres whom he had relied on to build up his political "machine" within the village. So he first singled out a number of minor production team cadres for denunciation and struggle.

Most of these targets were warehousemen, cashiers, and accountants: the officials in charge of directly overseeing each production team's public wealth. (A warehouseman administered the team's granaries and handled the distribution of grain rations to the team members. The cashier disbursed cash to the team members. The accountant kept the books for each team.) These were posts that provided few official rewards for their incumbents. Many of these cadres therefore supplemented their almost nonexistent official rewards with "unofficial" ones, diverting small sums of money for private use. The temptations inherent in such positions were enhanced by the very casual way some of the minor peasant cadres kept their accounts. They were not used to systematic accounting proce-

14. For a general discussion of the small Four Cleanups, see Baum, *Prelude to Revolution*, 81.

dures and little effort had been made to train them. For instance, the accountant of team no. 4 did not use an account book. For many of the peasants, precise record keeping was neglected, not simply because it was a difficult habit to acquire, but because it was not considered important: methodical accounting was not as significant as showing good human feelings towards friends and relatives by helping them (and oneself) a little more here and there than impersonal mathematics would allow.

Such team-level economic officials were thus logical and relatively easy targets for the campaign. Their misdeeds fit the government's guidelines about what had to be cleaned up. Their carelessness in keeping proper accounts was irritating to many peasants, especially those who had not benefitted from such irregularity. Moreover, they were relatively hapless people. They were mostly young, not, it seems, terribly clever, and without large loyal followings of local supporters. Peasants could attack them without worrying that they could someday mobilize strong local support to make political comebacks and thus be in a position to revenge themselves on their attackers. So it was relatively easy for the Chen Village Party branch to mobilize popular support for struggles against these minor officials. Investigations of their economic irregularities were duly carried out, and they were forced to write self-confessions, subjected to brigadewide denunciation or, in extreme cases, struggle sessions, and required to pay back the money they were supposed to have embezzled.

Such attacks on minor economic functionaries did not, however, constitute a vehicle for the comprehensive moral education that the rhetoric launching the Socialist Education Movement said was necessary. The rhetoric said that China's progress toward socialism was in serious danger, that China's old exploitative ruling classes and their thought were making a comeback. But if the only thing wrong with Chen Village was the petty corruption of a few minor cadres, then in what sense was there a plausible danger that Chen Village would "change color"? Such a danger could exist only if moral rottenness had crept into the ranks of the village's leading cadres. If some of the village's top political officials had come to define their vocation so as to make themselves exploiters of the people and if the way they defined their political vocation might influence future generations of cadres, then the village would indeed face a moral and political crisis. So if the intentions voiced in the campaign's rhetoric were to be carried out, the conduct of some of the village's leading cadres had to be scrutinized.

Since, however, the village's Party branch committee was in charge of directing the campaign at this time, it was unlikely that the top leadership of the village—all of whom were members of that branch committee—would come under systematic scrutiny. But for appearances at least one member of the village's top leadership should be "cleansed." What followed was a simple power play. Qingfa, who was directing the campaign, took this opportunity to get rid of his rival Longyong.

Qingfa's position within Chen Village was still considerably stronger than Longyong's. Most of the members of the brigade Party branch had been personally recruited into the Party by Qingfa. Most of the cadres on the brigade Party branch committee and brigade management committee belonged to this group of Qingfa recruits. Moreover, Qingfa's careful fostering of good relations with his political superiors had paid off. He was a good friend of the Party secretary of the commune who is reported to have considered him one of the best Party branch secretaries in the commune. Thus, when Qingfa decided to turn the Four Cleanups campaign against Longyong, the latter had little chance.

Longyong was not without fault. At the end of the Great Leap Forward, soon after he had risen to a top position in the brigade administration, he had used his public office to obtain personal benefit for himself. Some lumber had been left over from the construction of a brigade meeting hall. Longyong, a newly elected cadre, had asked Qingfa if he could buy some of the surplus lumber to build a small kitchen for his house. Since lumber was in short supply in Guangdong, this was considered a significant (though not extraordinary) privilege. To use one's political position to obtain such a privilege was a clear transgression of the strict standards officially set down to guide cadre conduct. Qingfa not only had been sympathetic to Longyong's request but had taken Longyong one step further: he let Longyong take the lumber free of charge, perhaps hoping that Longyong would show him some deference in return.

Now, during the small Four Cleanups campaign, Qingfa used this free lumber as a basis for attacking Longyong. He painted the incident as a flagrant abuse of authority. Longyong was dragged before a struggle session, denounced and verbally abused, stripped of his post, and sent home in disgrace. When he went home he tried to hang himself. His wife stopped him and stayed awake several nights watching him for fear he would try to kill himself again. There was probably more to Longyong's attempted suicide than a despairing response to a world fallen apart. Suicide in China can be a way for a person who has lost political power and social status to get back at those who have stripped him of that power and status. By committing suicide, a person who feels that his demise was unjustified can dramatize the degree to which he has been wronged and bring shame on those who have caused his downfall. At any rate, Longyong was to use his attempted suicide in years to come for such a purpose. He made it a public issue, telling the villagers how Qingfa's perfidy and their ingratitude had almost caused his death. "You elected me to be a cadre," he would tell them, "and I worked as hard as I could for you; but then you turned against me, and if it were not for my wife, I would have killed myself." The suicide was a grim private ritual aimed at exposing the moral emptiness of the public rituals in which he had been condemned.

And there was indeed a moral hollowness to the rituals of the small Four Cleanups. They were full of sound and fury, but they signified nothing. It was too obvious that the campaign had been shaped by purely political rather than by moral considerations. The small Four Cleanups could produce a healthy respect for Qingfa's political prowess, but because it was so patently a power struggle, it could not generate a profound respect for Maoist political virtue. The demise of Longyong—and even the demise of the lesser cadres attacked during the campaign—could be seen simply as a lesson about the occupational hazards of being a cadre in rural China. Their humiliation was not an effective means of conveying the moral standards that rural citizens should apply in judging the conduct of their local leaders or, for that matter, of themselves.

About five months after the small Four Cleanups, however, the work team arrived and made the announcements with which I opened this chapter. The rituals of political struggle that they organized were called the "big Four Cleanups." These rituals led by the work team were similar in form to those of the small Four Cleanups: there were investigations into the habits of brigade cadres, the extraction of self-confessions, and finally the denunciation and struggle sessions. But the big Four Cleanups made a much more powerful statement about the meaning and purpose of life in socialist China than the small Four Cleanups had, because the work team was able to insulate the symbolic actions that formed the heart of the big Four Cleanups from the contamination of local politics. The big Four Cleanups did not appear to be simply an instrument in a local power struggle. A cynic would have had a hard time plausibly explaining it away in those terms. Thus the campaign had to be accepted as a vehicle for conveying an orthodox statement about what constituted a good life and a good society, a statement that had to be listened to, even if not accepted.

The work team achieved this symbolic insulation by practicing the "Three Togethers": living, eating, and working together with the poor peasant masses. The work-team members could have stayed in special guest quarters in the brigade headquarters. But soon after they arrived, they asked the brigade leadership which families were the poorest in the village. Then they went to the families indicated by the brigade leadership and made still further inquiries to find out if there were in fact any households even poorer than those. From among the poorest families in the village they sought households in which to "sink roots." One team member attached himself or herself (one of the work-team members was a woman) to a poor family in each of the ten production teams. If the family had room in its house to keep a guest (in most cases they did not), the work-team member lived in the family's house and paid for his or her lodging. If there was no room, the work-team member found a place to sleep in a nearby abandoned house. But in any case, work-team members paid for and ate their meals with the families to which they were attached. Sharing the food from a common kitchen defines one's membership in a household in the villagers' scheme of things. So the work-team comrades made themselves symbolic members of some of the poorest of the village's households. In the morning, the work-team members met together to prepare their work, but in the afternoon they went into the fields to labor with the peasants. They worked hard and well at farm labor—a fact that favorably impressed the peasants.

Practicing the Three Togethers served some important political purposes. It enabled the work-team members to gather a wealth of information about cadre malpractice from people who had benefitted the least from the current political system in the village. It also allowed them to identify potential allies in the struggle against the old political system. But the symbolic dimension of the Three Togethers was at least as important as its instrumental dimensions. By practicing the Three Togethers, the work team made a statement about its relationship to the village's cadres and to the style of leadership they represented. The work team showed the villagers that it was completely independent of the local cadres, thus in no way an instrument of their political purposes. And perhaps even more significantly, the work team put itself forward as an exemplar of a leadership style that differed fundamentally from the cadres'. The work team did what Mao had called for in his essay "Serve the People": it completely identified with the experience, hopes, and aspirations of China's poor peasant masses.

One of our interviewees described how the work-team members shared the daily life of the village's poorest peasants but were so simple and pure that they "did not even take a needle or thread from the masses." This phrase was not just a product of raw observation. It was from the "Three Main Rules of Discipline" formulated for the People's Liberation Army in the early years of the revolution, and it had become an element of Chinese Communist propaganda's official sacred myths that described the honesty of revolutionary cadres during heroic periods like the war of liberation and land reform. Through the Three Togethers, the work team linked itself to the heroes of the Chinese Communist Party's glorious tradition. More specifically, the work team linked itself to the villagers' memories of land reform. The Three Togethers were practiced in the days of land reform, when the Communist Party led the village's poor in struggles to break the power of the landlords and redistribute the village's wealth. Whatever misgivings the village's poor and lower-middle peasants may have had about collectivization, the Great Leap Forward, and other government rural policies of the late 1950s and early 1960s, they had few such misgivings about land reform. For the poor and lower-middle peasants, land reform represented the beginnings of economic security and political power. It was a cherished event. In land reform, the pillars of the old social order were overturned by the power of the masses organized by selfless cadres coming from outside the community. By practicing the Three Togethers, the work team invoked the moral aura of land reform and suggested that it was time once again for another glorious, morally redemptive struggle against the pillars of the village's new social establishment—an establishment that had betrayed the moral hopes generated by land reform.

As we have noted, the village's local cadres inevitably shared the particularistic moral habits accepted as natural by most of the village's population. Moreover, to run the village smoothly, they could not afford to identify only with the poorest of the village population; they had to respond to the interests of a wide spectrum of the community. Also, feeling responsibility for their families and at least some desire for personal gratification, the cadres had inevitably allowed themselves—some more than others—to take advantage of their positions for private gain. In contrast to the village's cadres, the work team seemed to be purely devoted to the class interests of poor and lower-middle peasants and totally loyal to the orthodox teaching of Chairman Mao. To maintain this aura of ideological purity, the work-team members refused to tell any of the villagers anything about what they had done before they came to the village. The villagers were not permitted to ask them where they came from or even what their given names were. The villagers could thus judge them only in terms of their rigorously moral behavior within the village. "To cut through steel," a popular political slogan in China said, "you yourself must be hard." The work team developed an image of moral hardness that enabled it to cut through the steel of the old moral structure of the village.

Thus, to the work team's words about the need to root out dangerous manifestations of capitalist morality in the village was added the dramatic example of its public self-presentation. The villagers now had before them vivid images of correct forms of political behavior. Now the work team was ready to carry out vast public rituals to make the villagers fear and hate bad political behavior and love the socialist good that Mao proclaimed and the work team represented. Since the chief ministers of these rituals were (to all appearances) politically pure, the rituals were far more effective carriers of a new, ideologically orthodox moral teaching than those administered by local politicians all too obviously using them to further their own local ambitions.

The work team took about three months to "sink roots" in the village and to complete its investigations. In public, work-team members were very quiet and noncommittal about the village's leadership. But after about three months, there came a sudden change. "They smiled at genuine poor and lower-middle peasants. . . . But they had a very long face towards bad people. It was very clear."

The "bad" people included almost all of the village's cadres. Every one of the cadres had to "go down into the water," that is, undergo a purifying investigation. Most of the brigade and production team cadres were taken to a meeting in the commune headquarters, about five miles from Chen Village. With them went most of the work-team members and a group of specially picked poor and lower-middle peasants. The core of this group of poor and lower-middle peasants consisted of members of the ten poorest households to which the team members had attached themselves. The meeting lasted about twenty days. Information was systematically gathered from the poor peasant representatives about cadre malpractice and then used as a basis for interrogating the cadres. The cadres were interrogated about these problems in marathon sessions lasting all night if necessary. Fresh groups of questioners would be brought in every few hours to continue the interrogation. When the cadres—either out of a genuine sense of guilt or out of exhaustion—finally admitted what their interrogators demanded of them, their wrongdoing was considered proven. Then the cadres, exhausted, listless, and depressed, were brought back to the village.

Mass struggle sessions and denunciation sessions were prepared. One by one, the cadres ascended the village stage and confessed their transgressions. They confessed how they had misused public money, not "drawn a clear line" between themselves and class enemies, and given undue favors to the village's former landlords, rich peasants, counterrevolutionaries, and bad elements. They confessed how they had not been willing to work with all their hearts for the service of the poor and lower-middle peasants and had bullied the masses and disregarded their feelings and opinions. And the assembled peasants, led by carefully cultivated agitators, screamed condemnations at them.

Almost all of the brigade-level cadres underwent intense mass criticism; many of them were indeed subjected to struggle sessions. Most of the production team heads also came in for sharp criticism, though for varying reasons; none was criticized as fiercely as the leading brigade cadres. The most prominent target of public condemnation was Qingfa.

Qingfa had allegedly misused his power for personal gain. The most serious accusation concerned his having accepted a considerable sum of money to allow a family from Chen Village to emigrate to Hong Kong in 1962 (when border controls between China and Hong Kong were relatively relaxed). In addition, his accusers alleged a great number of smaller cases of accepting money and gifts in exchange for favors. He was one of those cadres, it was claimed, who had "eaten too much and owned too much." His attitude, moreover, was too harsh and undemocratic. He had regularly cursed and humiliated people who were outside his circle of friends and had beaten several teenagers who had neglected to carry out his orders. In addition, the work team claimed that he was lazy and refused to participate in the required amount of manual labor. He was also charged with neglecting to draw a clear line between himself and class enemies: specifically with maintaining friendly contact with his landlord relatives and his old guerrilla crony, who was now officially considered a bad element. He had committed the full range of errors that the propaganda said threatened to turn China back toward capitalism.

Whether he—or any of the other condemned cadres— was really as evil as the work team made him out to be, is of course another matter. He had undoubtedly used his public position to "eat well and live well." No doubt he had at times been more lenient toward certain members of the Four Bad Types—especially his former guerrilla fighter crony—than official regulations would permit. But whether he was so scandalously committed to such "evil" practices as seriously to threaten the village's socialist order is not at all clear. Interviews with persons familiar with other villages in Guangdong Province have turned up cases of cadre corruption far more flagrant and serious than anything attributable to Qingfa: cases of cadres embezzling very considerable sums of public money, demanding sex from village women in return for political favors, and so forth. In comparison with these examples of corruption, Qingfa's faults seem like minor peccadillos. In holding Qingfa up as a prime example of official misconduct, the work team was interpreting all of his actions in the worst possible light. It did so not in the interest of pursuing retributive justice but of carrying out a socialist education.

Following policies set by higher-level authorities, the work team seems to have wanted to make Qingfa and other leading village cadres into living symbols of certain "backward" themes in the village's customary moral order. The work team attacked the whole idea of placing positive moral value on the particularistic sensitivity to human feelings and on the patronage politics that flowed from such sensitivity. Qingfa's political persona was presented as a concrete paradigm of this moral theme and the villagers were mobilized to express hatred of the persona and thus of the moral themes it was made to represent. Qingfa was the logical target of a particularly intense struggle ritual, not because he was objectively the worst of the village's cadres, but because he was the most prominent official in whom the tendencies were manifested.

Most of the other brigade cadres underwent similar public trials by verbal fire. Longyong was denounced again, especially for his fierce, "undemocratic" style of work. The brigade's deputy Party secretary—a friend of Qingfa's—was attacked for faults similar to Qingfa's: petty corruption, laziness, and an overindulgent life-style. The brigade accountant was attacked for embezzling $1000 in public funds; the brigade militia head for indiscriminately cursing and humiliating people; the brigade secretarial clerk, an old man in rather poor health, for taking naps in the afternoon and not doing enough manual labor.

At the expense of their cadres, the villagers were being taught a moral lesson. A pure work team of righteous Communists was doing what the propaganda said was the will of Mao Zedong himself. Mao wanted his people to have the correct class consciousness and to take the correct class stand. One could tell whether people did so by measuring their behavior against a set of authoritative norms. By a thoroughly dispassionate investigation, the village's cadres had been measured against such norms and found lacking. No favoritism and no prejudice had been involved in choosing targets for the campaign. The work team had not spared any cadre a thorough investigation. It had spent months gathering information from the poorest of the village peasants. The cadres themselves had admitted their mistakes. If any mistakes had been made in attributing guilt to any of the cadres, it was certainly not the work team's fault; it was the fault of the people who had provided information to the work team.

Thus, unlike the small Four Cleanups, the big Four Cleanups had all the appearances of a moral struggle directed by genuine ministers of Maoist thought against the village's customary political morality. Many of the villagers might not appreciate the need for such a struggle. But the system of meanings expressed and created through the rituals of mass criticism of the big Four Cleanups stood before them as an objective fact. They were vigorously being taught a moral lesson. And this was not just an abstract textbook lesson that could be politely studied and conveniently forgotten; it was a lesson taught with vivid symbols infused with flaming emotions. The symbols centered on the public lives of their own familiar leaders. They had publicly cursed those leaders in sometimes frenzied mass meetings. Regardless of why they had individually decided to participate in that criticism and cursing, the process of criticizing, screaming, and cursing generated an emotionally charged atmosphere that tended to carry them away. And by word and symbolic deed, the work team told them that all of the anger, fear, and hatred pouring out of them was being evoked to do battle against manifestations of evil capitalist thought in their midst. They might never fully understand that message and never fully believe it, but they could never forget it and never totally ignore it. It was like a huge fiery stone falling unbidden onto the landscape of their consciousness. They might not welcome it, but they would have to reorganize their consciousness to take account of its presence.

Political Ritual and Village Culture

Rituals both express a certain vision of what is true and good and make that vision become powerfully alive for the performers of the ritual. They are sets of symbols that bring into being what they symbolize. Rituals accomplish this by inviting people personally to act out a particular model of the world, to pour their feelings and desires into a set of meaning-filled actions.[15] This is what I have argued happened during the big Four Cleanups phase of the Socialist Education Movement in Chen Village. But to what extent was the villagers' participation in the campaign authentic? To what extent were the feelings expressed in those performances genuine? When the villagers violently cursed their cadres for failing to live up to the standards of Maoist virtue, to what extent could they have been truly indignant? Without some attempt to answer these questions, we cannot assess the impact the political rituals had upon village culture.

I have already argued that the villagers customarily judged each other's behavior using different terms than those advocated by the work team; I have also argued that by village standards, most cadres were fairly good. If this is so, how could the villagers passionately condemn the cadres at the work team's bidding and *mean* it? Whence came the animus that made the campaign such an explosive event?

There was indeed a real animus generated by the campaign. From all accounts, the struggle sessions were awesome explosions of anger. It is difficult to believe that peasants were merely acting when they expressed these emotions. Clearly, the work team manipulated the expression of emotion by cultivating and organizing people who were naive or opportunistic or who felt vindictive toward some of the targets of the campaign for purely personal reasons. Before each struggle or denunciation session, the work team would assemble a carefully selected core of activists, tell them they would be counted on to lead the struggle, and fire them up with lurid descriptions of the target's crimes. Many of these activists were unmarried young people in their late teens and early twenties who, unlike adults, had not yet built up webs of personal alliances in the village and thus did not have to worry about offending anybody with their outspokenness. Young people tended to believe what their political lead-

---

15. See Clifford Geertz, "Religion as a Cultural System," in *The Interpretation of Cultures* (New York: Basic Books, 1973), especially 112–13.

ers told them more readily than older people. Also, young people in their teens and early twenties knew that if they "manifested themselves" well in a campaign, they would have a good chance of entering the Communist Party and eventually working their way into a position of power in the village.[16] Some adults were mobilized to speak out against the cadres, but these were mainly people who had special grudges against the village political establishment, grudges not necessarily shared by most people in the village. Thus, the heads of the poor peasant households with which the work team members had lived were made activists for the big Four Cleanups. But these were especially poor people, more bitter than most about the status quo in the village. Some of them saw their association with the work team as a way to gain new power and prestige. They were not acting out of pure indignation against the moral turpitude of the cadres, but the work team carefully used such people to create the correct atmosphere of indignation within the village.

Was the general outpouring of emotion that characterized the struggle sessions simply generated by the work team's manipulation? Were the peasants' feelings twisted so that most of them found themselves shouting curses at people who they did not believe had done anything wrong? The answer, at least in part, was yes. Yet I would argue that there did seem to be a reservoir of volatile hostility toward the village leaders that could flare up once the work team had made careful efforts to ignite it. Without the existence of such a current of hostility, it would be difficult to account for the explosions of anger that characterized some of the struggle rituals of the Four Cleanups.

I would suggest that the source of that undercurrent of resentment was the disjunction between the village's economic and political structures on the one hand and its cultural system on the other. The village's economy was socialist. The whole village was a single production brigade divided into ten production teams, the main units of the collective economy.[17] To form the production teams, the villagers had given up their

16. For a fuller account of the role played by young people during political campaigns in the village, see Richard Madsen, "Harnessing the Political Potential of Peasant Youth," in *State and Society in Contemporary China,* ed. Victor Nee and David Mozingo (Ithaca, N.Y.: Cornell University Press, 1983).

17. The relationships between production teams, production brigades, and people's communes are summarized in A. Doak Barnett with Ezra Vogel, *Cadres, Bureaucracy and Political Power in Communist China* (New York: Columbia University Press, 1967), pt. 3; Benedict Stavis, *People's Communes and Rural Development in China* (Ithaca, N.Y.: Cornell University Press, 1974); John Pelzel, "Economic Management of a Production Brigade in Post-Leap China" in *Economic Organization in Chinese Society,* ed. W.E. Willmott (Stanford: Stanford University Press, 1972); Byung-joon Ahn, "The Political Economy of the People's Commune in China: Changes and Continuities," *Journal of Asian Studies* 34 (1975):631–58; and William L. Parish and Martin King Whyte, *Village and Family in Contemporary China* (Chicago: University of Chicago Press, 1978), chap. 4.

privately owned land. If Chen Village is at all typical of most Chinese villages, many of the villagers were reluctant to relinquish their land; but in the end they had no choice.[18] The government promised the peasants that they would be better off if their land were collectively owned. Collectively owned farm land would produce more than privately owned land, and the benefits of that extra production would be shared among all members of the collective. But peasants worried about being cheated. A family that owned its own farmland possessed an important measure of control over its daily pattern of life and its economic destiny. Under the direction of its head, the family itself made decisions about how to cultivate its property and bore the responsibility for its economic growth or decline. Now, under collective ownership, a production team cadre told each team member what type of daily work to do; and an important measure of responsibility for each team member's economic well-being lay in the hands of the team's management committee.

How could a team member trust the production team leadership to be truly concerned for his or her well-being? Team members could have this basic trust only if they were sure that their team was being managed by utterly impartial officials who would reward each and every one of them according to an honest and accurate assessment of each person's contribution to the collective economy. Team members had to believe that their leaders were committed to a different kind of morality than they themselves were. They did not in general believe this was the case. Thus one gets the impression from our interviews that life in the village was marked by a constant bickering over matters like the assignment of work

18. For a general account of the process of collectivization, see Franz Schurmann, *Ideology and Organization in Communist China,* 2d ed. (Berkeley: University of California Press, 1968), 442–500; for collectivization in Guangdong Province, see Ezra Vogel, *Canton under Communism: Programs and Politics in a Provincial Capital, 1949–1968* (Cambridge, Mass.: Harvard University Press, 1969), 146–56; for collectivization in Chen Village, see Chan, Madsen, and Unger, *Chen Village,* chap. 1. In general, poor peasants favored full-fledged collectivization more than middle peasants, because poor peasants could take advantage of the extra land and draught animals owned by the middle peasants. But this is not to say that all poor peasants immediately and spontaneously embraced the new collective arrangements. For the reasons discussed in the text, many poor peasants, especially those middle-aged and older, were initially reluctant to join collectives. The government relied on carefully selected activists, usually ambitious young poor peasants, to drum up support from enough poor peasants to put pressure on their more "backward" peers. The first stages of the movement to form collectives were supposed to be voluntary; but by the end of 1957, the pressure to join the new collective units had become overwhelming. In spite of all of the political and social pressure employed to bring about collectivization, however, the Chinese Communist collectivization movement was less purely coercive than that in the Soviet Union. Reasons for this are given in Thomas P. Bernstein, "Leadership and Mass Mobilization in the Soviet and Chinese Collectivization Campaigns of 1929–1930 and 1955–1956: A Comparison" *The China Quarterly,* no. 31 (1967): 1–42.

and the allocation of work points. It was not uncommon to have heated arguments over differences in pay amounting to only one Chinese cent a day! The bickering was in response to expectations that unless each person was very vigilant about his or her rights, the system would favor some at the expense of others.

To the village's socialist economy, there corresponded a Leninist political administration. A Communist Party branch governed Chen Village brigade through the brigade management committee. This form of local government had much more power than any the village had known before Liberation. The brigade administration profoundly influenced the lives of villagers by organizing occasional rectification campaigns (like the small Four Cleanups), by routinely scrutinizing the lives of villagers for social and political deviance, by mobilizing villagers to take part in large public works projects during the agricultural slack season, by deciding who could join the Communist Party and thus have a chance at upward mobility in the village. The local village government, for all the inefficiencies we have alluded to from time to time, intruded much more deeply into the lives of the villagers than any other local government within memory. This new political system brought important benefits to the lives of the villagers, established a greater degree of public security than ever before possible, and organized more extensive projects for economic development than any in the past. The government's propaganda emphasized the positive side of this new political system. It was based on the principles of democratic centralism, the propaganda said. The local government was run by and for the poor and lower-middle peasants who formed the majority of the rural population. The village government was intimately in touch with the poor and lower-middle peasant masses and was bound to act in their interests. Therefore, the people of good class background had nothing to fear from the coercive power of the new government. They need only look forward to reaping its benefits.

But the villagers tended to be suspicious. Poor and lower-middle peasants would have little to fear *if* the brigade's cadres were totally impartial, *if* the cadres were totally devoted to the public welfare, and *if* the cadres were committed to consulting closely with the masses on all important issues. That is, ordinary poor and lower-middle peasants would have nothing to fear if their leaders were committed to a fundamentally different morality than most of them were. But villagers expected their cadres to play favorites and expected them to act in a commandistic fashion. That was only natural. But if cadres acted that way in the powerful new political system, many villagers would have to worry about being hurt or arbitrarily pushed around.

Thus, the village's new socialist economic and political structure needed a new, socialist morality—a morality like that advocated by the work team—to work smoothly, fairly, and benevolently. But it is relatively easy to impose a new set of political and economic structures upon a population and much more difficult to transform the centuries-old cultural system through which a people apprehends the meaning and purpose of life. Many of the basic traditions that governed the villagers' ways of understanding the difference between right and wrong had remained intact. Thus, the villagers expected their cadres to act in the same "natural" way that ordinary peasants acted: "There *should* be favoritism; it's *reasonable* that there be some. . . . But of course all cadres publicly deny this." And they denied it, of course, because their favoritism angered the same peasants who thought it reasonable.

It was that anger which the work team evoked, focused, and justified in the struggle rituals of the Four Cleanups. Participation in those rituals did not radically change the villagers' minds about the difference between right and wrong. The explosions of public anger against unsocialist morality tended to be confined to formal political rituals. To this day, people are expected to act with proper regard for good human feeling in their everyday lives. It is only, as one interviewee stated, in struggle meetings that one has to be "without feeling." In the end, the struggle meetings failed to effect a fundamental transformation in villagers' world views because the official political rhetoric used in those meetings was composed of categories alien to villagers' culture. The theory of class, class struggle, and the march of history toward a socialist utopia did not easily resonate with villagers' ordinary ways of understanding their world. Yet the struggle rituals were not without effect. They gave a name to certain very real resentments the villagers were feeling, resentments that the villagers' traditional moral culture could not fully account for. Thus, through political ritual, new symbolic elements were established within the moral lexicon of the villagers.

Chinese folk religion had long been cheerfully syncretic, commingling at least partially contradictory Buddhist, Taoist, and Confucian ideas into a casual unity. Now a new kind of moral syncretism was being attempted, as the socialist morality of Mao was added to the peasants' traditional moral system. The Maoist morality did not dominate the village's culture, but it did provide some new symbols that could be duly mixed with older symbols and brought into play on appropriate occasions for appropriate purposes.

A Moral Crossroads for Longyong and Qingfa

After the Four Cleanups campaign was completed, the work team did not attempt fundamentally to change the composition of the village's leadership. Nor did it essentially alter the village's political institutions, although it made some (largely symbolic) steps in that direction. There was in fact a shortage of good leadership material in the village, and the government could hardly afford to replace the old leaders with a whole new group. So the work team prepared to rehabilitate most of the cadres it had just deposed.

This was a somewhat difficult task to accomplish, given that the cadres had just been condemned as paragons of moral corruption. The work team gradually let it be known that the cadres were not quite as bad as it had seemed at first. Some of the accusations brought by the work team, it was now alleged, were not quite accurate, the inaccuracies being not the fault of the work team but of the faulty information provided by the villagers in the impassioned confusion of the campaign. Thus, the work team continued its search into the evidence against the cadres and let it be known that the brigade accountant seemed to have embezzled only $100 of public money rather than $1000 as originally charged. Forcing him to pay back $1000 would have totally bankrupted him; $100 was a sum he could afford, and if that was all he had taken, he might, having humbly confessed his error, be eligible for a position of public trust again. By measures such as these, the work team minimized the personal damage done to the village's cadres, while letting the lessons taught by their ordeals stand. The work team thus prepared the way for most former cadres to assume positions of leadership once again.

Elections were organized by the work team to select new cadres for the brigade management committee and the production teams' management committees. Working through carefully organized groups of local activists, the work team let villagers know who would be acceptable as new cadres. At the same time, ordinary poor and lower-middle peasants let the work team know who they would consider acceptable as leaders. A slate of candidates emerged and was then elected (by secret ballot) almost unanimously. These candidates met the requirements of the work team and fulfilled at least some of the wishes of the masses. A few old cadres who were either especially corrupt or particularly incompetent were eased out of the village's leadership in this process, and some "new blood" (mostly people who had been exceptionally helpful to the work team during the Four Cleanups) was brought into the management committees; but most of the old cadres had a chance to resume their posts.

To ensure that the new leaders would exercise their power properly, the work team made one institutional innovation: they reinvigorated an old institution—the Poor Peasants' Association.[19] During land reform

---

19. For an analysis of the political processes leading on the one hand to a reactivation of the Poor Peasants' Associations and on the other hand to the limitation of their influence, see Richard Baum, *Prelude to Revolution*, 28–31; and Ezra Vogel, *Canton under Communism*, 314–17.

such associations had been used to mobilize poor peasants against the landlords and rich peasants. In the years since land reform, however, the Poor Peasants' Associations had virtually withered away. In the early phases of the Four Cleanups, the work team had started to rebuild the village's Poor Peasants' Association, and after the struggle sessions were over, it tried to ensure that the Association would remain intact to represent the interests of the village's poor and lower-middle peasants, check the power of its cadres, and provide the vehicle for a new kind of participatory democracy in the village.

All poor and lower-middle peasants in the brigade who were not cadres were made members of the Association simply by virtue of their class status. The poor and lower-middle peasants of each production team constituted a unit of the Association and elected a three-member "leadership small group" to represent the poor and lower-middle peasants of the team. Each small group chose a group head who was supposed to represent the interests of the poor and lower-middle peasants at meetings of the team management committee and who sat on a committee of eleven persons (one from each team plus a committee head) charged with supervising the brigade cadres. Most of these Poor Peasants' Association representatives were, by arrangement of the work team, the heads of the households in which the work team members had lived while practicing the Three Togethers.

This revivified Poor Peasants' Association, however, was in the long run not very effective in checking the power of the cadres, mainly because the village's poor and lower-middle peasants never really saw themselves as having any collective interests to represent. The Poor Peasants' Association representatives were chosen by the work team because of their poverty and their willingness to take the lead in speaking out against the cadres. But many of those villagers officially classified as poor and lower-middle peasants were really not poor any longer by village standards, and many of them looked down on their officially appointed representatives as incompetent people with no social standing who were simply trying to move up in the world under the sponsorship of the work team. As a result, most of the Poor Peasants' Association representatives did not really have a great deal of support from the poor and lower-middle peasants in their production teams and therefore were not able to bring much leverage to bear against the village cadres. The reestablished Poor Peasants' Association symbolized the idea that a class struggle was in process and that the poor classes were charged with the historical task of completing China's revolution. But since that idea did not dominate the villagers' consciousness even after the Four Cleanups, the Poor Peasants' Association had little practical ability to check the power of the cadres.

So the village's political structure remained essentially unchanged. What had changed somewhat was the system of meanings the cadres had to use to justify their conduct. Cadres had to appear more impartial, more ascetic, even more democratic than they had in the past. Otherwise, the lessons of the Four Cleanups could be invoked against them. Some cadres were in a better position to accept this new moral discipline than others. Thus the character of Longyong and Qingfa, the two village strong men, developed and diverged as both chose different strands of meaning within the village's culture with which to weave the web of their fate.

Longyong, for instance had established a reputation for being relatively ascetic, relatively uncorrupt, and relatively devoted in an uncompromising way to the good of the village as a whole. True, he was harsh and "undemocratic." But the work team itself had, after all, been pretty harsh in its own right and in fact been forced to admit that it had acted a little too hastily in attributing guilt to some of the cadres. It was relatively easy for Longyong to "repent" and mold his conduct to the new standards of behavior the work team injected into the village. He accepted the opportunity to be reelected to his post as brigade chief. And from that time on, he eschewed even more rigorously than before the taking of any personal gifts and flaunted his personal poverty and lack of kinship connections. In the post-Four-Cleanups atmosphere such virtues made good political capital, and he was obviously determined to make the most of them.

But even as he embraced the newly emphasized virtues, he subtly changed their meaning. The work team had said that the austere virtues of socialism took their meaning and purpose from the task of leading China's workers and poor and lower-middle peasants in their struggle against the masters of the old society to create a glorious new Chinese nation. But those ideas and hopes did not really fit the villagers' experience. The virtues of austerity and impartiality made more sense if they were seen to serve the task of making the whole village one unified, powerful, and prosperous big family. As we shall see, that is how Longyong lived them. He turned his morally disciplined energy not to the service of poor and lower-middle peasant masses throughout China but to the glorification of Chen Village and, incidentally, the glorification of himself.

Qingfa, however, was unwilling to accept the discipline required by the new moral atmosphere. He too was given his job back; with high-quality leadership ability in short supply, the work team was not willing to cast aside someone as capable as he was. But he committed political suicide. While the work team was still in the village, he resumed some of his old arrogant ways. He quietly began developing networks of loyal supporters by hinting that he would give them small favors. He again tried to use his power to take advantage of villagers outside his circle of relatives and friends. His final undoing came when he tried to use his authority to bully a peasant into relinquishing a goose to him. The peasant complained to the work team, which then called Qingfa to account. Instead of being contrite, Qingfa exploded in anger against the work team: "You really think you are something," he said, "coming into our brigade and disrupting our life. But you don't know anything about our life here! You don't belong here!" After this outburst, the work team deposed him.

Qingfa may simply have been acting on undisciplined impulse, but I think there was more to his reckless behavior than that. Even though the work team gave him his job back, he could not accept such a post if it meant that his style of patronage politics would be crippled. Might it not be better, in the long run, to stand up for the old moral traditions in the face of this intrusion by an uninvited, self-righteous work team? Qingfa's defiance of the new political rectitude could bring into focus a theme that, despite the work team, still lived within the village's culture. Villagers would not forget this theme. And perhaps in the long run, Qingfa's defiance could be turned to his political advantage.

A Time of Crisis

In the last two chapters, I have argued that in the mid-1960s, the peasants of rural China were drawn into a great debate about the moral basis of social action. Parties to this debate used variations on both a Confucian and a Maoist paradigm of moral discourse. These paradigms contained different assumptions about the proper relationship between the individual and society and employed different modes of reasoning from basic assumptions to practical conclusions. Within the Confucian paradigm considerable debate about the appropriate style of conduct for a local political leader could occur as a result of two distinctive Confucian visions of the proper structure of a good village society. Leaders used their appeals to different Confucian visions to gain rival sorts of political capital. Neither of those visions was completely compatible with the Maoist vision presented by the Socialist Education Movement work team, although Longyong's vision of the village as a big family was closer to the Maoist paradigm than Qingfa's image of the village as a federation of families linked together by the flavor of human feeling.

My characterizations of "Confucian" and "Maoist" moral discourse do not draw directly on the writings of Confucian philosophers or of Mao but on the meanings implicit in the words and deeds of opposing village leaders. The "Confucian" moral discourse of the villagers can only be un-

derstood in the light of time-honored themes in China's Confucian tradition, but the peasants' discourse certainly cannot do full justice to the
range and subtlety of Confucianism. The same holds for the "Maoist"
words and deeds of the work team. The work team's insistence on the
moral dimensions of social class and class struggle came from the
thought of Mao, and indeed from those elements of Mao's Thought that
came to distinguish Mao from his rivals in the Chinese Communist leadership in the 1960s. But what the work team told the villagers did not
exhaust Mao's Thought and was only the tip of an ideological iceberg, an
iceberg that was constantly changing its shape in the swirling currents of
Chinese politics. In the next four chapters, we shall see how parts of that
iceberg not yet visible to the villagers collided with the villagers' moral
discourse with disastrous consequences.

Besides interpreting the different modes of moral discourse argued
about within the village, I have tried to show how different strands of
that discourse were fused together into a rough unity by political rituals
of struggle complemented by rituals of reconciliation. Even though I would
condemn the terrible cruelty with which this process was carried out, there
was something necessary about it. The Confucian paradigms for moral
discourse did not enable villagers to come to terms with the moral challenges of living in a collectivized economy governed by a powerful, dynamic state.[20] If one accepts the assumptions that some form of cooperative agriculture was necessary to increase China's productivity and that a
more powerful form of political apparatus than existed in imperial times
was necessary for China to maintain its integrity in the modern world,
then I think one must conclude that some fundamental changes in peasants' traditional moral discourse were also necessary. Peasants needed to
develop ways of judging their village leaders that would demand that those
leaders carry out public duties with impartial fairness, and it was important for the national government that villagers develop a civic sense that
would help them understand their responsibilities not only as members of
a local community but as citizens of a nation. The Socialist Education
Movement tried to use Maoist moral theory to instill such standards of
impartial fairness and to create such a civic sense.

But one cannot quickly, totally destroy a community's moral traditions without producing confusion and chaos. The promoters of the Socialist Education Movement had to allow peasants to retain important
elements of their old traditions. If they had not done so, villages would
have had no local village leadership. The most able leaders were persons

20. This line of argument was suggested by Clifford Geertz, "The Integrative
Revolution: Primordial Sentiments and Civil Politics in the New States," in *The
Interpretation of Cultures,* especially 254–79.

who had acquired leadership ability by affirming certain important values in their village's traditions. If most of those local leaders could not be retained, villages would face anarchy. But if those "natural" local leaders could regain their jobs only by totally denying the moral standards that had originally given them their political capital, then their ability to command a village following would be destroyed. To resolve such predicaments, the Party Central eventually directed work teams to affirm in deed, if not in word, the basic correctness of the moral stance taken by cadres like Longyong, even though this position was not completely congruent with the grand vision of commitment to class struggle demanded by the thought of Mao Zedong.

If the moral synthesis effected in the first stage of the Socialist Education Movement—the Four Cleanups—had held up, then Chen villagers might have learned to demand of themselves and their leaders a steady commitment to the village as a whole disciplined by a willingness sometimes to see the interests of the village in the context of those of the nation as a whole. But this was not to be. This moral synthesis was fatally flawed by fundamental defects in the ability of Maoist thought to be an adequate guide to a coherent public morality. The defects did not exist so much in those aspects of Maoist thought apparent to the villagers in early 1965. The poor and lower-middle peasant majority of the village might become reconciled to a version of that thought which emphasized the importance of commitment to a grand nationwide class struggle but which allowed them to interpret that class struggle in terms of their pursuit of the general welfare of their own community. But now there were other people in the village who were trying to devote themselves totally to that thought in ways not demanded of the ordinary villagers. These were members of a band of sent-down youth who arrived in the village at the end of 1964. Total devotion to Mao's Thought led these youth into painful predicaments and eventually the spectacle created by those predicaments destroyed the plausibility of Mao's Thought for the peasants of Chen Village.

PART TWO ▪ MAOIST MORALITY
AND ITS CONFUCIAN
TRANSFORMATION

4 Maoist Moralists and Their Predicaments

In the middle of September 1964, a youth brigade composed of fifty young people set out from Canton for Chen Village in three separate contingents.[1] One contingent of sixteen people was being sent to the countryside from a municipal street committee. These street committee youths generally had only a primary (sixth grade) education. They were about fifteen or sixteen years old—just the age when young people not in school would have to find a job. Since jobs were rather scarce in overpopulated Canton, street committees organized contingents of youth to go down to the countryside in order to lessen the pressure of finding employment for the people of their district. The young people who had accepted the call to go to the countryside from this particular street committee generally lacked outstanding skills and had little hope of being assigned to an especially satisfying job in the city.

The other two contingents of Canton youth were from middle schools. One of the middle schools was only a junior middle (up to the ninth grade), and the twelve persons from that school were all recent graduates, about sixteen years old. The other middle school combined junior middle and senior middle grades. Twenty-one students came from this school: about half were sixteen-year-old graduates of junior middle. This particular middle school had a large number of Overseas Chinese students, mostly from Indonesia; its sent-down youth contingent included about six Indonesian-born Chinese. Most of the students from the two middle schools had failed to be admitted to higher levels of

1. The social composition of the sent-down youth is also described in part 1 of chapter 4 of Anita Chan, Richard Madsen, and Jonathan Unger, *Chen Village: The Recent History of a Peasant Community in Mao's China* (Berkeley: University of California Press, 1984).

education. They could have stayed in Canton and reapplied to enter a school the following year, or they could have remained in the city and let themselves be assigned jobs in urban factories. But if they failed to continue their schooling, the jobs they might have obtained in the city would very likely not have been commensurate with the level of education they had attained. None of the youths, neither those from the street committee nor those from the middle schools, were forced to go to the countryside. They genuinely felt that they had made the decision of their own free will, against the advice and urging of their parents in many cases. Some of them hoped to return to Canton someday, but none of them could know for sure when—or if—they would be able to return.[2]

They bravely set off from Canton amid the enthusiastic banging of gongs and drums, "filled with revolutionary enthusiasm." But as they boarded the train out of Canton, many of them began to weep. The Young Communist League members among them, fighting back their own tears, led them in revolutionary songs to blot out their sorrow and bolster their resolve. An interviewee remembered particularly well a few lines from one of the songs they sang: "On a glorious morn, an army of heroes heads for afar. The train is carrying us youthful friends . . . to build up the land of our ancestors."

The group had been given a choice of two counties within Guangdong Province. One was close to Canton, the other far away. They knew that life would be considerably more difficult in the faraway county than in the one closer to home, but they chose the faraway place. The Young Communist League members among the youth brigade had made this decision in private meetings. But when the decision was presented to the larger group, the group members (even according to interviewees who never became part of the group's political elite) sincerely threw their support behind the decision. (The choice of exactly where to go in the county had already been made, however, by officials from the county.) When the young people reached the county seat, they were met by officials from the commune to which they had been assigned. The commune officials questioned them again about their resolve to go to a poor production brigade. If they wanted, they could work in a reforestation farm near the commune headquarters, or they could go to Chen Village, called the "Siberia" of the commune. They all said, "the further the better." When they finally reached Chen Village after a two-hour walk, they were exhausted.

2. For analyses of the political issues involved in sending urban youth to the countryside, see D. Gordon White, "The Politics of *Hsia-hsiang* Youth," *The China Quarterly*, no. 59 (1974):491–517; Thomas P. Bernstein, *Up to the Mountains and Down to the Villages: The Transfer of Youth from Urban to Rural China* (New Haven, Conn.: Yale University Press, 1977); and Peter Seybolt, ed., *The Rustification of Urban Youth in China* (White Plains, N.Y.: M. E. Sharpe, 1977).

The villagers had divided the village ancestral temple into sleeping units, each shared by several people; the youth were settled into this make-shift dormitory.

The youth from Canton would have a powerful impact on the village, though in a way they could never have predicted. Most of them were committed to making a supreme effort to live according to the current, official version of Mao's moral teachings and to use that teaching to "build up the land of our ancestors." But it turned out that their attempts to live out the Maoist ethic within Chen Village led them into unresolvable moral predicaments. Their experience in the village became their stumbling block, the stone of scandal that occasioned their disillusionment, confusion, and fall from Maoist grace. And their fall from Maoist grace helped precipitate the village's fall.

How could the problems of a group of immature urban youngsters have an important influence on the moral framework of a peasant village? Those problems eventually had such an impact because they exposed the villagers to the inadequacy of Maoism as a guide to life. Mao said that the class struggle continued, and it manifested itself now especially in moral terms. The true members of the good classes were those who lived by a particular kind of moral code, a code that demanded "total devotion to others without thought of self."[3] As we have seen, the work team had preached such ideas to the villagers, but it had softened their impact. Thus, for a peasant cadre to be truly on the side of the good classes, it was enough to be rigorously fair in public dealings with villagers and to be dedicated to improving the welfare of the community as a whole. One did not have to be so utterly forgetful of self that one cared nothing for the prosperity of one's community or for the feelings of one's fellow community members. It was unrealistic to think that peasants, embedded in the networks of responsibility that defined their personal identity in the village, could think of their moral responsibilities literally in terms of total devotion to others without thought of self. But they could accept Mao's doctrines as a set of ideals that might be good in themselves, although not fully practical within the routine of daily life in Chen Village. Those ideals could thereby have a genuine influence on village conduct, especially the behavior of the village's political leaders. They could encourage a kind of village-oriented selflessness and discourage the cruder manifestations of family-oriented selfishness.

But the sent-down youth tried to take Mao's moral teachings literally. For a while, they tried to live as if they were small cogs in a vast impersonal class machine, small screws in the great locomotive of the revolu-

3. This phrase is from Mao's essay "Serve the People," *Selected Works of Mao Tse-tung*, 4 vols. (Beijing: Foreign Languages Press, 1961–65), 3:177–79.

tion. And after a fairly short time, most of them failed because the Maoist moral demands were unrealistic and the Maoist doctrine insufficiently plausible to motivate heroic self-abnegation. Their failure showed the villagers that Mao's doctrines were not intrinsically good, and thus Mao's ideals lost their influence.

The First Year in Chen Village: Competitive Cooperation Within the Sent-Down Youth Team

During their first year in the village, the city youth were kept apart from the normal organization of Chen Village. They lived in their own dormitory (the old ancestral temple) and worked together on plots of land specially assigned to the youth brigade. Their day-to-day affairs were directed by the seven Young Communist League members among them, who were responsible to the village's leading cadres. (The urban Young Communist League members formed a subbranch of the village League, so that, although formally a part of the village League, they usually met as a separate group.) The young people from Canton met almost every night for incessant rounds of meetings directed by their Young Communist League subbranch through a three-person management committee. Besides dealing with the day-to-day organization of the youth brigade's affairs, these meetings dealt at exceedingly great length with the system of moral ideals that were to guide the conduct of the sent-down youth. Living and working apart from the peasants and kept from close personal contact with them by the need to attend a constant round of political discussions, the urban youth focused their attention on one another. In almost daily criticism and self-criticism meetings, culminating in intense monthly "evaluation sessions," they measured themselves against each other according to their peer group's common conceptions of ideal behavior for revolutionary youth in the countryside.

There was a desperate intensity in the way in which many of these urban youth strove for Maoist perfection. We can understand some of this desperate striving for political excellence by examining what the youth had lost in coming to the countryside, what they could hope to gain, and the ways they could hope to gain it.

All of the city youth, those from the street committee as well as those from the middle schools, felt that they were making a great sacrifice in coming to the countryside. They were leaving behind not only urban comforts but urban civilization. They were going *down* to the countryside, where not only life was harder than in the city but people were more ignorant, more superstitious, more narrow-minded, and more conservative than urban dwellers. Moreover, they were leaving behind families and friends. Some felt that they were making a greater sacrifice than others. In general, the more the youth pictured themselves as capable of achieving a high level of success in an urban setting, the more they felt deprived by coming to the countryside. Thus, the middle school graduates felt that they were giving up more than the street committee youth did as a rule. But all felt that they had given up some important goods, comforts, opportunities, and joys to come to Chen Village.[4]

This was experienced as a freely made sacrifice. The young people had made their choices without being directly threatened with clearly defined sanctions by any government authorities for refusing to go. They had not, however, been free from more subtle pressures. Given the economic situation prevailing in Canton at the time, it was going to be difficult for them to find challenging employment or educational opportunities in the city. In the middle schools, most graduating students who cared about making a good impression on their superiors had formally announced their intention to go to the countryside if the nation wanted them to go. Having made such a declaration and then failed the tests to continue their education, such students were under pressure not only from school authorities but also from their peers to live up to their declaration. Not to have gone would have tarnished their reputation for "Redness" and would have made them vulnerable to the charge of hypocrisy from their peers. But in 1964 these economic, social, and political pressures were not such as to ineluctably force any of them to go. Many young people in similar situations had successfully avoided going to the countryside. For instance, in the class of Ao Meihua, the sent-down youth who eventually became my research assistant in Hong Kong, about thirty students failed to be accepted to senior middle school, and most of these had at one time or another declared their intention to go to the countryside. But, in the end, only twelve students actually went, and those who did not go apparently suffered no serious consequences. Practically all of the young people who came to Chen Village, therefore, were conscious of doing so primarily not to avoid the negative consequences of staying in the city but to attain certain positive goals.

The young people could expect several types of rewards for their sacrifice. One reward was an increase in their personal political status, through which they might eventually obtain power, better job opportunities, more education, and perhaps a more comfortable level of social and political security. For instance, the teacher of one of the sent-down middle school students told him privately that if he went down he would be

4. My analysis in this and the following two paragraphs has been informed by Rosabeth Moss Kanter's discussion of the "commitment mechanisms" of "sacrifice and investment" in her *Commitment and Community: Communes and Utopias in Sociological Perspective* (Cambridge, Mass.: Harvard University Press, 1972), 75–83.

"worth much more" after a few years and would eventually be able to get into a good school. Like perhaps one-third of the sent-down youth, this student rather clearly viewed his sacrifice as a "gold plating" that in the relatively near future would bring him improved career opportunities. Another reward was the opportunity to pioneer in a new and exciting kind of work. Provincial and national newspapers were full of inspiring stories of sent-down city youth who were helping to change the face of the Chinese countryside, bringing literacy, scientific production methods, and the wonders of Mao Zedong's Thought to China's poor and lower-middle peasants. Here was an opportunity for city youth to use their courage and creativity to accomplish great deeds. But the greatest of all rewards that could be expected from the heroic sacrifice of city youth in going to the countryside was that of "revolutionary glory." For the Chinese Communist, "glory" is something like "salvation" for religious believers. It is the ultimate deliverance from the limitations of the human condition—the ability to transcend death. In Communist ideology, if a person through his strivings makes an important positive contribution to the progress of history, his individual, circumscribed, and transitory life acquires a significance that even death cannot destroy. As Mao said, "To die for the people is weightier than Mount Tai."[5] Chinese propaganda extolled the act of going to the countryside as a glorious sacrifice made for the good of the masses of Chinese people and for the revolution. The youth who made such a sacrifice could expect nothing less than what Robert Lifton has called "revolutionary immortality."[6]

Although it is possible to distinguish neatly between the various rewards that could have been sought by going down to the countryside, most of the sent-down youth were only conscious of a confused jumble of personal motives at the time. Young and idealistic, they saw their futures as an open-ended frontier, full of different kinds of exciting possibilities. Many of those who even harbored relatively clear careerist hopes still believed that they could change their political consciousness in the countryside, make creative contributions to their country, and perhaps achieve revolutionary glory. But whatever the exact mixture of distinctions the various young people were individually striving for, the rewards were all relatively scarce, and there was only one way to obtain any of them: to outdo one's fellow city youth in expressions of fervent com-

5. Mao, "Serve the People," 177.
6. Robert J. Lifton, *Revolutionary Immortality: Mao Tse-tung and the Chinese Cultural Revolution* (New York: Random House, 1968). Lifton, a psychohistorian, interprets Mao's motivation in launching the Cultural Revolution as the desire of an aging leader to find meaning in the face of his impending death by ensuring that the historical movement he has led will continue.

mitment to officially defined Maoist virtue. This set the stage for intense competition among the urban youth.

Whether one wanted to advance one's career, to exercise one's creativity in great and beneficial deeds, or to attain the transcendent joy of playing an important role in the revolution, a sent-down youth had to do more than simply become another peasant. The youth had to use the knowledge and skills he or she had gained in the city to make a significant contribution to the countryside, a contribution that could not have been made by the peasants themselves. As the sent-down youth settled into their new rural home, however, it became very clear to them that opportunities for making significant contributions to the village were going to be scarce. None of them was strong enough or skilled enough in farm work to be anything but an economic liability to the village for the time being. The village needed only a few mechanically minded people to help set up new machinery, since the mechanization of the village was proceeding at a slow pace. The largely illiterate village was going to need "cultural workers," but the farmers did not have the time to receive too much "culture" and were not going to require a major effort by all fifty youth in this regard. The socialist transformation of the village would require some literate propagandists, but the villagers would not let themselves be overwhelmed by immature city dwellers who presumed to preach to them about the virtues appropriate to a revolutionary society. They might listen to the political lectures of a few outstanding city youth—but just a few.

As it turned out, only about one-fourth of the sent-down youth had an opportunity to use their urban-developed skills to make any kind of important contribution to the village. The others were just ordinary farmhands, and some of the women became cheaply obtainable wives for Chen Village men. For those city youth with little education, few skills, and uncertain hopes of finding decent employment in the city, it might not be too bad to think of settling in the village as ordinary peasants. But the more one felt that he or she was making a great sacrifice in coming to Chen Village, the more one perceived the fate of becoming an ordinary peasant as disastrous. Such a fate might well mean the destruction not only of whatever personal career ambitions one might harbor but also of one's youthful hopes for becoming a glorious revolutionary hero.

Consequently a desperately intense competition quickly developed among the urban youth to determine who would gain the positions of highest political status in the youth brigade and thus an opportunity to undertake glorious deeds in Chen Village. The members of the Young Communist League monopolized the leading positions in the youth brigade. To join the League one had primarily to win not the admiration of the peasants but the respect of one's fellow youth—especially those who controlled access to the Young Communist League. To be considered worthy of acceptance into the League, an urban youth had to excel in devotion to the Five Goods defined by central government propaganda: enthusiasm for physical labor, dedication to political work, correct thought, concern for the collective, and concern for solidarity and friendship.

One knew what it meant to be a good person by listening to the voice of approved political authority—authority canonized by the approval of Chairman Mao. The young people's moral discourse thus centered around exegesis of official government moral imperatives and their application to the details of daily life. Such moral discourse only made sense, however, for people set apart from the mainstream of ordinary village life. People burdened with the responsibilities of making a living and raising a family within the village inevitably had to make compromises between devotion to the glorious goals of the Chinese revolution and their need to achieve social and economic security.[7] Taken literally, however, Maoist moral doctrine allowed for no such compromises. The spirit of the true Communist was one of "total devotion to others without any thought of self." In its pure form, this Maoist ethic was only workable for people whose sole responsibilities were to the pursuit of excellence in political virtue and whose sole hopes for the achievement of personal dignity lay in fervently following the official norms of political rectitude. Such were the sent-down urban youth—as long as they lived in their own tightly organized youth brigade. The urban youths' quest for Maoist virtue, therefore, turned them away from the concerns of ordinary villagers. When, inevitably, the urban youth became integrated into the mainstream of village life, their commitment to Maoist morality created major predicaments for them.

The Five Goods: Dimensions of Maoist Virtue

The urban youth interpreted the first of the Five Goods—enthusiasm for physical labor—in terms of a willingness to embrace as ends in themselves the values of hard work and abstemious living that official government propaganda told them were the essence of poor and lower-middle

7. In the terminology used by sociologists of religion, the young people's form of social organization was *sect*like rather than *church*like. My analysis of the relationship between ideological commitment and social organization among the sent-down youth has been informed by the extensive theoretical discussions of church and sect in the literature on the sociology of religion. See Ernst Troeltsch, *The Social Teaching of the Christian Churches*, trans. Olive Wyon, 2 vols. (New York: Harper, 1956), 1:331–49.

peasant virtue. Like the archetypically good poor and lower-middle peasants portrayed in official ideology, the youth strove to develop suntanned "black skins, red hearts, hard bones, and iron soles." Peasants did not wear shoes. None of the Canton youth wore shoes, even though in the beginning their feet were not yet properly calloused and thus quickly became cut and infected as they worked in the fields. Peasants wore simple, poor clothing. The sent-down youth vied with each other to wear the most ragged clothing possible. Peasants ate simple, meager food. Some of the young people literally almost starved themselves in order to become more truly peasant than the others. They ate less rice than most of the peasants. They did not even use soy sauce with their rice, because this was considered a luxury. Instead of ordinary vegetables they ate turnip leaves and spring bean leaves—little more than fibers. Anyone caught eating soy sauce or candy or cakes sent by their parents in Canton was severely criticized. "It was not so bad for the girls: two and a half ounces of rice for both breakfast and lunch and five ounces for dinner. We were just about satisfied with our share. But not the boys who expended such a lot of energy. They became *so* hungry. They had headaches and stomachaches. They became so thin." The young people pushed themselves to the point of exhaustion in their work. The health of several of them broke down. At least one caught tuberculosis; others contracted hepatitis; many others, especially the girls, developed rheumatic inflammations in their legs from standing too long in wet paddy fields; almost everyone developed infections in their cut, bare feet. When they became sick, their comrades brought them medicine and offered them encouragement in the fashion of proper revolutionary friendship, but their comrades also criticized them if they rested from their work because of their illness. As Ao Meihua said: "We were so stupid then! Our thoughts were so Red! We only thought about how to unite with the poor and lower-middle peasants, how to emulate the Red Army, how to train ourselves to endure all sorts of hardships, how to train ourselves to become revolutionary successors!" The goods of "dedication to political work" and "correct thought" came down to the same thing: intense study of Mao's works and constant criticism of oneself and others for not living up to them. In their spare moments, the young people read and reread Mao's works, especially such basic texts as the Three Constantly Read Articles ("Serve the People," "In Memory of Norman Bethune," "The Foolish Old Man Who Moved the Mountains"), "Combat Liberalism," "Rectify the Party's Style of Work," "On Correcting Mistaken Ideas in the Party," "Reform our Study," "On Practice," and "On Policy."[8] In their discussion

8. See chap. 1, n. 20.

groups they tried to outdo each other in showing how these articles applied to their present situation and in criticizing themselves and others for not living up the spirit of Mao's teaching. The brief Three Constantly Read Articles were studied again and again and memorized word for word. The young people were to be as self-sacrificing as Zhang Shide, the humble charcoal maker whose selfless life and death were celebrated in "Serve the People"; as internationally minded, warmhearted, and devoted to others as Norman Bethune who came from Canada to work and die for the Red Army; and as persevering as the foolish old man who began the generations-long task of digging away a mountain. They were to combat "liberal" tendencies to value comfortable friendship over critical comradeship. They were to combat such evils as lack of discipline, "subjectivism," "individualism," and "commandism." They were always to take care to live as they preached, to unite theory with practice. They constantly and anxiously watched themselves and each other to detect and to criticize subtle deviations from these norms. They were to emulate heroes like Lei Feng and Ouyang Hai.[9] A few of them even went so far as to mimic the stylized image of these heroes portrayed in revolutionary movies and plays. In plays the almost superhuman determination of revolutionary heroes was depicted in a stylized striding walk. A few of the sent-down youth imitated this heroic stride. A revolutionary hero was never portrayed as tired or downcast. Quite a few of the educated youth constantly tried to bury their feelings of exhaustion or discouragement and strained always to present an image of joyous enthusiasm.

The fourth and fifth of the Five Goods were "concern for the collective" and "concern for solidarity and friendship." The young people from Canton pooled all of their money in a fund controlled by their Young Communist League leaders under the supervision of the brigade authorities and involved themselves in caring for the collective affairs of their own youth brigade rather than going out and entering into private personal relationships with the local people. They tried to outdo each other in showing concern not only for each other's hardships and illnesses but also for each other's political development. Concern for each other's political development, as we have seen, often meant criticizing one another for slacking off or becoming discouraged. This political faultfinding tended to cancel out the potentially soothing aspects of the concern over

9. Like Lei Feng, Ouyang Hai was a young People's Liberation Army soldier who died in an accident in the course of duty and who by the mid-1960s was being praised in the official Chinese media as a model for nationwide emulation. See Mary Sheridan, "The Emulation of Heroes," *The China Quarterly*, no. 33 (1968): 47–72.

each other's hardships. The formation of particularistic friendship cliques was also scrutinized and criticized, so that the youth brigade was composed of fifty individuals bound together not by warm personal friendship but by principled revolutionary comradeship.

Those who strove most fervently to realize these revolutionary ideals paid a painful price: isolation from others and indeed from their own affective selves. Ao Meihua, for instance, cut herself off from all friendly communion with others. During her first year in the village, she had no friends among the sent-down youth. Her relationship with others was one of constant exhortation to practice revolutionary principles and constant criticism for failing to live up to those principles. "I trusted in myself but did not trust in others. This was not very good. I ordered them around as if I were a parent. It is understandable that they could not stand me. But I did not realize this at the time." She characterized her relations with others as completely lacking in "human feeling." One example she gave to illustrate this lack was the way she handled herself when she returned to Canton on vacation and visited her old friends. They threw a party at which everyone sat around a table preparing meat dumplings and chatting about old times. But Ao sat in a corner reading the works of Mao; she no longer had time for such friendly frivolity.

Besides being isolated from her friends, Ao was cut off from her inner self. Once, for instance, a few years after her arrival in Chen Village, as she looked at a photograph of Chairman Mao and Lin Biao, the thought flashed through her mind that Chairman Mao looked like a pig and Lin Biao like a Pekinese dog. Horrified, she pushed the thought away. Her main reaction was not guilt but fear. "You see, we often went on propaganda tours and all the women slept together, and I often talked in my sleep. I was afraid that I would voice these thoughts in my sleep and others would overhear them. . . . So every morning when I woke up, I asked the people around me whether I had said anything in my dream the night before." She also had some feelings of guilt. "This proved that my feelings for our great leader Chairman Mao were not deep enough. Other people loved him from the marrow of their bones, from the deepest recesses of their hearts. They would never think like me. I did not have much to be thankful for from the Chairman. My feelings did not come from my bones and heart. I asked myself why my feelings were different from the others. I shuddered." During her first year in the village, she also ran into difficulty because when she was acting in revolutionary dramas with the sent-down youth propaganda team, she could not cry no matter how hard she tried. The other youth criticized her for this, because it indicated that she did not have deep enough class feelings. She was by no means the only one among the sent-down youth who cut herself off from close personal relations and struggled fearfully to repress unorthodox feelings and to create orthodox ones by exerting her reason and will.

Ao Meihua's behavior was typical of a progressive minority consisting of about one-fifth of the sent-down youth who pushed themselves past their other Canton colleagues into an enduring fever of revolutionary enthusiasm. The ones who reached this plateau were individuals who could withstand the physical and mental rigors required, who turned out to have a chance of crowning their efforts with political status and power, and who deeply valued this kind of success. Practically all of the young people started out trying to reach this high plateau, but after a few months, many quickly fell by the wayside. Some simply could not take the mental strain involved. Others, who seemed genuinely willing to endure the efforts required to "make progress," had their health break down. When they could no longer work as hard as a "true poor and lower-middle peasant," they were criticized by their peers for being backward, came to realize that they could never be considered as progressive as their most advanced comrades, and eventually gave up trying. Still others felt that, for them, the rewards of scaling the revolutionary heights were not sufficient to repay the suffering entailed. Most of those from the street committee had not given up as much as the middle school graduates in coming to the village, and because their sacrifice in coming to the village was less, their need to have that sacrifice rewarded through political preeminence was correspondingly less. Thus, most of them eventually stopped exerting themselves with the desperate intensity of the middle school youth.

The chief concrete sign that one's ascetic efforts were being rewarded with political success was admittance into the Young Communist League. Over half of the non-League members applied to enter the League during their first year in the village, but only three new members were admitted in that year. It was Communist policy that League recruitment proceed slowly, but the slowness of recruitment in the Chen Village youth brigade was also due in part to the seven Cantonese League members' delay in admitting new members. Managing the affairs of the sent-down youth, directing political study, and acting as liaisons between sent-down youth and village cadres, the Young Communist League members were too busy making contributions to the village and achieving personal revolutionary glory to take time to sponsor new members. Moreover, they may have been reluctant to recruit too many new League members for fear of diluting their own power. People whose applications for League membership were not being acted upon quickly, began to grow extremely resentful. In evaluation sessions, they sharply criticized

League members for not caring enough for them politically. Many of those who had reason to believe that they would never be allowed to enter the Young Communist League began to abandon their intense revolutionary zeal.

Another obstacle to having one's hard work and ascetic endeavor rewarded by recognized political status and power was one's official class background. About four-fifths of the sent-down youth had poor class backgrounds. They did not come from worker or revolutionary cadre families, but from petit bourgeois families or even worse. When they had gone down to the village, the official slogan was that class background was not as important as political performance. Upon reaching the countryside, they were given an official poor and lower-middle peasant identification card, which they could use to go to the front of lines in state-run clinics and to gain other such privileges. But their family backgrounds were still noted by the authorities. As the Four Cleanups started in the village and ever greater stress was laid on the importance of being a poor or lower-middle peasant, a shadow began to fall on their ambitions. Six of the original seven Young Communist League members in their group had poor class backgrounds. But the three new members who were admitted into the League at the end of their first year in the village were all from genuine proletarian backgrounds. The other youth began to suspect that no matter how hard they worked, their poor class status might keep them from receiving official political trust. This too produced a decline in political fervor and the beginnings of a hostility toward those persons who had already reached a high plateau of political success.

Many of the former sent-down youth whom I and my colleagues interviewed spoke of their first months in Chen Village in enthusiastic, almost idyllic terms. Those days had been physically hard, mentally exhausting, and emotionally draining. But they had been filled with excitement from the discovery of a new environment and the prospects of accomplishing great deeds for the revolution. There was happiness from learning new things and trying out a new life and joy from expending one's energies to the fullest for a glorious cause. But after a few months in the village, the atmosphere became more and more strained as competition among the youth intensified, hunger and exhaustion took their toll, and about ten of the youths moved into solid control of positions of high political status and influence. The Redness of many of the youth began to fade. For that first year in Chen Village, there was no path to social or political success except the one controlled by the youth brigade's Young Communist League—the path that demanded intense study of the thought of Chairman Mao and rigorous practice of his teachings. Those who had failed to advance along this path were angry and discouraged.

The First Year in the Village: Relations between
Sent-Down Youth and Peasants

As we have seen, the sent-down youth saw their vocation as one of unit-ing wholeheartedly with the poor and lower-middle peasants of Chen Village. During their first year in Chen Village, however, their under-standing of the poor and lower-middle peasants was based more on reading and discussing Maoist thought than on observing the poor and lower-middle peasants around them. Maoist thought had taught them that the poor and lower-middle peasants were the backbone of the revo-lution and that their values were the essence of revolutionary rectitude. These peasants lived plainly, worked hard, and steadfastly supported the revolution. In their enthusiasm to excel in learning from the peasants, some sent-down youth lived more poorly, labored harder, and rested less than practically any of the real poor and lower-middle peasants of Chen Village. The city youth believed that all of this manifested their deep love for the peasants.

The image they got when they did actually observe the peasants, however, was often at variance with the peasant ideals they so ardently emulated. These peasants lived poorly because they had to not because they wanted to for the glory of the revolution; they often sought every possible opportunity to augment their income through their private plots and sideline production, even when this distracted them from their col-lective duties. They did not usually enjoy attending political meetings, could not discuss Mao's works, and did not seem especially anxious to learn how to. The men liked to squat in several meeting places after din-ner not to discuss revolutionary politics but to tell feudalistic stories from the *Water Margin* and the *Romance of the Three Kingdoms*. Sometimes they even talked and joked in a crude way about sex! Many of the women seemed to talk about nothing but the most provincial gossip, and even they sprinkled their talk with frequent references to sex. The peasants' brand of poverty, moreover, led not only to a simple, austere life but also to a sloppy, unhygienic one. In the eyes of well-bred city youth, their houses were often disgustingly dirty. The family pig usually slept in the kitchen; the family living quarters were often a shambles. The peasants not only dressed in ragged clothes but were always disheveled and dirty. The sent-down youth might emulate the poverty of the peasants, but they at least kept their dormitory tidy and themselves neat. They might emulate the very open and direct way in which peasants spoke to each other, but they at least kept their language clean.

Soon after their arrival in the village, the sent-down youth leaders formally criticized the village cadres for allowing the people to use such vulgar language. They set up a Learn from Norman Bethune Team to help the peasants become like Norman Bethune, "noble-minded and pure, persons of integrity and above vulgar interests."[10] The Learn from Norman Bethune Team was a story-telling unit that tried to entertain the peasants by telling them uplifting stories about people like Lei Feng rather than the feudalistic nonsense they seemed to enjoy so much. A few people came to hear the Norman Bethune storytellers out of curiosity, but, as one interviewee put it, "the stories weren't all that good." Few people returned to listen and the Learn from Norman Bethune Team disbanded. In a less quixotic vein, the sent-down youth set up a team to teach peasants proper hygiene. This had some small initial success, but more than the lectures of a few city youth were needed to change the habits of the villagers. The peasants were, however, interested in some of the modern medicines the youth had brought from Canton, and their introduction initiated a process that would lead them away from some of the superstitious practices they still used to cure the sick. The young people also set up teams to read the newspaper to the peasants. The peasants were not too interested in the editorials, but some were fairly interested in learning about the events of the larger world and especially about progress made by other production brigades.

This was the villagers' first experience with a contingent of sent-down youth. They had been pressured by the county government into accepting this group; most of the production teams in their commune had a youth brigade. They saw no liability for themselves in taking in the youth. The government had given them money to turn their ancestral hall into a dormitory, and they had done so in such a way that the dormitory could easily be converted into a school if the youth left. When the young people first came to the village, they were given six months living expenses by the government, and the plots of land they were given to support themselves were reclaimed land. They were no burden to the village. The city people could be of use in teaching the peasants to read and in helping them to learn about the outside world. True, their self-righteous Redness was a little strange, and their puritanical criticisms of peasant language and habits a bit obnoxious. But on balance, during the first year the city youth lived in the village, the peasants probably felt them to be more of a benefit than a burden. Peasant attitudes toward them changed, however, when the youth brigade was disbanded and its members settled into the village's various production teams.

10. From Mao Zedong, "In Memory of Norman Bethune," *Selected Works,* 2: 337–39.

Dispersion of the Youth into Village Production Teams

In late 1965, after the urban youth had been in the village for about a year, the youth brigade was broken up and its members assigned to Chen Village's ten production teams. This change was made because the urban youth had not been able to produce enough collectively to provide for their needs without subsidies from the government or the rest of the village. When the youth brigade's existence as an organization structurally separate from the village was ended and its members were assigned to production teams, the power of the urban subbranch of the Young Communist League to control the lives of the urban youth was broken. There were no more daily political study meetings, no more opportunities for the fifty youth constantly to scrutinize one another. The urban youth could now establish their own personal relationships with individual peasant families and through these relationships begin to achieve other kinds of success within the village than that dictated by the thought of Chairman Mao and controlled by the League. The attitudes and habits they had developed and the political positions they had achieved during their first year, however, helped to determine the ties they now forged with the peasants, the moral discourse they adopted, and the moral predicaments they encountered as political circumstances changed.

After the urban youth had been in the village production teams for about a year—that is, by the end of 1965—they began to fall into three main types, according to the kinds of commitments they had made to the village inhabitants. The first type comprised those who developed close social ties to the ordinary peasant masses; the second, those who forged close political alliances with the village's leading cadres—especially Longyong—and helped those cadres push through their programs; the third, those who developed close ties neither to cadres nor to the masses within the village and, becoming restless and unruly, were regarded essentially as troublemakers.

The youth regarded as most acceptable to the ordinary peasants were those of the first type: the ones who abandoned a large measure of their urban identity. These youth gave up the hope of returning to the city, at least for the near future, and the desire to change the village socially or politically according to the ideals they had learned in the city. These city youth were mostly persons who had failed to attain a position among the political elite of the youth brigade and who had little immediate hope of obtaining a good job and a tolerable social position in the city. Many of these youth had come from the street committee. Having abandoned the hope of becoming revolutionary heroes by becoming more peasant than the actual peasants of the village, they quickly settled into the village routines of hard work, friendly gossip, and the patient building of secure relationships based upon exchange of favors according to the principles of "human feeling." They began to speak the kind of moral language traditional to the village; they abandoned the Maoist mode of moral discourse.

The young women of this type had an especially easy time becoming thoroughly rusticated. There was a shortage of women in the area, and many families were having a hard time finding wives for their sons. Really desirable wives—women who came from secure families of good official class status, were physically healthy and capable of hard farm work, had a docile temperament, and if possible were reasonably pretty—were hard to come by. If a local young man's official class status was undesirable (upper-middle peasant or worse), his physical ability lacking, and his family poor, he could have extreme difficulty finding a wife. The city girls who were genuinely interested in staying in the village were connubial bargains. Even if their families had a relatively poor official class status, they were, after all, officially considered poor and lower-middle peasants because they had moved to the countryside. Although they were not good farm workers, they were still young, and if reasonably healthy, they could be taught agricultural and domestic skills. Most important, village peasants could marry them without having to pay a high bride price. Their families in Canton were not as accustomed to demanding high bride prices as families in the countryside; moreover, since their daughters were stuck in the village with little chance of returning to the city, it was in the interests of their families to marry them off as best they could in the village. Thus the urban families were in no position to strike a hard connubial bargain. Within two years after the youth brigade had disbanded, six of the girls had married into local peasant families. Five of these girls were from the street committee, one from junior middle school. They quickly lost their urban primness and youthful good looks. They aged quickly, usually appeared disheveled, and grew adept at arguing and gossiping in the vulgar slang of the village. Their fate was viewed with sadness by those sent-down youth who clung more firmly to their urban values. Four other girls, all junior middle school graduates, married young men of peasant background (not from Chen Village) who had received an education and had gained white-collar jobs within the commune: two of these men were teachers, one a post office clerk, and one a worker in the commune broadcasting station. These girls then moved to their husbands' family villages elsewhere in the commune. Although they became deeply rusticated, their lot in life was considerably easier than that of those who had married peasants.

Young men who had no realistic hope of returning to the city in the foreseeable future and were not willing or able to join the political elite of sent-down youth had a much harder time becoming thoroughly rusticated, because they were not able to join a local family network through marriage. Thus few of the urban young men reconciled themselves to staying in the village. Some, however, realizing that they could not return to Canton in the near future, settled down to a life of hard work among the ordinary peasants, hoping that by gradually winning the respect of the peasants and cultivating friendships with influential local families they might eventually find a way to return to the city. Five young men fit this category: three were poorly educated youth from the street committee and two were middle school graduates who could not dare think of returning home by any illegal means because this would hurt their parents, who were in a vulnerable political position.

A second type of sent-down youth comprised those who became deeply involved in Chen Village politics by performing important services for the village's leading cadres—especially for Longyong. These young people were mostly from the political elite of the youth brigade. They had distinguished themselves by their righteous Redness. Most of them were Young Communist League members. When the members of the youth brigade were scattered among Chen Village's production teams, the village was still being run by the Socialist Education Movement work team, which was preparing to set up new village organizations to help the peasants study Mao's works; carry out propaganda through the performance of skits, songs, and dances; and operate the wired broadcasting system being set up in the village. To play leading roles in the propagation of Maoist virtue, the work team was looking for politically fervent, articulate young people without any close personal ties to local power factions. It naturally turned to some of the most zealous of the sent-down youth. By the time the work team left the village at the end of 1966, Longyong came to appreciate the value of some of these Red city youth. He saw how their political righteousness and lack of personal ties in the village might help him beat down the factions that opposed him. He understood how their ability to do propaganda work might tip the community's ideological scales in favor of the austere vision of community life to which he was committed. He recognized that their educational and cultural work might make Chen Village a more enlightened place, a community more ready to undertake a leap forward in technological innovation, and hence a community able to surpass its neighbors in wealth and prestige. So Longyong supported, encouraged, and promoted those Canton youth who were the most fervent, the most articulate, and the most willing to do as he told.

After their dispersal among the production teams, about twelve of the sent-down youth were quickly given jobs that, at least in their eyes, conferred high levels of political status and influence. The most prestigious of these jobs was that of Mao Zedong Thought Counselor (*Mao Zedong sixiang fudao yuan*). These counselors were responsible for "teaching the peasants philosophy," that is, for directing them in the study of Mao's sayings in an attempt to make them more committed to the moral ideals of socialism. In terms of the value bestowed on this post by official propaganda and the real influence it conferred, it entailed a high degree of responsibility and power and provided the highest position of status available to a politically minded sent-down youth in Chen Village at the time. Eleven of the twelve members of the political elite of sent-down youth were such Mao Thought Counselors. The twelfth person was very busy helping the village cadres carry out the electrification of the village. Nine of these twelve outstanding urban youth were Young Communist League members.

From these twelve emerged a group of four who demonstrated exceptional ability and effectiveness. The other eight lagged behind because of sickness, a relative lack of intelligence and personal drive, or other personal handicaps that precluded their playing a leading role within the village. The city youth who was the secretary of the sent-down youth subbranch of the Young Communist League, for instance, was an Overseas Chinese from Indonesia who manifested a great deal of Redness but was handicapped by the fact that he could not speak Cantonese fluently—a failing for which he earned the nickname "International Phonetic Alphabet." In spite of his language limitations, he worked diligently and steadily as a Mao Zedong Thought Counselor, and he was widely respected by both the sent-down youth and some of the lower-level village cadres. But once forced to seek his political glory outside the confines of the youth brigade, among the peasants of Chen Village, he never attained a position of preeminence.

The four young people who did the work required in new posts with exceptional effectiveness and enthusiasm were carefully scrutinized by Longyong. In the end, he only chose two to work at his right hand. The two he rejected were not docile enough for his purposes and tastes. The brigade chief liked to have hard-driving articulate people as his associates only if they would do as he told them. The two people who had these qualifications were Ao Meihua and the young man who was eventually to become her fiancé, Red Cheng. The two city youth who, after a quick jump into prominence, were rejected by Longyong, were Overseas Deng and Stocky Wang. They were bitterly disappointed by their rejection. It was a major moral crisis for them.

Their rejection constituted such a crisis because they could no longer consider themselves good in terms of the Maoist moral discourse to which they had so firmly committed themselves. For those youth committed to Maoist moral discourse, doing good was, as we have seen, intimately connected with getting ahead. Although a person was not supposed to do good deeds *in order* to get ahead, truly good people should expect to advance in political rank. If not, then they could logically conclude either that there was something fundamentally wrong with the political system or with their conception of goodness. In late 1965 and early 1966, it was impossible for young Maoists in the position of the sent-down urban youth to make the case in Maoist terms that there was something fundamentally wrong with China's political system. To justify their lives, they were committed to looking to the words of Chairman Mao as interpreted by government authorities. And the Maoist orthodoxy that reached their ears told them that they were to do what their approved political superiors commanded. Thus they could not blame their political failure on a corrupt political system. The current version of Maoist orthodoxy compelled them to admit, therefore, that their failure was attributable to their lack of Maoist moral virtue. When applied to their failure to achieve political success, Maoist moral discourse created a painful moral predicament for them.

The more deeply one had theoretically and practically committed oneself to Maoist morality, the more painful was one's predicament when the path to upward political mobility was blocked. Those youth who had dropped out of the quest for status through the pursuit of moral Redness early on had resolved their dilemmas; those youth whose pursuit of moral virtue had been crowned with political success felt none as yet. But Overseas Deng and Stocky Wang, the two youth who by virtue of their zeal and skill had climbed the highest before falling, experienced an extraordinarily painful kind of impasse. And they were not alone. By mid-1966, the majority of the sent-down youth—about thirty of them—had shared similar predicaments. These included most of the young men and many of the better educated young women who had not attained hoped-for positions of political prominence and saw no meaningful future in becoming like ordinary peasants in the village. They formed the third type of village youth—the restless malcontents.

But by the autumn of 1966 news of the Cultural Revolution reached Chen Village. And in the moral propaganda that launched the Cultural Revolution, Mao himself offered the malcontents a way out of their dilemmas. Mao himself said that the "orthodox" interpretation of Maoism—the one that demanded unflagging obedience to established authority—was wrong. Mao said that rebellion against China's established political institutions was justified, because these institutions were perverted by those who had "taken the capitalist road." This teaching offered salvation to the zealous Maoists among the sent-down youth who had so recently tasted political failure. They could now believe that they had indeed been righteously good but that the political system had failed them, had indeed been unworthy of them. Thus, in the name of goodness itself, they could turn against the system with fury. Overseas Deng and Stocky Wang became their leaders.

But we are getting ahead of ourselves; we shall discuss the moral dynamics of the Cultural Revolution in Chapter 6. This chapter will conclude with brief profiles of the character and careers of the four sent-down youth who had tried the hardest to become committed Maoists by mid-1966.

Overseas Deng

Overseas Deng was an Indonesian-born Chinese who could have gone on to the university after graduation from middle school but decided to temper himself by heeding Mao Zedong's call to go to the countryside. He came from a very wealthy family in Indonesia. His father had deposited large sums of money in the People's Bank in Canton, and Deng had access to this money. Even though he ate and dressed as poorly as any of the sent-down youth during the first year of revolutionary fervor in the youth brigade, he let everyone know that he was indeed very wealthy. For instance he bought an expensive tape recorder (a commodity far beyond the reach of most people in China at that time) that he shared with people to aid in the study of Mao's Thought but that also testified to his financial resources. He was very good at working with machinery, especially electronic equipment. Soon after the youth brigade had arrived in Chen Village, while Qingfa was still in power, Qingfa got him to help in the first phases of the electrification of the village. Thus he became known as Qingfa's man.

A member of the Young Communist League, Deng was one of the most politically fervent of the sent-down youth during his first year in the village. A senior middle school graduate, he was also one of the oldest, about twenty years old. His relative age and his outstanding speaking ability made him one of the most prominent of the youth brigade's leaders. But Overseas Deng was a very stubborn person who would defer to no one. His foreign connections and his evident wealth made him appear sinister to many of the villagers. His stubborn pride and his early association with Qingfa left an especially bad impression on Longyong. When Longyong sought out city youth to play an important role in the village, he bypassed Deng. During the Cultural Revolution, Deng became one of the boldest and most articulate leaders of those discontented city youth who had been excluded from positions of political responsibility in the village and who saw no future in an ordinary peasant life within the village. After the Cultural Revolution he was to pay a harsh penalty for his rebelliousness. He was "struggled against" in a campaign to "cleanse the class ranks" and locked up for a year in a makeshift village jail.

Stocky Wang

Stocky Wang was a junior middle school graduate, one of the most elo-quent members of his class. His father had been a minor official for the Guomindang but had died just before Liberation, and his mother had remarried. His stepfather had fought in Korea and was considered a war hero. Wang's official class status was that of his stepfather, and it was an extremely good class status. After arriving in Chen Village, Wang tried to change his name to Lin, the name of his stepfather, so that he could even more fully take advantage of his stepfather's glory, but everybody contin-ued to call him Wang.

Wang had given up an opportunity to continue his education in a teachers' college in order to come to Chen Village. During his first year in the village he distinguished himself for his Maoist Redness and was ad-mitted into the Young Communist League. Less haughty than Overseas Deng, he in general enjoyed better relations with ordinary peasants. Soon after he had been assigned to a production team, however, he be-came involved in a factional struggle against his team head. A brash, ar-ticulate person, Wang took the lead in criticizing his team head's work methods. Some of the peasants rallied behind him, using him as a spokesperson. Because of this, Longyong regarded him as a trouble-maker. With Longyong against him, there was little hope of advancing into the village "aristocracy." Along with Overseas Deng, he soon became one of the principal youth leaders to criticize the village cadres for their handling of the city youth, and during the Cultural Revolution he led a band of rebellious youth back to Canton. Unlike Overseas Deng, Stocky Wang took an active part in the Red Guard movement in Canton. Like Overseas Deng, however, he was severely punished when forced back to the village.

Ao Meihua

Ao Meihua, my research assistant in Hong Kong, was a young woman of enormous determination from an intermediate class background: her fa-ther was a physician. The fact that she had an inferior class status and was younger than such leaders as Overseas Deng put her at an initial disadvantage in her striving to accomplish glorious deeds and to gain status and power. But these initial disadvantages may have worked to her long-term advantage after the youth brigade was disbanded. Being enor-mously determined to succeed politically but slightly handicapped be-cause of her age, sex, and class background, she was perhaps more prone than Overseas Deng and Stocky Wang to defer to Longyong's direction. At any rate, Longyong made her one of his main assistants. Besides being the head of the Mao Zedong Thought Counselors in the village, she became the announcer for the village's wired broadcasting system, a member of the public security committee, a member of the village's propaganda team, and a cashier for her production team. As we shall see, when a power vacuum was created in the village during the Cultural Revolution, she and her fiancé Red Cheng became two of the most politically powerful people in Chen Village.

Red Cheng

Red Cheng came from a politically active proletarian family. His father was a factory laborer who constantly won citations for being a model worker. His older brother was a Communist Party member and a schoolteacher. In middle school Cheng was not respected as much as Ao Meihua because his grades were not as good and his proletarian manners not polite enough for his refined teachers. To his family's dismay, he became involved with a group of Overseas Chinese students who had a good deal of money and enjoyed good food and expensive entertainment. To keep up with his friends' life-style, Cheng stole some blankets from the school dormitory and sold them. He was caught and received a "major demerit." His parents and his elder brother were furious and berated him for not living up to the dignity of his proletarian background. He seems to have had deep feelings of guilt and shame over this incident. Although he was admitted into a Canton technical school after graduation from junior middle school, he passed up this opportunity to go to the countryside. As Ao Meihua put it: "He wanted to make himself into a new person."

In the village, he developed into an extraordinarily intense young person. Of all the sent-down youth, he was perhaps the hardest on himself, wearing the poorest clothing, eating the most abstemiously, laboring with the most fanatical intensity. In political discussions he spoke out with all his might, not carefully weighing his words like many of the sent-down youth, but brashly making big political issues out of small incidents. After a year he was allowed to join the Young Communist League. Although he was in the youth brigade, he remained only in the second echelon of the brigade's political elite. Such established League members as Overseas Deng and Ao Meihua clearly ranked above him in prestige and power. But when he was assigned to a production team, "he was like a fish let loose in the sea." He found an environment perfectly tailored to his abilities, and he responded with tremendous energy. In his first two years in the village, he rapidly grew into a tall, strapping young man. He became an excellent farm laborer and an extremely articulate speaker. He was exceptionally outspoken in defense of brigade policy within his production team. For instance, his team was responsible for farming a very small plot of land about three hours' walk from the village center; the team members had reached a tacit agreement not to farm this land, but Cheng publicly berated them for their laziness, bringing this issue out into the open. The team members disliked him and called him an "immature kid" who should mind his own business. But such actions won him the approval of Longyong. Of all the sent-down youth, he became Longyong's favorite. Longyong liked him not only because he worked immensely hard in support of Longyong's policies but also because, unlike most of the sent-down youth, he did not wilt under Longyong's fierce tongue. Longyong liked people to do as he said, but he did not respect people who cringed before him.

More than any of the other city youth, Red Cheng seems to have acted out of a fierce desire for revolutionary immortality. The furious passion of his striving seemed to be something much more than could be explained by a mere desire to advance his career. He seemed to be atoning for a deeply felt guilt at his theft of the blankets and did so under the shadow of death. In early 1966, he suddenly became extremely ill and was taken to the county hospital where his illness was diagnosed as leukemia. Doctors believed that his death was imminent, and his parents were called to the county seat to see their son before he died. But instead of dying, he quickly made an extraordinary recovery. The doctors decided that their diagnosis had been incorrect and that he was completely cured. He returned from the hospital to Chen Village just as the harvest season was beginning and, instead of resting, plunged into ten hours of work a day. After this brush with death, he drove himself harder and harder. He not only worked tremendously hard at farm work but stayed awake late into the night studying the works of Chairman Mao. This awesome display of dedication was rewarded and hence abetted by Longyong's encouragement and by the attainment of high political prestige in the village. During the Cultural Revolution, when many of the village's cadres "lay down and refused to work," Cheng became vice-chairman of the "Cultural Revolution Small Group," which took over the management of the village. He had reached the highest political position any sent-down youth could reach in Chen Village. In 1968, he was admitted into the Communist Party. But a year later, while stationed with his army unit in northern China, he became ill again—apparently with leukemia. In October 1969 he died.

The development of Red Cheng's character highlights the most important theme running through the account of the sent-down youth presented in this chapter: the interaction between Maoist moral commitments and social situational constraints in the formation of the character of the youth. It is impossible to explain the way Cheng struggled and died only with reference to personal career interests. If he were simply a person rationally pursuing clearly defined self-interests, he would have husbanded his energy, taken better care of himself, and not exhausted himself trying heroically to "serve the people." His conduct, as well as that of other city youth, is only understandable in the context of Maoist moral ideology of the mid-1960s.

Yet this is not to say that shifting career opportunities, tied to shifts in Chinese social structure, played no part in shaping the characters of the young people portrayed in this chapter. Maoist ideology told the youth how to live in order to have a good and glorious life. To become glorious, Mao said, they had to pursue a political calling successfully. Sent from their homes in the city to the unfamiliar and "backward" countryside, the young people were in varying degrees stripped of the opportunities to achieve a meaningful life other than through the pursuit of Maoist virtue. They could not become learned scholars, skilled technocrats, competent bureaucrats, or even capable factory workers. Most of them saw no other choice but to become idealistic revolutionaries in the Maoist mold or ordinary peasants. Those "street committee youth" who had only minimal education might accept becoming ordinary peasants. But the more educated one was, and the higher one had hoped to climb among the privileged levels of the urban environment, the more becoming an ordinary peasant seemed—as Ao Meihua put it—like being "thrown into the garbage can of history." The problem was that only a few of the youth had any chance of becoming a success in Maoist terms. Those who did, like Red Cheng and, for a while, Ao Meihua, pushed themselves to extraordinary heights of self-sacrificing zeal. But those who could not achieve what the ideology said they must experienced a tremendous moral tension—a tension that exploded into rebellion during the Cultural Revolution.

5 Maoist Rituals

WORSHIP OF AN IDOL WITH FEET OF CLAY

Under orders from above, the Socialist Education Movement work team launched a Mao Study campaign, the high tide of which lasted from the middle of 1965 to the middle of 1966.[1] This was the second half—the most positive half—of the Socialist Education Movement. In the first half of that movement, the peasants had been harshly taught how not to live through rituals of struggle. At the end of the Four Cleanups, the work team had effected the beginnings of a synthesis between the new Maoist moral discourse and themes from the older Confucian discourse. Now, in the Mao Study campaign, it was going to try to deepen that synthesis. The work team was going to make Mao into a sacred symbol of all the deep hopes and aspirations potentially uniting the villagers into a moral community. This sacred symbol could link the villagers' hopes and aspirations to those of the great public community that was the Chinese nation. This endeavor was doomed to failure, however, because the religion of Mao was fatally flawed. Mao was an idol with feet of clay.

The problem was that there were two inseparable parts to the Mao cult: a veneration of the person of Mao himself and of his teachings. They were inseparable because Mao was presented as a great person precisely because of his great teachings. He was almost godlike because his teachings were the Truth itself.[2] In the long run it might have been possible to

1. The Mao Study campaign is also described in Anita Chan, Richard Madsen, and Jonathan Unger, *Chen Village: The Recent History of a Peasant Community in Mao's China* (Berkeley: University of California Press, 1984), chap. 3.

2. For examples of the devotional literature produced in connection with the veneration of Mao, see George Urban, ed., *The Miracles of Chairman Mao* (London: Tom Stacey, 1971). A good analysis of the quasi-religious aspects of Maoist ideology in the mid-1960s can be found in Richard Baum, "Ideology Redivivus," *Problems of Communism* 16, no. 3 (1967):1–11.

venerate the person of Mao as a great leader who summed up the most glorious accomplishments and the best hopes of the Chinese revolution. But in the short run, it proved clearly impossible to worship Mao's teachings. Because it was so obviously absurd to make those teachings into sacred dogma, Mao's teachings became his feet of clay.

In the beginning of the Mao Study campaign the peasants did not notice the feet of clay. They saw only the halo of revolutionary accomplishment surrounding the person of Mao. Most of the peasants, however, were illiterate. They could not learn much more than a few slogans of Mao's doctrines. When they participated in solemn rituals to study Mao's teaching, they were really focusing their attention on the person of Mao himself and on a few of Mao's more noble-minded ideas. As we shall see, this could and did lead to a heightened sense of unity and common purpose, at least for a time. And it promoted the loose integration between traditional moral discourse and the basic principles of Maoist teaching. For the villagers, the Mao personality cult was a ceremony of innocence.

However, the integrative spell cast by the worship of Mao could last only as long as the peasants believed that Mao's image was noncontroversial. As long as the image of Mao was that of a wise teacher who had expressed some lofty general teachings that practically every villager could give lip service to and many villagers could quietly interpret in somewhat different ways, the villagers might remain united around that image. But when educated people who should be able to *understand* Mao's teaching started arguing violently about that teaching, the controversy toppled the image of Mao and destroyed the fledgling moral order within the village. As we shall see, this is what happened when some of the village's sent-down youth who had been pressed into service as official teachers of Mao's Thought began to realize the absurdity of Mao's teachings.

Ministers of Maoist Ritual: the Mao Zedong Thought Counselors

By the fall of 1965, the campaign to study the works of Chairman Mao was building up a tremendous momentum all over China. The People's Liberation Army, controlled by Lin Biao, had taken the lead in studying Mao's works. The lessons of its experience were now being applied throughout the country. In the process, Mao's Thought and Mao himself were becoming apotheosized. Mao's Thought was becoming not only an important theoretical guide to correct political action but a sacred Word, awesome and magically powerful. Mao was on his way to becoming almost universally venerated as a quasi-divine supreme teacher, the emotion-charged symbol of the revolution's goodness and power.

To assist in preaching Maoist Thought, the work team set up an organization of Mao Zedong Thought Counselors. Since the goals of this organization were to communicate Mao's Thought and to ensure behavioral compliance with it, its members had to be literate and articulate, familiar with village life, personally devoted to living according to Mao's Thought, and unafraid to criticize fellow villagers for not living up to its principles. In Chen Village, the persons who best met these requirements were politically zealous sent-down youth. In most neighboring villages, many of the Mao Zedong Thought Counselors were educated peasant youth. But because of Chen Village's poverty, it contained few local educated young people. Since the task of directing Mao study required an ability to read Mao's works and to talk coherently about the ideas contained in them, most local youth were excluded from being leaders among the counselors.

Furthermore, the job of counselor required that one preach a Maoist ideal of total devotion to the collective and indifference to "selfish" economic interests. Only a sent-down youth could be completely indifferent to such mundane concerns as the cultivation of a private plot. Anyone who was married had to be concerned with such matters to some extent. Even unmarried local youth had to help their parents care for the family's private enterprises. The sent-down youth had no one to support but themselves. Having minimal economic needs, they could afford to practice and preach Maoist indifference to "selfish" economic interests more easily than any other group of village residents. The job of counselor required that one constantly criticize one's neighbors for failing to live up to the rigorous standards of Mao's Thought. The sent-down youth were practically the only villagers who did not—or initially thought they did not—need any of the social security that came from being on friendly terms with large numbers of people in the village. The job of counselor required one to have an intimate knowledge of conditions in the village, so that one might know how Maoist virtue ought concretely to be manifested in the village and recognize who was and was not demonstrating that virtue. Here the sent-down youth were at a disadvantage that could be fairly easily overcome. In a small place like Chen Village, practically everyone knew everyone else's business. Once out of their youth brigade, the sent-down youth quickly learned the business of the village, although they did not sympathize with it like most other villagers. They thus made excellent Mao Thought Counselors—for a while. Later they came to lose their effectiveness.

Within each of Chen Village's ten production teams, a small group of four or five counselors was chosen by the work team. "The work team asked the masses for ideas, but they had none." So the masses "spontaneously" elected those persons whom the work team suggested to them. About half of the members of each small group were young peasant activists who were literate and had distinguished themselves in struggles against the cadres during the first phase of the Four Cleanups. But the head of each small group—and therefore the person who set the pace for the work of each team—was a sent-down youth. Shortly after the election of the small groups, the work team chose a brigade counselor from the small group heads: Ao Meihua. She was in charge of coordinating the work of the small groups under the direction of the work team.

In the winter of 1965–66, all of the Mao Thought Counselor group heads attended a ten-day-long meeting in the county seat where they were trained for their role. At this meeting, they memorized and discussed the Maoist texts to be used for the initial phase of Mao study within their village: the Three Constantly Read Articles, "Combat Liberalism," and selections from "On New Democracy." They also studied manuals published by the People's Liberation Army that outlined the main points to be drawn from the Maoist classics and suggested stories that might be used to illustrate each of the various points. By studying examples of model brigades that had already carried out exceptionally effective programs of Mao study, they learned how to organize study sessions among the peasants and how to present the material so that the peasants would see the relevance of the abstract Maoist ideas to their own life situation.

The Mao Thought Training Sessions

When they returned to Chen Village, they helped the work team organize a series of political rituals to begin the process of transforming peasant consciousness. These meetings, Mao Zedong Thought Training Sessions, had primarily a kerygmatic rather than a didactic purpose. Like religious revival meetings in the United States, they aimed not to teach a rationally coherent system of abstract doctrines but to proclaim a few fundamental ideas, to endow them with compelling moral and emotional power, and to call for personal and communal conversion to a life structured around them. These ideas were not the clearly defined concepts of the philosopher or scientist but the multivocal symbols of the prophet and the poet. The ideas were encased in the stories of humble, self-sacrificing Zhang Shide; of broad-minded, warmhearted, selfless, and courageous Norman Bethune; and of the resolutely persevering old man who moved the mountains. One could speak of these stories in terms of abstract concepts of altruism, diligence, and perseverance, but the work team and the counselors wanted people to *feel* these stories as paradigmatic symbols of the meaning and purpose of life.

To accomplish this, the work team and the counselors had first to implant the stories indelibly in the memories of the Chen villagers. To do this, they put the stories and slogans that summarized their meaning into songs and taught them to the peasants. To ensure that people actually memorized the stories, they called on individual peasants to recite passages from them, duly rewarding those who succeeded with praise and mildly criticizing those who failed. Along with this process of instilling the paradigmatic ideas of Maoist ideology in the minds of the peasants went the process of charging those ideas with emotional and moral value, making them fundamental symbols of the meaning of life. This was done by evoking deep feelings of gratitude for the Liberation wrought by Chairman Mao and by linking these feelings with the Maoist stories. Then the stories, filled with a deeply felt sacred value, were used to criticize the normal "selfish" patterns of life engaged in by most villagers and to evoke resolutions of repentance.

The "training sessions" at which this was accomplished took place in the crude, dirt-floored pavilion that was the brigade's meeting hall—"our great school for communism," Ao Meihua said with nostalgia and pride. The first training sessions took place after the winter planting in 1966. Each session lasted five days, and one-fifth of the village attended. The participants at each session included roughly equal numbers of known "progressive" and "backward" elements, men and women, old, middle-aged, and young people. The sessions ran from eight in the morning until five or six in the evening and began every morning with a general meeting. Participants squatted on bricks placed on the dirt floor; according to traditional custom, men and women squatted on opposite sides of the hall. The meeting opened with a song session; usually a woman counselor stood on the stage enthusiastically leading the peasants line by line through a musical rendition of one of the Three Constantly Read Articles. The peasants were completely unaccustomed to choral singing, and most of them sang hesitantly and reluctantly. But as Ao Meihua said: "Even if they couldn't sing, we forced them to open their mouths and sing. They sang very slowly; it was like teaching a child to sing." The only people really enthusiastic about singing were children and adolescents. Adult women were somewhat less reluctant to sing than the men. Choral singing was a new, but not unpleasant, activity that broke through familiar patterns of expression and helped open the villagers to receive a new ideology. Rough as it was, the singing generated a collective enthusiasm among the assembly and created a mood of anticipation for the new doctrine that was to be preached.

After the song session, the work team member directing the training session gave a short talk on the purpose of the session and the schedule of study to be followed. This was followed by a lecture on the "national and international situation" usually given by one of the counselors. (The content of this lecture would mainly be drawn from study materials published by the People's Liberation Army.) Filled with vivid stories, the lecture proclaimed China's glorious progress under the banner of Mao Zedong's Thought and the nation's daily increasing wealth and strength in the face of American imperialism's and Russian revisionism's increasing weakness. At the end, the lecture touched upon the progress of Chen Village: how rich the village had become, how many new buildings and new grain-drying yards had been built since Liberation, how much its population had increased, how its standard of living had improved. The lecture lasted about forty-five minutes; some of the peasants complained that their backsides hurt from sitting so long, but no one dared to doze off or obviously cease paying attention. The counselors kept a close eye on the audience and criticized anyone who did not pay attention. At the very end of the lecture, the speaker made a brief self-confession: he should be supremely grateful to Chairman Mao for all of these wonderful things, but sometimes he still thought more of his own selfish needs than of the good of the collective. He resolved to do better in the future.

After the lecture, the villagers were divided into discussion groups of twenty persons each; the composition of each group was carefully matched according to political progressiveness, age, and sex. Each group was led by a work team member, a counselor, or both. On the first day, the group leaders directed the discussions along fairly general lines to get the peasants accustomed to talking with each other about Mao's Thought, the revolution, the progress of Chen Village; they did not make them discuss matters of deep emotional resonance. Gradually, however, the leaders led the discussions into a more personal vein. They got some staunch old peasant to say something like: "Our life now is so wonderful compared to the old days, but we're not satisfied, think it is too hard, pay too much attention to how many work points we get, don't want to do hard, dirty jobs like taking care of the pigs or cows." The group leaders acknowledged that they too had been ungrateful to Mao and led the other members of the group to make similar confessions.

On the second and third days of the training sessions, the lectures became more and more personal and emotional. Some old peasants were eventually brought up to recall the past and compare it to the present. These recitations of past bitterness were clothed in solemn gestures to make them profoundly moving events. The sessions were held at night with almost all the lights in the meeting hall extinguished to evoke the darkness of the past. Peasants who had suffered the most terrible personal degradations ascended the stage to tell about their past. They usually wept as they told their stories and sometimes could not even finish their accounts. From the darkness, people in the audience punctuated the speaker's accounts of bitterness with shouted slogans: "Down with the old society! Down with the Guomindang reactionaries! Down with the landlord class! Long live Chairman Mao!" In the small discussion groups, people poured out their grief over the bitterness of the past and expressed their deep-felt sorrow for their ingratitude to Chairman Mao. The group leaders helped the discussants catalogue all of the little ways in which they shirked their responsibility to the collective and failed to advance along the glorious road to socialism. At the end of the training sessions, a special meal to remember the bitterness of the past was presented: the bitter wild herbs that poor peasants often ate in the old days when they could not afford better food. Some of the old people actually wept as they ate the bitter food.

Thus the training session rituals imbued the parables containing Mao's moral teachings with an aura of holy goodness and made Mao himself a symbol of salvation. Expressed in richly vague compact sayings, the Maoist teachings came to represent a wide range of profound human experiences for those hearing them: the peasants' memories of deliverance from fear and oppression and their hopes for making their ancestral home a prosperous and proud community, the dreams of the sent-down youth for revolutionary glory, the desires of the work team to accomplish a job well done. In the training session rituals, all of these memories, wishes, dreams, and hopes were fused into a common set of symbols—the vaguely presented teachings of Mao and the person of Mao. These symbols became the emblems of a single moral community uniting the peasants, the sent-down youth, and the work team.[3] All of these different groups felt that they were part of a common holy enterprise, even though they might think about the meaning of that enterprise in somewhat different ways. Their differences remained, but because of this fundamental unity around Maoist symbols, their different streams of moral discourse flowed into, influenced, and adapted themselves to one another.

Mao's appeals for a renunciation of self in favor of the collective thus genuinely transformed the conduct of many of Chen Village's poor and

3. This is paraphrased from Emile Durkheim's famous definition of religion: "A religion is a unified system of beliefs and practices relative to sacred things, that is to say, things set apart and forbidden—beliefs and practices which unite into one single moral community called a Church, all those who adhere to them" (*The Elementary Forms of the Religious Life,* trans. Joseph Ward Swain [New York: Free Press, 1965], 62). Durkheim's *Elementary Forms* remains the classic sociological treatment of the importance of religious ritual in creating the moral foundations of social solidarity.

lower-middle peasants. It did not result in a permanent commitment on their part to lives less devoted to private interests and more devoted to the collective, but it did develop a sufficient degree of emotion-laden respect for Mao's ethical ideals to make the peasants temporarily susceptible to the urgings of the work team and to cause the sent-down youth to work harder and faster on collective undertakings and to devote less time to private affairs.

Praising the Good and Criticizing the Bad

For most people, greater enthusiasm for collective endeavors and less attention to private interests did not automatically follow from participation in the training sessions. But the work team followed up the training sessions with systematic programs for criticizing individual laziness and selfishness and praising individual public-spiritedness. The Mao Thought Counselors were chiefly responsible for this praise and criticism. The main goal of the revivalistic training sessions was to legitimate the work of the counselors in praising the progressive and criticizing the backward. When a counselor criticized a villager for failing to live up to the ideals of Norman Bethune, the remark could not be passed off as the censure of a brash, self-righteous youngster. The counselor was speaking in the name of Chairman Mao, and the criticism had to be taken seriously; it produced shame and perhaps some degree of guilt. Similarly, praise from one of the counselors could not be simply dismissed as a type of flattery designed to make one work harder but could give one a sense of honor in the eyes of one's peers. For the time being, the peasants of Chen Village were morally vulnerable to the counselors' praise or criticism.

Under the direction of the work-team member in charge of propaganda, the counselors met together at least once every five days. During these meetings, they earnestly discussed passages from Mao's works and sang revolutionary songs, criticized themselves and others for failing to live up to Mao's teaching, and reported on the extent to which people in their production teams were or were not selflessly abiding by Mao's Thought. The head of each small group of counselors also met with the group's production team management committee almost every day to become acquainted with the main production tasks facing the team and the primary way selfless adherence to Mao's Thought could further those tasks. Armed with this knowledge, the counselors then formulated tactics for promoting a socialist spirit in their teams and advancing production by systematically praising the good and criticizing the bad.

One of the main opportunities for carrying out this praise and criticism came during a half-hour Mao study ritual that took place every afternoon during the peasants' lunch break. Every afternoon between 12:30 and 2:00 p.m., the peasants stopped work for lunch. Since most of their fields were far from home, they brought their lunches with them and ate at their work places. After a half hour of eating, they normally rested under a shady tree or ran up into the hills to cut burnable grass that could be sold to the brickworks as fuel for a tidy profit. But now they had to participate in a half hour of Mao study. Every work squad was assigned a counselor who read the workers a passage from one of Mao's works for them to discuss. The passages were carefully chosen to correspond to concrete problems that arose in the production squads. For instance, if some peasants did a sloppy job of transplanting rice shoots, the counselor might read the following passage from "In Memory of Norman Bethune": "Comrade Bethune's spirit, his utter devotion to others without any thought of self, was shown in his great sense of responsibility in his work. There are not a few people who are irresponsible in their work, preferring the light and shirking the heavy, passing the burdensome tasks on to others, and choosing the easy way for themselves."[4] The counselor would then deliver a little homily on this passage, saying how certain people by doing a careless job of rice transplanting were failing to live up to this teaching and were failing to be duly grateful to Chairman Mao. The squad head would then say a few words about the importance of doing an efficient job of transplanting the rice, and the workers would discuss this problem. Although no names would be mentioned, everyone would know who the lazy person was. The young militia members in the squad might then add their support to Mao's Word and express the hope that everyone in the squad would work hard in accordance with Mao's teaching. Other squad members, including the guilty persons themselves, would then feel pressured to speak out against poor workmanship.

Besides criticizing the backward, the counselors made a point of praising anyone who had worked harder than usual for the collective on any given day. In giving such praise, they often named names. This praise was not just a positive encouragement for good behavior but also a subtle means of threatening shame for backsliding. The praise was often slightly exaggerated and was directed at relatively backward people who had recently made some progress. The slightly exaggerated praise reminded everyone how backward such persons had been before and opened them to criticism from their peers if they began to slack off.

In addition to routinely praising and criticizing during the daily Mao study sessions, the counselors directed more intensely focused thought

4. Mao Zedong, "In Memory of Norman Bethune," *Selected Works of Mao Tsetung*, 4 vols. (Beijing: Foreign Languages Press, 1961–65), 2:337–39.

reform efforts at people whose backwardness was deemed to be especially detrimental to the collective. For instance, the counselors in production team no. 7 decided that the wife of the team head was proving to be a major obstacle to her husband's effective exercise of authority. Although her husband had a reputation as a hard, relatively selfless worker and a skillful manager, his authority was being undermined by his wife's reputation as a lazy, contentious person given to petty theft and spiteful damaging of collective property. To avoid having to follow the team head's orders, the team members said that their leader was not worthy of their respect since he could not even control his own wife. The counselors from his team proposed a major effort to reform this woman (who seems to have been a bit mentally unbalanced). The team head cooperated because, besides undermining his authority, his wife was making life miserable for him at home, constantly nagging him for spending too much time at his job and not enough time on his private plots. As Ao Meihua explained: "We expended a great deal of time helping his wife reform. If she did anything well, we immediately praised her during general team meetings. When we went to her house, we told her her good points, encouraging her to become good in other respects. It was the same process that a school uses to make small children Red. So after a fairly short period of time, she was very good. She didn't steal things and was more manageable. So the team head was very happy."

In addition to face-to-face criticism of backward elements and praise of progressive elements, the counselors had a powerful new medium of communication through which to propagate Maoist virtue: the production brigade's wired broadcasting system.[5] Installed at the beginning of 1966, this system consisted of thirty loudspeakers positioned throughout the village. The job of broadcaster was given to Ao Meihua, the head of the brigade's counselors. The broadcasts ran for two hours in the morning and two hours at night. Half of the time was devoted to programs and announcements conceived by Ao Meihua in collaboration with the other counselors. Every evening she went around to the heads of each production team's small group of counselors and found out who was acting in an especially progressive or an especially backward way. She then used this material to broadcast reports on various teams and the different personalities within each team. Any workers who were lagging behind would soon hear their laziness, selfishness, and lack of appreciation for Chairman Mao's Thought broadcast over the loudspeakers. Even though Ao

5. By 1975, according to an official Chinese source, 92.7 percent of the production teams throughout China were reached by wired broadcasting. Cited in William L. Parish and Martin King Whyte, *Village and Family in Contemporary China* (Chicago: University of Chicago Press, 1978), 363.

Meihua did not usually criticize people by name, everyone in the village knew who was being referred to in her broadcasts. Ao Meihua also made extensive use of fulsome praise in her broadcasting. She praised by name—usually exaggeratedly—anyone who showed any significant improvement in attitude or work. In the course of a year, she so commended about half of the adults in the village. She also praised whole production teams for leading the way in the struggle to learn from Mao's Thought. She never criticized cadres over the broadcasting system but she often praised them. They had been hurt enough during the first part of the Four Cleanups, she and her work-team leaders reasoned. Now it was appropriate that their authority and will to continue in their posts be bolstered rather than weakened. Her use of praise, however, not only rewarded cadres and ordinary peasants for moving ahead but also tended to make them fearful of falling back. As people used to say to her half-seriously and half-jokingly, "Little Sparrow [her nickname, given because of her thinness], who told you to praise us? Now I'll have to work even harder."

The kind of praise and criticism Ao Meihua and the other counselors gave to the villagers was somewhat similar to the kind the sent-down youth gave to each other in their private small group study sessions. Yet there were important differences: when criticizing each other, the zealous sent-down youth scrutinized every small detail of their conduct and discussed how that conduct might be measured against the small details of Mao's doctrine. Thus their almost absurd preoccupation with the trivia of personal life-style. When praising and criticizing the peasants in the name of Mao, they focused on relatively large manifestations of one's socialist commitment, on whether villagers worked hard at their collective labor, took proper care of collective property, and so forth. The Maoist doctrines they emphasized to the villagers called for a general commitment to the public good, not a total regulation of one's life-style. It was easy for peasants to accept this in principle even though they might not be inclined to follow it in practice. It was especially easy to accept this concern for the public welfare if in practice it meant concern for the good of one's neighborhood or one's village as a whole. Here Mao's appeals to serve the people could easily resonate with the tradition-based sense of responsibility toward the community as a whole that was advocated by local leaders such as Longyong. The villagers may have thought it bizarre that the sent-down youth counselors were so concerned with their own individual righteousness. But as long as the counselors told the villagers that Maoist virtue implied not that they too must practice such rigorous self-scrutiny but that they must be concerned about the village's public good, they could easily accept that doctrine.

And for a while at least, they accepted it not only in principle but in practice. The praise and criticism showered on the population of Chen Village in the name of fidelity to Mao's Thought initially had clear behavioral effects. People showed up for work more promptly and instead of quitting early even stayed past quitting time. While at work, they worked harder. In some production teams, fields that used to take five days to harvest could now be harvested in three. During the agricultural slack season, production teams found it easier to convince people to work on public works projects. There was less pilferage of collective night soil for use on private plots.

Toward a More Socialist Economy: The Dazhai Work-point System

According to the propaganda issued by the Party's central leadership, the study of Mao's Thought was supposed to provide a blueprint for economic and social change in China as well as the "philosophical weapon" for bringing such changes about. The study of Mao's Thought would produce "spiritual changes" in the consciousness of the Chinese people; this transformation of consciousness would make the people willing to accept socialist transformations in the economy and the social structure; these structural changes would in turn bolster new socialist modes of consciousness. Turning Marx on his head, the Maoist propaganda proclaimed that "spirit" would transform "matter"; changes in social consciousness would transform China's economic base.

At the height of the Mao Study campaign, the work team began putting this theory into practice. It tried to use the greater commitment to public welfare induced by the Mao Study rituals to introduce important structural changes into the village's collective economy.

The heart of these changes was the Dazhai work-point system. Named after Dazhai, the production brigade in Shanxi Province that Maoists proclaimed as a model for the whole country, the Dazhai workpoint system made collective agriculture more of a cooperative enterprise than it had ever been in the 1960s.[6] Prior to the adoption of the Dazhai system, workers in the village's production teams were paid for their labor using various piece rates. The number of work points (that is shares in the net profit of the production team) one received from collective labor was directly tied to the measurable quantity of one's work: how

---

6. On the intended purposes and the actual consequences of the Dazhai workpoint system in Guangdong villages, see Parish and Whyte, *Village and Family*, 62–72.

many rice shoots one planted, how many pounds of grain one harvested, and so forth. The overall quality of an individual's cooperation with his or her teammates was not taken into account. Moreover, exceptionally strong individuals could earn considerably more income than weak ones. Under the Dazhai system, workers were paid according to a collective judgment of the overall quality of their contribution to their production team. These judgments were made by one's production team peers in regular appraisal meetings. At these meetings, each worker was given a work-point ranking that determined how many work points he or she would be entitled to for a full day's work. The best male workers received 10 work points a day, the worst about 8.5. In practice, most adult males received between 9 and 10. The best females received 7.5, the worst 6.

The Dazhai system encouraged each worker to cooperate more closely with the other members of his or her production team. Moreover, under the Dazhai system the differentials between the highest and the lowest paid workers were much smaller than those under the piece-rate system. So the Dazhai system was more truly socialist, maximizing the importance of collective cooperation and minimizing the difference in material reward.

According to Maoist theory, the Dazhai system was an improvement over the piece-rate system primarily because the pursuit of self-interest was intrinsically bad; therefore collective cooperation was inherently better than individualist competition, and equality of income inherently better than inequality. But Maoists believed that the Dazhai system was also better because it would help the villagers become more productive and thus eventually increase their overall standard of living. However, for villagers who understood the world in terms of a Confucian moral discourse, maximum cooperation in production teams was not necessarily good in itself. It was good only insofar as it was appropriate to think of one's team as one's "big family." Moreover, equality of income was not necessarily good in itself. Certain people might very well deserve more than others. If, on the other hand, the Dazhai system could indeed make everyone in the village better off economically, even traditional villagers could accept it.

But the Dazhai system could fulfill its promise of increasing overall productivity only if the villagers consistently followed particular rules. First, when judging how many work points each individual should receive, they had to apply the general criteria impartially. Otherwise, the system would produce great resentment, lower morale, probably undermine cooperation, and lower productivity. However, we have already seen how the villagers' traditional ethos did not dispose them to apply such impersonal criteria strictly and how before the Socialist Education Movement they could not even trust accountants to follow the simple rules of arithmetic when calculating things that were quantifiable. Now they had to make impartial judgments about matters that were not easily quantifiable. To do this required a resolute suspension of their traditional modes of moral discourse.

For the Dazhai system eventually to increase productivity, the villagers also had to commit themselves to working hard even when this would not clearly benefit them in the short run. Under a piece-rate system, strong workers might push themselves to the point of exhaustion if they saw that every extra drop of sweat expended would bring them extra income. But under the Dazhai system, one's work points depended on how hard one worked relative to the other people in one's unit. If most of the others were not working especially hard, one could also slack off and still achieve a maximum number of work points. And since the differential between the best and the worst workers was rather small, especially strong and skilled workers were essentially subsidizing their weaker teammates by their extra labor rather than directly benefitting themselves. To increase productivity effectively, the Dazhai system required workers to put the relatively long-term collective good above their desires for immediate personal gain. If they did that, they might indeed benefit individually through increased income in the long run.

The key to making the Dazhai system work was maintaining the public spirit generated in the Mao Study rituals. As long as this spirit lasted, the villagers might be inclined to treat one another as revolutionary comrades engaged in a common public venture, and they might be willing to carry out the Dazhai work point evaluations in an impartial way. And as long as they were willing to work hard for the public good and not simply for personal benefit, they might labor with energetic enthusiasm even though they might not be sure of reaping immediate material rewards.

The Dazhai work-point system was introduced in the beginning of 1966, and for the first six months of its operation at least, it worked well. The village's cadres could count on the counselors aggressively preaching the need for principled fairness in assigning work points. They could also rely on the young men of the village militia to set a fast pace of work and thus keep the standard for the greatest number of work points high. The village's "basic militia" was composed of unmarried young men and women in their late teens and early twenties. As they reached their full adult strength, the young men especially liked to show off their physical prowess; if they could be convinced to show off that physical strength in hard farm labor in the name of serving the people, they could set a furious pace in their work and drive up the standard other villagers would have to reach to acquire the maximum number of work points. In the general enthusiasm created by the Mao Study campaign, it was indeed possible to organize the militia to set such a pace; villagers worked as hard under the Dazhai system as they had under the piece-rate system.[7]

In appearance at least, the Dazhai system was leading the village toward prosperity. With the introduction of the new system, village productivity began to climb. By the end of 1966, the output of most production teams was almost double that of 1964. And village standards of living were on the rise. In 1964 top-ranked laborers received only about forty-five pounds of grain a month. By 1966 they were getting almost eighty pounds, which was more than enough to eat and could in part be used as feed for pigs and fowl. These animals added significant amounts of meat to the villagers' diet for the first time. How much of this was really caused by the new work-point system is hard to say. Production was certainly helped somewhat by the fact that in the charged atmosphere of the time the peasants were working harder and in a more organized manner for the collective than ever before. While instituting the Dazhai system, the work team also helped the village install an electric water pump, made available improved strains of seed grain, and provided new fertilizers. Much of the increase may have come from these new technologies. Indeed one might suspect that the work team accompanied the establishment of the Dazhai system with the introduction of these new technologies in order to legitimize the new system by making it appear to cause miracles of productivity. If so, the work team had some success.

The increase in productivity meant different things to different members of the village community. For the zealous Mao Thought Counselors it was a sign of the validity of Mao's Thought, a proof, as Ao put it, that "spirit can really transform matter." For most peasants it offered a welcome opportunity to build a materially better life for themselves and their families. For some villagers, especially people like Longyong, it provided a chance to make the whole village a proud and prosperous modern community. These different views were not totally congruent. But because of the integrative effects of the Mao Study rituals and the general happiness over the increased productivity of the village, they overlapped enough to sustain a busy round of effective collective cooperation. A former production team leader expressed it this way: "When production increased and things did not turn bad [the peasants] began to believe in Mao Zedong Thought. Even the old generation had to believe because they had eyes to see that since the work team had come, production had increased. The increase in production proved that the campaign had been successful."

7. See Richard Madsen, "Harnessing the Political Potential of Peasant Youth," in *State and Society in Contemporary China,* ed. Victor Nee and David Mozingo (Ithaca, N.Y.: Cornell University Press, 1983).

Tensions within the Village's Moral Unity

But there were clearly tensions within this unity of purpose. Eager to prove their heroic devotion to Mao's Thought, the counselors had little sympathy for the peasants' desires to further the welfare of their own families. They tended to generate resentment among the peasants by pushing them harder than they thought reasonable. None of the peasants, of course, dared directly to criticize the sacred message of Maoist thought. Any such criticism would be quickly punished by the work team. As time went by, it would also be punished by the criticism of one's peers as the sacred aura surrounding Mao's Thought intensified and made that Thought increasingly unassailable. And if one felt reluctant to live by the high standards of Mao's Thought and grew tired of being hectored by a band of righteous youngsters, one might look for a way out. Unable to attack the preaching, one might attack the preachers and thus undermine their legitimate authority righteously to tell one how to live.

Perhaps the most effective way to attack a righteous preacher is to point out his hypocrisy, his failure to practice what he preaches. Thus in talking with their more backward friends, peasants grumbled that the counselors spent half their time (an exaggeration) going to meetings preparing to tell others how hard they should work and only half their time doing hard physical labor themselves. If they had to spend all day working like an ordinary peasant, they might change their tune. They would not be able to pass the test. Any counselor who took an undue amount of time off from work was especially vulnerable to this criticism; these counselors' legitimacy could be completely undermined.

The sad case of Li Jiali provided a clear example of how what Ao Meihua called a group of "mischievous" peasants could destroy the legitimacy of a counselor and thus partially avoid having to respond to the counselors' preaching. Li Jiali was the head of the small group of counselors for production team no. 1. This production team was the most backward team in the brigade. While the members of team no. 7, the most progressive team (in 1966 at any rate), used to start work around 7:00 a.m. during the agricultural slack season (6:00 a.m. during the busy planting and harvest seasons), the members of team no. 1 often did not start work until 10:00 a.m. When the members of team no. 1 did get to work, they worked slowly and carelessly. It took them almost one-third again as long as team no. 7 to complete basic collective tasks. While the women of team no. 7 usually took part in collective farm labor, the women of team no. 1 usually stayed at home, taking care of the family pigs and other private sidelines. In her role as counselor, Li was an especially vocal critic of the dilatory work habits of her fellow team members. But like many of the young women from Canton, she had the misfortune to contract a severe case of rheumatism in her legs, the result of standing too often and too long in wet paddy fields. Her case of rheumatoid swelling was especially painful and so serious that she often had to quit work early and go home where she would lay on her bed and cry. Because of her ailment she had to be given light work, picking vegetables during the harvest season, instead of cutting rice, or gathering medicinal herbs from the hills, instead of weeding the fields. One important men's gossip network in the village was centered around two poor peasants who worked in the brigade's farm-tool repair shop. Many men from Li's production team used to gather in front of this repair shop to discuss local affairs, share rumors, and express complaints. The two men who worked in the shop were especially witty speakers and generally set the tone for the discussions of this group. The men in the repair shop christened Li the village "light-work department head," and the appellation stuck. Soon people all over the village were talking about Li's inability to do heavy farm work, especially the members of her production team. Thus, "Although [Li] herself often talked about the need to go to the most difficult place, to be unafraid of sacrifice, and so on, what she said didn't have any force behind it because she couldn't do it herself. People used to say, 'She often conducts meetings, and what she says sounds very fine, but she doesn't live up to any of it very well.' So she had a lot of ideological problems. The whole village used to laugh at her; they didn't have any sympathy for her." The other counselors, however, banded together to encourage her to stay. As a result, she "thickened her skin and kept on doing her job."

The brigade cadres eventually became worried about the way the two men in the repair shop were encouraging resistance to the work of the counselors. Since the two men were of impeccable class status—poor peasants—and were widely respected in the village, they could not be stopped by heavy-handed punishment. So they were co-opted, made brigade cadres in charge of the fledgling brigade industries team. When this happened, Ao Meihua and the other counselors made a special point of praising them over the brigade's broadcasting system, extolling the importance of their work and expressing the hope that under the banner of Mao Zedong's Thought they would continue to make important contributions to Chen Village and to the Chinese revolution. As a result, the two men stopped being so "mischievous" and joined the brigade cadres in relentlessly pushing people to work harder and faster. Apparently realizing that the counselors could help them in this regard, they stopped attacking the counselors.

This vignette illustrates how ordinary villagers sought to undermine the counselors' moral authority. It also illustrates the delicacy of such a task. Criticizing the validity of Maoist moral demands was out of the question. Criticism could only be directed against the counselors' inability to live up to those demands themselves. Although such criticisms were widely muttered, the leading role in articulating them could only be taken by persons of good class status. An upper-middle peasant would not have dared to coin and publicly circulate the phrase "light-work department head." Such an act would have inevitably created political trouble for a person of bad class status. But once such a phrase was coined and circulated, many people might use it to undermine the authority of a counselor without serious fear of reprisal. If anyone got into trouble, it would be the people who had originated the phrase. In calling Li the "light-work department head," her detractors were implying that she was a hypocrite. The villagers were not unaware of the distinction between poor performance caused by bad intentions and that caused by physical weakness. But the very high standards of Mao's ideals, as conveyed in the parables of revolutionary heroism that epitomized his thought, demanded that people surmount all obstacles, even physical handicaps, through unflagging determination. Even though Li might have had good intentions, these could not really be proven unless she overcame her handicap through a heroic exercise of willpower. As long as she was not engaged in the bothersome business of badgering people to live according to Mao's standards, she was generally given the benefit of the doubt. Indeed, when she gave up the job of counselor several years later, she gained the affection of a large group of peasants; they even contributed money to buy a sewing machine for her so she could do something constructive besides farm work. But as long as she was a counselor, her conduct came under the most intense scrutiny. To give her the benefit of the doubt meant laying oneself open to her righteous, Maoist-inspired criticism.

The counselors were hurt by the peasants' attacks. In addition to Li, at least six of the original heads of the small groups of counselors proved vulnerable to the criticism that they did not deserve to be listened to because they could not pass the test of hard, persevering labor themselves. Some of the counselors responded to these attacks by driving themselves all the harder, striving to make themselves immune to such criticism. We have already seen how Red Cheng refused to rest after a serious illness and worked as hard as any of the peasants during the harvest season. Ao Meihua similarly pushed herself to the limit of her physical capacities. Although physically small and therefore not able to produce as much as a stronger person, she worked as hard as any of the peasants and produced as much as anyone of her size and weight. But others, like Stocky Wang, began to fall behind.

The motivation impelling the young urban counselors to work furiously hard was fundamentally different from that impelling most of the peasants. The peasants worked hard for economic reasons. Living very poor lives, they could all use the extra income that came from amassing high work-point totals. Even those who, like Longyong, worked hard without being deeply concerned about the number of work-points they would amass seem to have done so largely because they thought such labor would eventually increase the general prosperity of the village as a whole. But the urban counselors worked hard, not because they needed the income or were concerned about increasing the prosperity of Chen Village as such, but because they wanted to maintain the effectiveness of their political preaching. Through hard physical labor they secured the legitimacy of their authority, furthered the revolutionization of the nation according to Mao's Thought, and fulfilled their ambitions for power, status, and glory. But this political motivation was a rather fragile basis for unremitting hard work. When they had to slow down their pace of work because of particular physical infirmities or general exhaustion, their political effectiveness quickly began to disappear. As they lost hope of maintaining a pace of work that would enable them to play preeminent political roles in the village, their desire to work hard deteriorated very rapidly. Ordinary peasants who, for whatever reason, could not maintain an exceptionally energetic pace of work became moderately hard workers. Urban counselors who could not maintain an exceptionally energetic pace often quickly became backward, lazy workers. Having become discouraged, they no longer dared to criticize other villagers. Instead they began to think of ways of returning to Canton. The counselor system began to lose its teeth.

Ao Meihua, Red Cheng, and the two or three other counselors who had been able to maintain a hard pace of physical labor and who thus continued on the path to political power and glory through the preaching of Mao's Thought, tried to encourage their flagging colleagues by giving them a dose of righteous criticism. As Ao Meihua explained:

> We used to have heart-to-heart talks with them, point out things from the newspapers [about the need for self-sacrifice, perseverance, etc.] to them, get them together to sing songs. We used to give them Mao Thought lessons! They didn't like this—didn't like our giving them lessons, teaching them songs, and so forth. They didn't like our being their commanders. We used to often have meetings with them. I was so arrogant! I wasn't united with the educated youth.

Thus the encouragement of the more successful counselors often increased the backwardness of their lagging colleagues. The stage was set for the development of bitterly opposed factions among the urban youth. As this factional fighting progressed, over half of the original counselors began to drop out of their roles, as we described in the last chapter. In most cases their places were taken by local youth who, though relatively committed to Chairman Mao's Thought, had too many friends and relatives in the village to criticize people as thoroughly and as intensely as the original counselors. As the counselor system began to decline and the emotional fervor created by the first phase of the Maoist political revival began to wane, the villagers moved back toward their normal "selfish" ways.

An Idol with Feet of Clay

The rituals of the Mao Study campaign thus made an important contribution to Chen Village's ethos but did so in a fatally flawed way. The rituals created a new framework for moral discourse within the village, a framework that combined traditional and modern modes of moral thinking in a loose synthesis.

The Mao Study rituals in effect allowed the peasants to keep some of their old moral traditions—for instance, the idea that a good person was one who treated the entire village like his big family—and integrate them into some of Mao's teachings about the goodness of selflessly serving the people as a whole. They did this by making Mao Zedong and some of his moral slogans into a sacred symbol of the highest hopes and aspirations of the villagers and the whole Chinese people. The problem with this was not so much that Mao was being venerated as a great person and a great leader. Practically all nations attach a sacred aura to their greatest leaders, making them stand for the deepest shared hopes of the nation.[8] The problem with China was that the Mao personality cult involved not only veneration of Mao's person but worship of his specific teachings, not only respect for Mao as a wise person who told the Chinese to serve the people but also blind obedience to a complicated set of dogmas attributed to Mao. These doctrines were Mao's feet of clay.

Mao's moral teachings were too heroic; they left no legitimate room for self-interested behavior. People who took Mao's teachings seriously, therefore, had to deny any concern for themselves. But people are inevitably concerned with themselves to some extent. People who took Mao seriously and admitted their self-interests had to give up pretending to be good Maoists. People who did not admit to self-interests had to fool themselves and others. Thus under the guise of selflessly serving the people, the zealous sent-down youth counselors began to look more and more like self-righteous careerist hypocrites. Mao's teachings, moreover,

8. For a classic analysis of how this has been done in the United States, see Robert N. Bellah, "Civil Religion in America," in *Beyond Belief* (New York: Harper and Row, 1970), 168–89.

were too rigid. In their pure form, they were not a set of flexible principles that could be applied to complex moral situations in the light of informed common sense but doctrines to be memorized, exegeted, and forced to apply to ambiguous situations. Since it was difficult to make the doctrines fit perfectly, this process could result in tremendous factional arguments. What kept these arguments from breaking out was that in the early 1960s one's legitimate political superiors were supposed to be able to give an authoritative interpretation of the doctrine. If that authority broke down, Maoism would be destroyed as a medium for coherent moral discourse.

Most ordinary peasants did not at first have to pay attention to the inadequacies of Maoist teaching. They could concentrate on the image of Mao as a venerable leader who uttered some general principles about denying selfish instincts to serve the people. But the peasants could see people among them who were supposed to be "experts" in Maoist thought; if that Thought led the experts to live absurd lives, then the feet of clay would be broken, Mao's image would topple, and it would bring down with it the newly established framework of moral meanings. By mid-1966 some villagers were, as we have seen, citing the weaknesses of some of the counselors as an excuse not to be too concerned with restraining self-interest for the good of the collective. In the coming Cultural Revolution, the inadequacy of the moral discourse of the urban youth would become even more obvious, and the spectacle of that inadequacy would destroy the village's fragile moral order.

6 Cultural Revolution and Moral Conflict

It is well known that the Mao personality cult of the early 1960s was a symptom of a power struggle within the top echelons of the Chinese government. Partially discredited by his ill-conceived Great Leap Forward in 1958, Mao was being edged away from the levers of political power by rivals like Liu Shaoqi and Deng Xiaoping. In the struggle to regain power, Mao launched an ideological offensive. He emphasized the differences between his interpretation of Marxism-Leninism and that of his rivals. Blocked by his rivals from using the ordinary Communist Party propaganda apparatus for broadcasting his ideas, he turned to the propaganda apparatus of the People's Liberation Army, commanded by his ally at that time, Lin Biao. The propaganda apparatus of the People's Liberation Army flooded the country with Mao's peculiar, highly moralistic interpretation of Marxism-Leninism and with Mao's encouragement went on to suggest that Mao, the "Great Helmsman," the "Great Teacher," the "Red Sun that Shines in Our Hearts," was almost divine. The Communist Party propaganda apparatus, dominated by Mao's rivals, tried to counterattack by encouraging certain well-known intellectuals to publish allegorical stories and plays subtly criticizing Mao.

For most ordinary citizens throughout China, the din of Maoist propaganda drowned out the quiet voice of propaganda subtly critical of Mao. The message of the latter could only be attended to and understood by relatively sophisticated officials and intellectuals. But Mao was furious about this propaganda critical of him. In the autumn of 1965, he tried to get the official Party paper, the *People's Daily*, to publish an attack against Wu Han, the playwright who had written a play that Mao interpreted as a particularly offensive criticism of himself. The *People's Daily*, controlled by officials unsympathetic to Mao, would not cooperate. Mao eventually went outside normal Party channels and persuaded a newspaper in

Shanghai to publish a scathing critique of Wu Han. The literary critiques eventually escalated into political critiques. Mao used the vast popular prestige created by his personality cult to mobilize mass revolts against the major governmental and cultural institutions in China. The Cultural Revolution had begun.

One short-term result of the Cultural Revolution was political anarchy; another was moral anarchy. The political anarchy was eventually overcome, and basic law and order were restored in China. Now, a decade and a half after the beginning of the Cultural Revolution, China's political system has returned to the basic shape it had before the Cultural Revolution. But, I will argue, the moral anarchy of the Cultural Revolution has done more permanent damage. The experience of Chen Village suggests that it has become more difficult now for rural people in China to arrive at a meaningful moral basis for constructive political activism.[1]

The first public signs of the political struggle within the central government that would lead to the Cultural Revolution came in the form of Maoist-directed attacks in the Chinese press against the playwright Wu Han and his literary colleagues.[2] These attacks began in November 1965 and increased in intensity throughout the first part of 1966. However, the ordinary peasants and cadres of Chen Village barely noticed these literary debates. Disputes over national policies with regard to literature and education were quite outside the scope of their interests and quite beyond their understanding. Moreover, the Socialist Education Movement gave the peasants more than enough to occupy their full attention. But as the literary debates in the Chinese newspapers increased in intensity, the work team seemed to sense that something important was happening. The work team began to hold more private meetings than usual, meetings that seemed very mysterious to the villagers. As the rhetoric of the literary debates grew more shrill, with references to "poisonous weeds," "black gangs," and anti-Party and antisocialist activities, some of the urban youth within the village began to realize that the matter was indeed serious, and they began to discuss it frequently among themselves. But

1. The impact of the Cultural Revolution on Chen Village is described in more detail in Anita Chan, Richard Madsen, and Jonathan Unger, *Chen Village: The Recent History of a Peasant Community in Mao's China* (Berkeley: University of California Press, 1984), chap. 4.

2. For a concise general survey of the history of the Cultural Revolution, see Jean Daubier, *A History of the Chinese Cultural Revolution* (New York: Vintage Books, 1974). For a detailed political analysis see Hong Yung Lee, *The Politics of the Chinese Cultural Revolution: A Case Study* (Berkeley: University of California Press, 1978); and Stanley Rosen, *Red Guard Factionalism and the Cultural Revolution in Guangzhou* (Boulder, Colorado: Westview Press, 1982).

in general, the peasants were not interested enough in these matters to want to participate in such discussions.

In May 1966, overt political struggle erupted. There were violent attacks against Peng Zhen, the mayor of Beijing, and against the "black municipal Party committee" of Beijing. But Beijing was far away from Chen Village. With the exception of about five local youths who now began to approach the urban youth to discuss the Cultural Revolution, most of the peasants, masses and cadres alike, viewed the events with only mild curiosity.

Then the political ferment that had begun in Beijing began to boil over and spread throughout China. In late May and early June, groups of student proto–Red Guards, encouraged by Mao and his supporters, began to go outside Party channels to make revolution and to attack "powerholders following the capitalist road." At the beginning of August, a Maoist-controlled Eleventh Plenum of the Central Committee of the Communist Party was held in Beijing. At the end of the plenum, a sixteen-point directive was issued, formally proclaiming the launching of the Great Proletarian Cultural Revolution. In mid-August, Mao addressed a huge rally of Red Guards in Beijing, urging them to make revolution throughout the country and inviting other revolutionary youths to visit Beijing. As soon as Mao announced the formation of the Red Guards in Beijing, many local people in Canton, apparently with a minimum of supervision, began wearing red arm bands marked with Red Guard insignia and moved out into the streets to share the glory of criticizing evil Party and government officials. Cantonese officials tried to counter the threat of these independent Red Guards by forming rival Red Guard groups under their control. But the Maoists in Beijing sent thousands of Red Guards from the nation's capital and other parts of China into Canton to struggle against entrenched officials in Guangdong Province. As more Red Guards streamed into Canton and more local students joined them, the struggle in Canton became increasingly acute.[3]

When the peasants of Chen Village heard about the Red Guards, their initial reaction seemed to be one of admiration. "The peasants thought that the Red Guards must be very daring, that they must have the guts to act in society. Since not everyone could become a Red Guard, these must be people very concerned with the country's affairs." The peasants

---

3. This account is based on Ezra F. Vogel, *Canton Under Communism: Programs and Politics in a Provincial Capital, 1949–1968* (Cambridge, Mass.: Harvard University Press, 1969), 325–28. For a vivid account of the Cultural Revolution by an active participant in Red Guard movements, see Gordon Bennett and Ronald Montaperto, *Red Guard: The Political Biography of Dai Hsiao-ai* (Garden City, New York: Doubleday, 1971).

seemed to assume that the attack on bureaucrats who had taken the capitalist road must be commendable—as long as the bureaucrats under attack were in the cities. The villagers had no immediate reason to believe that the Cultural Revolution was going to come to Chen Village. After all, they had just completed their own revolution against social evil in the form of the Four Cleanups campaign. And indeed, the Sixteen Points promulgating the nature and purpose of the Cultural Revolution explicitly said that whereas the Socialist Education Movement was "currently being conducted in rural villages," the Cultural Revolution was to take as its focus the "cultural and educational units and leading Party and government organs in the large and medium-sized cities."

But precisely because the Socialist Education Movement had with some degree of success "taught the peasants philosophy," the Cultural Revolution was bound to have an effect on the village. The work team, assisted by the young urban counselors, had attempted to tear apart the village's traditional culture and to replace it with a new socialist culture. As we have seen, they had not obliterated the old culture and had not won anything like widespread acceptance for their brand of socialist consciousness. But after creating a devastating tornado of fear, confusion, and anger in the village, they had managed to pull together the beginnings of a new village moral order. The villagers were discussing the meaning of their common life together coherently; they were working together productively. Their discourse on how to live and work still contained many old elements. But a new element had been injected into their discourse—the idea of reliance on the Thought of Mao Zedong. Now, however, the Maoist orthodoxy they had learned was under attack in the cities. Red Guards—inspired by Mao himself—were saying that the Communist Party leaders who had been in charge of propaganda, who had therefore been the very guardians of Communist orthodoxy, were evil: what had passed for Maoist orthodoxy had been too oriented toward social order; the true meaning of Maoism was to be found in anarchic rebellion. This was bound to create confusion in the village. During the Cultural Revolution in Chen Village, the village's moral order broke down. This led to various crises in the village's economic, political, and social orders and to transformations in the character of the village's main political activists.

Breakdown in Moral Discourse

Clifford Geertz once said that man is "suspended in webs of significance which he himself has spun."[4] Such webs, however, are rarely seamless.

---

4. Clifford Geertz, "Ideology as a Cultural System," in *The Interpretation of Cultures* (New York: Basic Books, 1973), 5.

The web of meaning that constituted the fabric of moral discourse in Chen Village was at best a fragile patchwork. Before the Socialist Education Movement came to the village, the villagers lacked a solid consensus about what constituted proper public conduct for a village leader. Contradictory images of proper conduct were appealed to by leaders like Qingfa and Longyong. And with the Socialist Education Movement, a new, alien vision had been carried into the village by the work team and the counselors.

But by the latter stages of the Socialist Education Movement, the images had been forced into a fragile synthesis. The villagers had learned some of the vocabulary of what at the time constituted orthodox Maoist thought; they increasingly began to pepper their speech with such phrases (not always appropriately used) as "feudalistic customs," "bourgeois thinking," "contradictions," and "the spirit of the foolish old man who moved the mountains." Even though some of them did not fully understand those phrases—amid fits of laughter some peasant interviewees recalled the woman activist who used to criticize Qingfa for "nonbourgeois thought" when she should have said "bourgeois thought"—they understood that they had to give at least lip service and a certain minimum of outward commitment to that thought or else expect a variety of sanctions. The work team and the sent-down youth, for their part, realized that the villagers could not be expected to change their traditional world views overnight. The work team had let most of the old cadres back into office and had given implicit approval to Longyong's style of leadership, even though his style favored a more localistic pattern of loyalties than pure Maoism allowed. Longyong's patriarchal political style resonated more with the new Maoist orthodoxy than did Qingfa's style with its sensitivity to human feeling. But Qingfa's particularistic ethic was not excluded from the new moral fabric. Qingfa had, after all, been invited to take up a leadership role again, although he had refused in his dramatic way. And the work team had itself been willing to take account of human feelings to accomplish certain political ends, as when it arranged for certain critics of the counselors to be "bought off" by being given improved jobs.

Thus from the diverse visions of moral order available to the villagers, a delicate framework for moral discourse was patched together. The thread that held the framework together was the idea of serving the people. Work-team members, urban youth counselors, and different factions of villagers all publicly professed to be serving the people. They all meant something different by this profession and vaguely recognized this. But for the time being, all the parties to this profession were willing or at least resigned to partially modify their behavior to accommodate the others. And all parties were willing, within certain limits, to accept each other's hypocrisy.

One result of all this was that the village's political activists were beginning to develop similar styles of public conduct. Work-team members, counselors, and brigade cadres like Longyong were talking and acting in a similar way: they were hard-driving, self-righteous, unsentimental, impartial, dedicated to the advancement of the village as a whole but insistent on the idea that striving for the welfare of the village was a means of contributing to the nation's glory. Young people within the village who wanted to rise to positions of leadership adopted the same style. During Dazhai work-point appraisal meetings, activist young peasants could confess that: "On such and such occasions I didn't try my hardest. I should study Chairman Mao more, speak up more in meetings, be quicker to obey my labor assignments, and be more progressive in my thinking. I shall try to do better in the future." And according to all of our interviewees, most of them genuinely meant it! Older cadres who had once tended to favor Qingfa's leadership style began to mold their conduct to the new requirements. A unified image of what it meant to be an outstanding village leader began to emerge, even though that image was formed by a complex pattern of different shades of conduct. This set a moral tone for the village as a whole. Villagers opposed to this image of leadership kept quiet about their opposition. Villagers who were ambivalent tended to orient themselves toward respect for the new image of leadership for the time being.

The most important social consequence of this common moral tone was that it encouraged villagers to put aside concern for their immediate self-interests and to cooperate in common projects for long-term village improvement. Selfishness certainly did not go away. Fundamental disagreements over matters of public policy still existed. But concern for narrow self interests was not officially legitimate. If people did not care for the common good of the whole village out of conviction, at least they were moved to pretend to care out of fear of criticism. This made some contribution to the productivity of the village, and there was a dynamic order to the community. As a peasant interviewee recalled, "By the end of the Four Cleanups, production had been grasped well and everything was well managed. For the first time since Liberation, our countryside had really been given a chance to develop steadily."

But the common framework for moral discourse that made this dynamic order possible was extremely fragile. The accusations flung around and the humiliations inflicted during the Four Cleanups campaign had undermined trust and generated bitterness. Many villagers had ample reason to hate one another and plenty of excuses for seeking revenge. Some of this mistrust and this desire for revenge surfaced in the disputes over work points under the Dazhai work-point system[5] or in the backbiting gossip directed against some of the counselors. But most of it was forced beneath the surface, held in check but still ready to explode. Although it might be argued that the economic and political innovations of the latter part of the Socialist Education Movement had helped advance the prosperity and stability of the village as a whole, these innovations had hurt many individuals and groups within the village. Strong farm workers who had done well under the piece-rate remuneration system had lost out under the Dazhai system. Some villagers who had hoped to gain power and prestige under the new political system had been left out. In particular, many of the sent-down urban youth were seeing their initial hopes of rising to positions of importance in the village frustrated. The villagers' public moral discourse expressed their willingness to bury their personal resentments and disappointments for the good of the village as a whole, but the resentments and disappointments remained. Many people were looking for an excuse to vent their frustrations and pursue their own interests. Only a slight tear in the village's moral fabric was needed to give them that excuse.

The village's moral fabric was being held together by a version of Maoist orthodoxy, an officially sanctioned interpretation of what it meant to serve the people. To serve the people meant to be committed first and foremost to working toward the economic prosperity of the village as a whole and then to have some concern for the welfare of the nation as a whole. Many of the idealistic sent-down youth were much more concerned with the nation as a whole than with the village but were willing to serve the village to serve the nation. Most of the peasants were much more concerned with the village than with the nation but were willing to

5. As a team leader during the introduction of the Dazhai system recalled: "Originally the people were very enthusiastic." But "it only took a few months" for their enthusiasm to weaken. A sign of this was that the appraisal meetings quickly became exceedingly disruptive. Terrific arguments developed over differences in work-point appraisals worth only one Chinese cent a day. (The women were the most vociferous in these matters.) Sometimes the meetings lasted all through the night, leaving team members furious with each other as well as physically exhausted. The requirement that, besides the quality of one's work, one's political attitude was also to be taken into account made reaching a consensus at these meetings especially difficult. The evaluation of political attitudes involved highly subjective judgments that increased the possibility of arguments. For this reason, within a year after the Dazhai system had been initiated, the political consideration was quietly dropped, and villagers were evaluated solely on the basis of their laboring ability. Nobody publicly stated that the political criterion was being withdrawn; it was simply mentioned less and less at the evaluation meetings, and no effort was made to bring it up more frequently.

make some concessions to national welfare. The work-team members—representatives of official orthodoxy—were willing to stress the village-oriented aspects of serving the people. But what if Mao himself now cast doubt on that interpretation?

Now Mao was saying that "to rebel is justified." The most urgent political task, the noblest human endeavor was to join in a vast crusade to attack established authorities throughout the country, because most of those authorities had "taken the capitalist road." The image of a good Communist was shifting from that of a disciplined soldier committed to defending and building up the country to that of a passionate rebel bent on disruption and chaos as a prelude to some future, purer, national social and political order. No matter that the Sixteen Points said that the Cultural Revolution was to be confined to the cities. That was simply a policy directive. Basic changes in world view do not simply travel the routes neatly established by policy directives. If there were people in the village whose vision of life would be affected by that change in world view, then the Cultural Revolution would come to Chen Village, regardless of what official policy said.

And there were some people who were ready to be affected—some of the sent-down youth. Once they enthusiastically accepted the new world view, other villagers were forced to react to them, forced to take the new ideas into consideration. And then the village's moral fabric started to fall apart.

As the revolutionary hymn the sent-down youth had sung on their departure from Canton stated, they were "an army of heroes" who had traveled afar to build up the land of their ancestors. That metaphor neatly summed up their conceptions of what they ought to become. They were each a small part of a vast army of the forces of proletarian goodness arrayed against the forces of bourgeois evil. Their primary commitments were not to the private responsibilities imposed by family and friends but to the public, historical mission entrusted to this vast army. The value of their lives would be determined by the quality of their service to this army. But it was not an army of faceless persons who each made an anonymous contribution to the workings of a vast juggernaut. It was an army of *heroes:* bold, dynamic, creative individuals who were each supposed to distinguish themselves in a unique way. "Rank" within the army was determined by one's degree of personal heroism. The youthful members of this army had "traveled afar" from the city to Chen Village. The village was no home for them, only a temporary field of battle.

But this army was so vast that its structure was only vaguely defined. Its mission was so lofty that the responsibilities of its members were indistinct. How could one know how to become a hero? How could one tell if one was really on the way to becoming one? Propagandists in the cities had given the youth some initial guidelines. They were to excel in furthering the socialist transformation of the villages to which they had been sent and to follow the direction of duly constituted local authorities. One could tell if one was becoming a hero if one excelled politically within the battlefield constituted by Chen Village. But, as we have seen, only a few of the sent-down youth had been able to excel politically. About two-thirds of them had dropped out of the competition to become glorious revolutionary heroes in the village after their first year in the countryside. They had done so because their lack of intense self-discipline and articulateness and the handicaps of unfavorable official class backgrounds had made it seem that their efforts to excel politically were going to be fruitless. Thus they had settled down to more or less satisfactory lives as ordinary peasants within the village. The remaining urban youth had seen their hard work, study, and self-discipline partially validated by their positions as counselors, propaganda team members, or minor production team cadres and by either being admitted to the Young Communist League or being given some hope that they would one day be able to join. From this group of politically successful urban youth had arisen an "aristocracy" of four persons (later narrowed to two) who had gained a special degree of support from Longyong and encouragement from the work team, or both. All of the members of this political aristocracy were members of the Young Communist League. The members of this aristocracy were for the most part thoroughly dedicated to becoming revolutionary heroes by working under the aegis of the work team and the direction of Longyong. They were too busy attending to their various jobs to pay much attention to the calls for rebellion sweeping through Canton. They had achieved their positions by acting in accord with official Party directives, and since there was nothing in the official Party directives about bringing the Cultural Revolution to China's villages, they showed no interest in doing so.

But for the urban youth who had already made some significant advances along the path toward glorious revolutionary heroism but had failed to make it into the urban youth aristocracy, the Cultural Revolution had a different meaning. Such urban youth found themselves in a painful predicament. They had sacrificed a great deal to come this far on the path to revolutionary heroism. But the quest for such heroism was like an addiction: the more one achieved, the more one needed. For pouring so much energy and discipline into the search for heroism, they had been rewarded by officially granted political power and prestige. But these rewards only made them hungry for more. Revolutionary heroism was not something one could attain once and for all. Not to continue moving ahead was to fall behind. And the further one had advanced, the harder one's fall. So for these urban youth to have failed to make it into the small charmed circle of urban youth aristocrats was more than just a painful disappointment; it was an excruciating threat to their conception of their self-worth. Their very idealism made the achievement of ever-increasing degrees of political success vital to their sense of dignity. Their failure was now threatening to demolish that all-important sense of dignity. They were getting desperate. As one of them said: "I saw myself getting up every morning and taking a hoe and going to dig in the fields. I began to think: does it mean that for the rest of my life I'll be working like this? I looked around, and this place was so backward. . . . It wasn't that I shunned difficulties, but *I found my efforts meaningless*" (emphasis added).

But now the changes in the meaning of Maoist orthodoxy were giving them a new lease on life. The meaning of being a member of China's vast army of revolutionary heroes was changing. Mao's call to rebellion and the iconoclastic zeal of the urban Red Guards both suggested that the army of revolutionary heroes was not like a disciplined military machine but like a coalition of bands of free-floating rebels. One could become a hero now not by accepting the discipline of a tightly structured Party apparatus but by joining loosely knit bands of enthusiasts who would overthrow all discipline. The reason idealistic young people had been halted in their quest for revolutionary glory was that the rules for success were wrong, and the people who created those rules were evil. One could become a revolutionary hero now by boldly overturning all rules and all authorities. By becoming a rebel, one could rescue one's endangered dignity.

In late August 1966, many of the urban youth returned home to Canton for brief vacations. There they watched the proto–Red Guards demonstrating in the streets against public authorities, saw the "big character posters," and heard the rhetoric about dragging out persons within the Party who had taken the capitalist road. It was a heady experience, especially for those would-be revolutionary heroes who had failed to enter the sent-down youth aristocracy. One of them explained that through this experience he "got the Scriptures." In Chinese, that phrase (*qu jing*) refers to the acquisition of Buddhist doctrine by the group of Chinese scholars who made a celebrated journey to India during the Tang Dynasty—a portentous event that initiated profound cultural changes and eventual social unrest within the Middle Kingdom. The sent-down youth became missionaries bringing the new doctrine of Cultural Revolution to the village, and in the end this missionary activity caused not just important cultural changes but profound social unrest within the community.

For several weeks after their return to the village, the ten individuals who had been profoundly moved by the revolutionary excitement in Canton gathered after work in an informal group to discuss the political currents sweeping China's cities and to decide how they should respond to them. Their ideas were exceedingly vague. They knew that they would be called upon to criticize "powerholders taking the capitalist road," but they had no concrete idea about what they should do about this. (They assumed that all powerholders were on the capitalist road unless proven otherwise.) Then, in September, the forces of the Cultural Revolution drew near the village. In the commune seat, students in the commune middle school put up big character posters denouncing the principal of the school. But this was puny, mild criticism in comparison with what was happening in Canton. The sent-down urban youth were convinced that the thrust of the Cultural Revolution was being systematically thwarted in their rural area. So their discussion group became an action group. They put up a truly inflammatory big character poster, "Naming names and asking the work team and commune leadership what the hell they were doing." They signed the poster, "The Maoism Red Guards."[6]

The cadres both at the commune seat and in Chen Village were predictably furious at this. While not quite so threatened by the urban youth, most ordinary peasants were shocked by their audacity. "They could only say: 'Wow, what nerve! Really? So much nerve!'" Hostility from cadres and work-team members led the rebellious urban youth to band even more closely together. They became better organized and more disruptive. Although annoyed at these youth, local village cadres were afraid to crush them. The youth after all claimed to be carrying out the Cultural Revolution in the name of Mao. Even though the Sixteen Points said the Cultural Revolution was confined to the cities, the rebellious sent-down youth could point to the Maoist-approved Red Guards in the cities as exemplars of their conduct. If one attacked them and the wrong people got into power at the national level, then someday one might be accused of disrupting Mao's wishes for the promotion of the Cultural Revolution, of being a "capitalist roader." The cadres had just been through that sort of thing with the Socialist Education Movement and did not want any more. It was best to be cautious. So they tried to compromise with the rebellious youth, but the youth rebuffed their advances.

In November and December, as radical Red Guards from outside Guangdong Province were engulfing Canton and directing increasingly severe attacks against Guangdong powerholders, the crisis in the village began to worsen. Directives were issued by the Maoist leadership in Beijing that ended the policy of isolating the Cultural Revolution from the

6. For a detailed discussion of the behavior of sent-down youth during the Cultural Revolution, see Stanley Rosen, *The Role of Sent Down Youth in the Chinese Cultural Revolution: The Case of Guangzhou* (Berkeley: University of California Center for Chinese Studies, 1981).

countryside. Contrary to the stipulations of the Sixteen Points, the Cultural Revolution was now to be universally extended from the cities into factories and farms. Official directives also hinted that the Socialist Education work teams had unjustly attacked a good many cadres in the Four Cleanups campaign. So attacks against the work team were legitimated, and the Chen Village Maoism Red Guards enthusiastically joined the struggle. It was a heady experience. As one of them said: "We never realized that we could suddenly have so much power."

But the Maoism Red Guards did not know what to do with that power. In the end, the only revolutionary goal they could come up with was a program of attacking work-team members for allegedly writing unfavorable official reports about them. They increasingly turned their attention inward, focusing on real or imagined grievances that they themselves had suffered rather than upon any program of reform for rural China as a whole. Ordinary peasants became increasingly disgusted with them.

The village cadres needed to find a way to counter these obnoxious upstarts.[7] They could not dare claim to be opposed to the Cultural Revolution. But perhaps in the boiling cauldron of ideas that now passed for Maoism, they could find some justification for opposing the Maoism Red Guards. The only substantiation of the Maoism Red Guards' claim to be the legitimate preachers of Maoist virtue was their raw enthusiasm, their willingness to make vague, outrageous accusations. Anybody could do that. Surely there must be a better test of moral authenticity. A current of thought was emerging from the Red Guard groups in the cities which said that one could tell a true Maoist by his class background.[8] Only the "pure" classes—proletarians, poor peasants, and so forth—could be authentic spokespersons for Mao. One could judge the authenticity of one's complaints against the established leadership not by their content—for the official ideology was so vague and confused that there was no clear criterion for distinguishing true from false ideas—but by their source. Most of the Maoism Red Guards came not from poor class backgrounds but from intermediate backgrounds—they were the sons and daughters of doctors, educators, and the petite bourgeoisie. There were plenty of poor peasant youth in the village who shared the cadres' hopes of making the village a prosperous and stable place. Why not organize them into a new group of Red Guards who could counter the outrageous

7. For a general discussion of the impact of the Cultural Revolution on rural China, see Richard Baum, "The Cultural Revolution in the Countryside: Anatomy of a Limited Rebellion," in *The Cultural Revolution in China,* ed. Thomas W. Robinson (Berkeley: University of California Press, 1971).

8. See D. Gordon White, *Class Background in Modern Chinese Politics: The Case of the Cultural Revolution* (Canberra: Australian National University Press, 1975); see also Bennett and Montaperto, *Red Guard,* 131–46.

claims of the Maoism Red Guards by virtue of their class purity? Thus, following a strategy employed by local cadres throughout Guangdong, the village cadres encouraged the formation of an organization of local youths. It was called the "Mao *Thought* Red Guards." The new Red Guard organization had about forty members, most of whom were local peasant youth of poor and lower-middle peasant class backgrounds. (There were also several of the sent-down youth who had good class backgrounds and had become part of the sent-down youth "aristocracy.") The first thing the Mao Thought Red Guards did was to put up a big character poster telling the Maoism Red Guards to disband because they did not come from pure class backgrounds. In this way, the Maoism Red Guards were forced to turn their attention away from struggling against the village cadres to confronting the Mao Thought Red Guards, and the pressure was taken off the village cadres.

National politics—and with it village politics—continued to become more chaotic. In early December, the Socialist Education work team left Chen Village. Its members were called back to their local units to be struggled against by "revolutionary rebels" for alleged mismanagement of the Socialist Education Movement. Without the work team to back them up, Longyong and the brigade cadres were vulnerable. Then, in January 1967, an alliance of Red Guard and revolutionary rebel organizations in Canton seized power from the leading officials of the provincial government. Guangdong was in the hands of rebels who were calling for similar seizures of power at all levels of the province. The Maoism Red Guards, filled with boundless enthusiasm to follow the rebellious actions of their revolutionary comrades, went to the brigade cadres to seize authority from them. The cadres immediately gave in, handed over the official seal of the brigade, and quit their jobs. But the Maoism Red Guards had absolutely no idea about how to run the brigade. They did not take charge but retreated in some confusion.

The village's formal political institutions at the brigade level had thus collapsed. (The organization of the production teams remained intact, and the production team cadres retained their posts.) A temporary form of political organization was soon established to maintain a minimum of order. But the moral fabric of the community had been torn apart and would not so easily be repaired. This created a crisis in the village.

The villagers had slowly begun to come to terms with the orthodox version of Maoism preached by the work team with the aid of the counselors. But now the dissatisfied sent-down youth, taking their inspiration from Mao's pronouncements and from the chaotic events in the cities, had put forth a new heretical version of Maoism. The villagers had begun to live with the old version, but this new heresy was deeply repugnant to them. According to this newest version of Maoism, the rebellious urban youth were bearers of a new, higher gnosis, which made them not servants of the village but persons who would destroy its order for the sake of plunging it into the kind of chaos that existed in the cities. The cadres tried to form a Mao Thought Red Guard group to oppose the Maoism Red Guards. But a moral authority capable of clearly defining which of the two versions of Maoist virtue was correct no longer existed. The work team tried to support the Mao Thought Red Guards, but now the work team itself was disbanded and, it appeared, discredited. There was no longer a coherent framework for villagewide discourse about revolutionary morality. Different factions within the village could no longer discuss or even debate different possible interpretations of Mao's Thought. They could only argue past each other. Each faction was hermetically locked within a semantic cocoon.

When, as William Butler Yeats poetically expressed it, a moral center can no longer hold: ". . . The ceremony of innocence is drowned; / The best lack all conviction, while the worst / Are filled with passionate intensity."[9] That is a good description of what happened when the framework for moral discourse within Chen Village collapsed. Commitment to moral ideals did not disappear. Such commitments, in fact, often became more passionate than ever. The Maoism Red Guards, the Mao Thought Red Guards, and eventually Longyong and his associates passionately poured their lives into the defense of moral principles. But the ceremony of innocence was gone. Villagers no longer had the ability to celebrate collective rituals that blurred the boundaries of their different beliefs and hopes and thus kept people with different interests and varying ideals from challenging one another's integrity and devastating one another's claims to innocence. Without these ceremonies of innocence, moral commitments became so intense that they threatened to destroy themselves and thus become immoral. The moral conduct of the village's main political antagonists took on a consistency that eventually became self-defeating and self-destructive. It might well be argued that the best people under these circumstances were those who abstained from any deep convictions.

The Purification and the Destruction of Moral Character: The Maoism Red Guards

The Maoism Red Guards continued to preach the need to rebel against all local authority in the name of Mao. They could not compromise with local cadres or reconcile themselves to the pattern of life in the village.

9. William Butler Yeats, "The Second Coming," in *The Collected Poems of W. B. Yeats* (London: MacMillan, 1933), 211.

And thus they could not transform the village into a better place. They could only criticize. But having lost touch with village life, they were unable to put any meaningful content into their criticism. They continued to put up big character posters to "expose" the cadres, but the posters did not reveal anything new. They simply repeated the complaints that had been aired in the early stages of the Four Cleanups campaign: cadres had engaged in petty corruption and been overly harsh on the masses. Although big character posters were an important way of raising issues in the cities, they were not very good for communicating with the peasants, since most of the middle-aged and older peasants could not read. Before long, the Maoism Red Guards ran out of things to say against the cadres. "Since there were not really many instances of capitalist roading in the village, . . . after a while the whole campaign quieted down."

As the Maoism Red Guards ran out of criticisms of the cadres and heard their protests fall on deaf ears, they turned increasingly inward. In their private discussions and public criticisms, they began to dwell more on the mistreatment of urban youth who had come to settle in the countryside. They claimed that they had been given poor housing and inadequate help in adjusting to rural life and that they were looked down upon by the local peasants. These complaints echoed similar complaints voiced by sent-down youth throughout China. Many of these youth left their villages and returned to the cities to join urban Red Guard organizations. The policy of sending urban youth to the countryside was attributed to Liu Shaoqi's "black line." When the Maoism Red Guards began to raise these issues in Chen Village, they found a ready response in many of their urban friends within the village. Almost two-thirds of the urban youth began to rally around the leaders of the Maoism Red Guards and to talk of leaving Chen Village to return to Canton. Bitter arguments broke out between these dissatisfied urban youth and the satisfied members of the urban youth "aristocracy." In the summer of 1967, about two-thirds of the urban youth, led by the leaders of the Maoism Red Guards, went back to Canton. There, a few of the rebellious Maoism Red Guards joined Red Guard organizations in the city. But most of them simply stayed at home and passively watched events in the chaotic urban scene unfold around them. Thus, for the Maoism Red Guards, the pure wrath of revolutionary idealism isolated them from any constituency but people like themselves and degenerated into a simple expression of their own personal interests.

Longyong

Longyong was once again out of office, along with all the other members of the brigade management committee. He could no longer claim to be an official representative of a Communist government dedicated to serving the people of China and, for that matter, the whole world. But the villagers now desperately needed someone with enough forcefulness, a reputation for fairness, and an image of concern for the common good of the village as a whole to make them transcend their narrow self-interests and become in some respects like a big family. The village needed someone like Longyong to take the lead.

Even though many villagers may have disliked Longyong and the political vision he represented, they needed a leader like him because of the nature of the village economy. If, as in the past, the main unit of agricultural production had been the individual household independently working its own piece of land, there would not have been such a pressing economic crisis in Chen Village. Even though village political authority had collapsed, the villagers could have retreated to their households and continued to manage their families' affairs. But agriculture had been collectivized. The success of the grain harvest depended on how well the members of the various production teams worked together. Such cooperative work inevitably meant transcending immediate short-term interests for the common good. Under the piece-rate system of remuneration, the tension between individual and collective interests had been minimized, for an individual's reward was in direct proportion to the quantity of his or her work for the collective. But under the Dazhai system, the tension between individual and collective interests was maximized (see above, pp. 141–144). Tendencies to laziness were countered by the presence within each team of an organized group of activist pacesetters who set the standard for a high level of work points and were usually drawn from the ranks of the village militia. Their enthusiasm was fostered and their activities coordinated by the brigade militia commander in conjunction with the brigade Party branch committee and the other members of the brigade management committee. As long as the Dazhai system remained in effect, the peasants needed a central brigade authority that could stimulate, organize, and coordinate the energies of militia "shock troops," as well as organize and coordinate the production plans of each team. The development of the spirit of collective dedication could also be helped by the dynamic preaching of the need for selflessness that the Mao Thought Counselors carried out in the name of the Thought of Mao Zedong. To do these things, the brigade leadership had to possess a compelling moral authority, and it had to use that authority to foster a spirit of moral commitment throughout the village.

By the end of 1966, many peasants were losing their enthusiasm for the Dazhai work-point system, despite the fact that production had improved. But in January 1967, harvest time was rapidly approaching, and it was impossible to abandon it in the immediate future. If brigade leaders did not stimulate a spirit of cooperation for the common good, production would decline and villagers would go hungry. An enlightened awareness of self-interest made villagers look for leaders who could help them transcend their immediate self-interests—especially in economic affairs. Longyong helped to fill this need by becoming an informal village leader.

Soon after the seizure of power from the brigade leaders, a detachment of several People's Liberation Army soldiers entered the village to set up a new local governing body to maintain social order and agricultural productivity. (This was part of a general pattern throughout Guangdong Province.) The soldiers stayed for several weeks and set up the Cultural Revolution Leadership Small Group, a committee of ten persons, each of whom represented one of the brigade's production teams. None of the deposed village cadres was eligible for membership. As it turned out, eight out of the ten members were the production team representatives of the Poor Peasants' Association. Such people were logical candidates for membership in the small group because its official purpose was to represent the revolutionary will of the poor and lower-middle peasants against the village's political establishment. But in fact the small group was responsible not for revolution but for production. For this it was ill equipped. As discussed in Chapter 3, the Poor Peasants' Association representatives did not in general enjoy the respect and confidence of most of the villagers, even the village's poor and lower-middle peasants. It would have been difficult for a body composed mainly of these representatives adequately to manage the affairs of the village, especially under the tense circumstances at that time. The Cultural Revolution Leadership Small Group could serve as a forum in which the interests of different production teams could be articulated; but it was difficult for it to function as an overriding authority that could reconcile competing interests, instill a spirit of collective devotion, and impose a general order upon the village.

Besides lacking a clear moral authority that would enable it to command the ready respect of the village as a whole, the small group lacked administrative machinery to enforce its authority. The brigade management committee in coordination with the Party branch committee had been able to use the Party and Young Communist League branches, the militia, public security committee, and the counselor-directed propaganda organization to impose its will upon the village. But now the Party and League cells no longer met, the militia training sessions had ceased, the public security committee only met in response to emergencies, and many of the lower-level counselors had given up their jobs and were planning to return to Canton. The Cultural Revolution Leadership Small Group had no effective control over the "organizational weapons" that had given the former brigade authorities so much of their power.

Lacking the moral authority and organizational resources to maintain public order and to motivate collective production, the small group had to rely heavily on informal sources of authority in the village. The key source of informal authority that could be called upon to help the small group fulfill its task was Longyong. Even though he had abdicated his cadre post, he still retained a residual political legitimacy. He had not been barred from office as Qingfa had. His prestige within the village was such that people still looked up to him as a natural leader. If they were not so ready to look upon the members of the small group as their natural leaders, they might be willing to accept them if Longyong gave the nod.

Moreover, Longyong had encouraged the formation of the Mao Thought Red Guard organization, which was composed of the most zealous members of the village militia. Indeed, the head of the Mao Thought Red Guards was fiercely loyal to Longyong. If Longyong was firmly behind the Cultural Revolution Leadership Small Group, he could help the Mao Thought Red Guards play the pacesetting role in production that the militia had been playing. Also, Ao Meihua and several other members of the sent-down youth "aristocracy" were still fiercely loyal to Longyong and angry at the other sent-down youth who had tried to upset the village. With Longyong's encouragement, what remained of the sent-down youth "aristocracy" could thus continue to function as Mao Thought Counselors. Ao Meihua could get on the village's wired broadcasting system and, ignoring news about Red Guard activity in the cities, zealously preach the need for villagers to give up their selfish habits in order to serve the people, especially by selflessly cooperating in their farm work. Thus, even though Longyong had abdicated his post and was officially only an ordinary peasant, the leaders of the small group continually went to his house to ask his advice on running the brigade and to obtain his approval for their actions. He in turn used his connections with the Mao Thought Red Guards and the remaining counselors to help fire up the collective spirit needed if the village's economy was to flourish.

So Longyong continued to lord it over the village, like a patriarch over his family, even though he had no official mandate to do so. Assuming a position of leadership was a generous act of great benefit to the village as a whole. It was an act that contributed to maintaining an efficient organization of collective production. Blessed by good weather, Chen Village had perhaps one of the best harvests in the village's history in spite of the chaos. But there was probably more to Longyong's assumption of leadership than a generous concern for the village as a whole. He was a man who loved power, loved to be in control of things. The crisis in village moral order had led him to make a generous effort to overcome that crisis and to instill a new spirit of collective endeavor in the village. But this crisis also removed some of the moral constraints that had kept his love for power somewhat in check. Without those constraints he could become a very dangerous man.

As long as Longyong was acting in his capacity as a Communist Party member and as head of the brigade management committee, he was bound to some extent by Party discipline and by the practical need to achieve workable compromises with the other members of the brigade administration. He had been forced to modify some of his harshness and to temper his domineering ways. But now that he was functioning in a purely unofficial capacity, the only constraints upon him were the exigencies of the situation. The situation was too chaotic for him to grab hold of it in a tyrannical way. But in a year, the situation stabilized somewhat, as the chaos of the Cultural Revolution subsided in the cities and the beginnings of a new national political order were established. Then Longyong got his official position back, but with the national and provincial political orders still shaky, he was relatively unsupervised. Under those circumstances, the generous aspects of his patriarchal stance toward the village were overwhelmed and the potentially tyrannical aspects came into full bloom. Longyong was developing his character in accordance with the logic of a vision that saw the village as a single big family. Untempered by a vision that recognized the need for the flavor of human feeling or one that saw the village as a small part in a fabric of national responsibilities, Longyong's vision became very destructive. But that is a story for the next chapter.

Qingfa

While Longyong was trying to make the village into a big family, Qingfa was again on the move, practicing the politics of human feeling. The networks of relatives and friends through whom Qingfa had once exercised so much of his influence still remained. His former clients had dutifully gone through the motions of struggling against him at the work team's command, but their loyalty to him and their human feeling for him had remained essentially intact. When the political tide clearly went against a cadre in the village, friends and clients of the condemned were under particular pressure to manifest their loyalty to the government against him. The villagers considered it perfectly acceptable for people to follow the political tide in such cases. But they believed that a person called upon to attack a friend should do so only to the extent demanded by higher political authorities. It was considered morally wrong for a person to attack a friend and benefactor more severely than was actually demanded. It was considered natural for someone to retain a loyalty to the condemned person after he had fallen and inevitable that the friends and beneficiaries of a fallen cadre would rally to his support when and if the political tide turned.[10] Qingfa now began to make use of his old loyalties to shape the life of the village and to get himself back into power.

The head of Qingfa's production team was his brother-in-law: the husband of his wife's older sister. This man had gotten his post in the early 1960s through Qingfa's influence and had consistently been one of his staunchest supporters. The prestige and power of this brother-in-law had been intensified by the fact that Qingfa had secured many special benefits for his production team. Thus when Qingfa returned to his production team as an ordinary peasant, the team rallied around him in a quiet way. The brother-in-law had retained his post as team head, and he led the team as Qingfa told him. Though excluded from formal power, Qingfa was the real leader of production team no. 6.

After the work team had left Chen Village, but even before Longyong and his colleagues had relinquished their power, production team no. 6 had begun to resist the authority of Longyong and the brigade management committee. When they tried to get the various production teams in the village to contribute able-bodied laborers to help improve the road that ran by the brigade, to dig new irrigation ditches of eventual benefit to the community as a whole, or to carry out other such projects, production team no. 6, at Qingfa's instigation, refused to participate in any projects that were not for its own immediate benefit. When this production team resisted the authority of the brigade, the other teams also refused to obey. If team no. 6 did not contribute its fair share of the labor, they said, they would not take part in the brigade's projects either. Thus the authority of Longyong and his colleagues on the brigade management committee diminished. Since their authority was coming under a cloud as the Maoism Red Guards proclaimed appeals to drag out powerholders who had been taking the capitalist road, Longyong and his cadre associates could do little to counter Qingfa's divisive influence. Longyong could in-

10. A good example of the informal norms regulating criticism of a friend during a campaign is the case of Stocky Wang and Four Eyes Wu, narrated in Chan, Madsen, and Unger, *Chen Village*, chap. 7. Wu had befriended Stocky Wang during hard times. Then in 1971 Wu got into political trouble and a denunciation session was prepared against him. Each of Wu's friends was brought forth to denounce Wu's "crimes," but—except for Stocky Wang—his friends brought up only those incidents already known to the authorities. Stocky Wang, however, went further than the authorities were demanding. He brought up the fact that Wu's grandfather had been a landlord, an accusation that in the context of the times could only make matters much worse for Wu. Stocky Wang's acquaintances despised him for this: "They couldn't forgive him. . . . They felt he had no sense of righteousness."

veigh against Qingfa, but he could not follow up his protest with concrete sanctions. It was partially disgust at this situation as well as at the actions of the Red Guards that led Longyong and his associates to relinquish their power in January 1967.

Once Longyong and the other brigade cadres had given up their posts, Qingfa became even bolder than before. Through the village gossip network, he spread the opinion that the brigade cadres had been inept. What he said struck some responsive chords and weakened the village authority Longyong and his followers were trying to establish through the Cultural Revolution Leadership Small Group. To his subversive words, Qingfa added rebellious actions. He persuaded his production team to advance its interests through a variety of illegal activities. For example, since Chen Village was in a mountainous region with plenty of wild grass growing on uncultivable hillsides, it was relatively inexpensive to raise draft oxen in the region. Someone with the proper connections could buy oxen rather cheaply from the area around the village and sell them in the lowlands for a tidy profit. Such trading was supposed to be illegal, but Qingfa, using the connections he had acquired during his tenure as Party branch secretary, engaged in this lucrative trade on behalf of his team. The money thus obtained considerably augmented the income of the production team as a whole, raised the value of the team's work points, and in the process helped to secure the team's loyalty to Qingfa. Thus, Qingfa's words gave many people a convenient excuse for disobeying the village's central authorities and furthering their short-term interests. And his actions gave them courage to resist that authority, because everyone knew that if anyone would eventually be punished for such resistance, it would be the leader, Qingfa, not the followers. In this way, Qingfa's example set a tone for political action in the village as a whole. Each production team began to go its own way, concerned only with maximizing its own profit, regardless of the larger interests of the brigade as a whole.

The concept of social morality exemplified by Qingfa had considerable appeal for many villagers, even as they recognized the reasonableness of some of Longyong's appeals. The villagers realized that they had to sacrifice their immediate self-interests to the good of the collective in order to make the collective economy work, and thus they could follow Longyong. But many of them were not at all sure that they wanted to follow the vision of Longyong all the way through to its logical conclusions. They were willing to think of the public good as taking precedence over the well-being of themselves, their families, and their friends insofar as this was necessary to maximize the output of their production teams. But they were not necessarily willing to go further than that and were not willing to subordinate the welfare of their production teams to the good of the village as a whole. Thus many of them responded to Qingfa's appeals to consider their relatives, their neighborhoods, and their production teams more important than the brigade as a whole.

The problem with Qingfa's brand of morality, however, was that if taken to its logical conclusion, it would narrow the villagers' focus of concern to the point where the interests of families, friends, and neighbors would drown out public concerns. And in the broken moral world created by the Cultural Revolution, Qingfa's moral vision was being pushed to such radical conclusions. Qingfa himself showed disregard for established laws and a selfish lack of concern for the public welfare. He apparently hoped that when the dust of the Cultural Revolution settled, relatives, friends, neighbors, and production team members would help rehabilitate him and return him to formal political office. To prepare for that he was willing to deepen, not mitigate, the confusion troubling the public life of the village. Other villagers were affected by this example of disregard for the public good. Although villagers worked well together on collective production, there was an alarming increase in petty crime, especially of people stealing one another's chickens and ducks. There was also an increase in sexual harassment: for example, young women were increasingly bothered by peeping toms while taking their baths. The village's civic order, the order of mutual respect for private property and personal security, generally deteriorated. It was not simply Qingfa's example that created this, of course. But his disregard for the public good certainly did not discourage such activity. As we shall see, Longyong later developed a plausible case for accusing Qingfa of undermining the village's civic order. And villagers—irritated and anxious about the rise of petty theft, voyeurism, and the general disregard for community concerns—were made to turn their anger on Qingfa.

Social Order, Cultural Confusion, and Moral Character

When talking about the Cultural Revolution in Chen Village, Ao Meihua told me that it was a time of great chaos. But that impression needs to be qualified. There was no major breakdown of law and order such as occurred in China's cities. Rival Red Guard factions fought each other with words, not with physical violence as in the cities. Agricultural production flourished. Petty crime increased to an annoying degree, enough to cause villagers anxiety but not terror. The social and economic order remained intact, even though their foundations may have become a little shaky.

The chaos was mostly confined to the cultural realm. That realm had never been characterized by simple consensus. There had always been disagreements about exactly what constituted a good life, a desirable community, and a worthy style of political leadership. We have already spoken of some of the major ambivalences in the villagers' conceptions of the proper bases for social order and of the role a person in authority should play in that order. We have shown how the moral appeals made by Qingfa and Longyong spoke to two different poles within the villagers' ambivalent world view and how Qingfa's appeals to the flavor of human feeling could, if pushed to extremes, result in a subordination of the public welfare of the village to the private good of small families while Longyong's appeals were more in keeping with the subordination of private welfare to the collective welfare of the village as a whole. But these different visions had been made to resonate together in such a way that villagers could carry on some sort of coherent public discussion about the issues facing them. Now no constructive discussion was possible. The visions had broken apart.

The immediate effect of this was on the development of the moral characters of would-be political leaders in the village. People became polarized. Different key figures on the village stage developed sharply contrasting styles of political conduct. Some of the sent-down youth tended to become pure rebels. Longyong became a pure local patriarch; Qingfa a pure patronage politician. But if one's vocation is politics, it is immoral to be too singlemindedly moral. As Max Weber suggested in his essay "Politics as a Vocation," the morally appropriate stance for a politician involves both a commitment to principle and a willingness to compromise one's principles in order to achieve one's political ends, and a politician's moral task involves a continual effort to reconcile commitment to principle and the need to compromise.[11] But now the sent-down youth in the Maoism Red Guards tended to become uncompromisingly committed to rebellion, Longyong and his associates to glorifying the village as a whole, and Qingfa and his followers to celebrating particularistic loyalties within the village. In the end, this unwillingness to compromise made them leave behind the work of politics and focus on their own personal aggrandizement.

When the rebellious urban youth found no one in the village at all sympathetic with their idealistic but vague hopes for the socially redemptive possibilities of rebellion, they focused more and more not on saving society, but on simply saving themselves. When Qingfa took up the cause of personal concern for the particular needs of those close to him in such a way as flagrantly to oppose both established laws and the concerns of those who wished to strengthen the solidarity of the village as a whole, he began to become an opportunist who took advantage of a

---

11. Max Weber, "Politics as a Vocation," in *From Max Weber: Essays in Sociology,* trans. H. H. Gerth and C. Wright Mills (New York: Oxford University Press, 1946).

troubled situation to further his own ambitions. And when Longyong asserted himself as a stern village leader dedicated to the solidarity and prosperity of the village as a whole at the expense of any larger national project and of the needs of any particular groups within the village, he started to become a dictatorial demagogue. In the end, because of an inflexibility that made all these people unwilling to compromise their principles, in their own way they each became mainly concerned with personal aggrandizement; they became immoral politicians.

The village can survive as a social unit if its web of moral meanings has broken and its politicians have become immoral. Planting and harvesting can continue; children can be raised, marriages contracted, a family's old and sick taken care of; a semblance of public security can even be maintained. But the quality of life might greatly deteriorate. Public life might simply be reduced to an arena where people motivated by ambition, passion, or greed fight each other rather than a forum where those everpresent impulses are in part transformed into a collective search for the common good.

7 The Cleansing of the Class Ranks Campaign

MORAL EXPLOSION AND MORAL DISINTEGRATION

Throughout China in the fall of 1967, the Cultural Revolution entered a moderate phase. Mao and Lin Biao called for an end to factionalism between rival revolutionary groups, for the reinstatement of cadres who had erred, and for the establishment of new ruling structures called "revolutionary committees" at all levels of the Chinese polity. The army then moved in to take control of most of the revolutionary committees. The violence in the cities subsided.

But the violence in Chen Village was just beginning. It was now time for Longyong to appeal to the villagers' conception of themselves as members of a single big family and to make that conception into practically the sole basis for social action within the village. We shall see how this conception, when pursued with relentless logic, led to an explosion of moralistic zeal that in the end destroyed the moral basis for social order in the village. Political action based solely on this conception tended to make the village a demoralized place and Longyong an immoral person.[1]

Setting the Stage for Moral Violence

In the fall of 1967, a revolutionary committee was established in Guangdong Province to take the place of the old provincial administration. As in most of China's provinces, the leading positions in the new provincial government bodies went to the military. Military domination

---

1. The Cleansing of the Class Ranks campaign is described in more detail in Anita Chan, Richard Madsen, and Jonathan Unger, *Chen Village: The Recent History of a Peasant Community in Mao's China* (Berkeley: University of California Press, 1984).

extended all the way down to the commune level. The People's Liberation Army controlled the administration of the county in which Chen Village was located, and three army officers from northern China controlled the administration of Chen Village's commune. Stability and order were restored to the political life of the commune.

A young army officer was dispatched to Chen Village to supervise the establishment of a new village governing organization. But the soldier was a northern Chinese, unable to speak Cantonese. Backed by the authority of his military superiors in control of the commune, he was able to ensure that stability prevailed on the surface of political life in the village, but handicapped by his unfamiliarity with local affairs and his inability to speak the local language, he was in no position to control the jockeying for power that proceeded beneath the surface.

Under the direction of the young officer, village elections were held to create a Revolution Leadership Small Group to replace the Cultural Revolution Leadership Small Group. This new group was supposed to be the precursor of a full-fledged brigade revolutionary committee, the organ of government that was supposed to assume all the functions of the old brigade management committee in the post–Cultural Revolutionary era. The new Revolution Leadership Small Group was to consist of nine people, the same number that had made up the former brigade management committee. For most practical purposes, the functions of the Revolution Leadership Small Group were the same as those of the old management committee.

The elections to this new village governing body were, however, conducted differently from the elections to the old brigade governing body. These new elections were characterized by what one of our interviewees called a "great democratic atmosphere." This time, the elections were not carefully controlled from behind the scenes by small groups of local activists who were in turn carefully controlled by the local Party branch that was in its turn controlled by agents of higher levels of government. This was not an indication of a new commitment to democratic principles on the part of the central government, but rather a symptom of the practical inability of the commune government to control affairs in the village. The Party could not control the election, because the Party was still in disarray. The Chen Village Party branch still did not meet regularly and could not be expected to function as a disciplined force behind the election. And the hapless young People's Liberation Army soldier was the only contact between the village and higher-level authorities.

If a stable commune government working through a disciplined village Party branch had carefully "guided" the village election, the new Revolution Leadership Small Group might have gained a more balanced membership than it did. But as it was, Longyong and his associates managed to gain almost complete control over the small group. Six of the nine members of the small group were in Longyong's camp. The others held posts like women's association head and secretarial clerk—positions with little influence on the shaping of brigade policy.

The elections for the Revolution Leadership Small Group took place in January and February of 1968. In early March, the soldier who had been sent to the village returned to his army unit. Order and stability prevailed in the village, but it was an order dominated by Longyong. Since the new village political system had been established under the aegis of the commune authorities controlled by the People's Liberation Army and since those authorities were unwilling to tolerate any further factional fighting in the village, Longyong's position was secure. No one dared to challenge him. And since the commune authorities were in no position carefully to supervise Longyong's actions, he had a largely free hand in shaping the events that followed. Longyong could now, as the saying went, "jump very high." He could try to shape the whole community around his vision of what a good village should be. In the process he could try to satisfy his own desire for personal power. This would make him a very dangerous man.

As the new village governing bodies were being established, the central government was starting to send down directives for a new political campaign, the Cleansing of the Class Ranks campaign. For China's central leadership, the purpose of this campaign seems to have been to tighten discipline throughout China by punishing the unruly elements who had been responsible for so much of the Cultural Revolution's urban chaos. For the people of Chen Village, the violence of the Cleansing of the Class Ranks campaign was overwhelming, terrifying, and in the end demoralizing because of the way Chen Village's leadership—dominated by Longyong—interpreted and implemented the campaign's official directives.

Those directives were vague and not adapted to the realities of village life. According to the official directives, the campaign was to have six targets: (1) those who had spoken out against Chairman Mao and Vice-Chairman Lin Biao during the Cultural Revolution; (2) "black hands" (those who had manipulated others to do evil things during the Cultural Revolution); (3) "bad Cultural Revolutionary leaders" (Red Guards and revolutionary rebels who had caused excessive disruption during the Cultural Revolution); (4) "hidden counterrevolutionaries" (persons of bad class background who through various subterfuges had been able to avoid receiving a bad official class status after Liberation and had been secretly working to undermine the revolution ever since); (5) "criminal elements" (persons who had committed crimes such as arson and homicide during the Cultural Revolution); and (6) unreformed members of the

Four Bad Types. In the cities the most unruly people who had taken advantage of the Cultural Revolution were considered targets: the leaders of Red Guard gangs that had destroyed and looted property, for example. The Cultural Revolution had spawned plenty of people who were clearly guilty of antisocial acts in the cities. If these individuals were now punished in the campaign, public opinion would probably consider the punishments reasonable and just.

But in Chen Village, there had been no such extreme unruliness. Accordingly, there were few people in the village who were outstanding candidates for punishment. Thus more imagination was required in the village to determine exactly who should be "hit" during the campaign. The village leaders seem to have been given quotas: about 3 percent of the adult villagers—about twenty-five people—were to be targeted.[2] But commune and county authorities were not in a position to carefully supervise the process of selecting the targets. Instead, the imagination of Longyong and his close associates pointed the way from the vague official directives to particular residents of the village.

In the pages to follow, I will explicate the main lines of moral reasoning employed by Longyong and his associates to decide who should be punished in the campaign and to justify their decisions. The village leaders guided and justified their work by the idea that a good village should be like a big family. On the one hand, this conception of the good village led to a deep suspicion of the objective kinship ties that linked villagers to particular small families within the village and to the subjective human feelings that turned those objective ties into bonds of loyalty. On the other hand, it led to a profound suspicion of outsiders. In interpreting the campaign's official directives, the village leaders transformed them, on the one hand, into a mandate to affirm the dangers of kinship and to call upon villagers to forsake all particularistic loyalties for a zealous commitment to the collective welfare of the village as a whole. This moral theme was most discernable in Longyong's and his associates' understanding of who a hidden counterrevolutionary was. On the other hand, the village leaders transformed the campaign's official directives into a mandate to attack the bearers of any outside ideology that clashed with the villagers' commitments to the prosperity and stability of their own community. This moral theme was most discernable in the village leaders' attacks on the rebellious urban youth who were spreading Maoist heresy. These moral themes resonated enough with villagers' ideas and sentiments to enable Longyong to gain important support for his conduct of the campaign. But they diverged enough from village reality to enable Longyong

2. For evidence about the existence of such quotas, see Chan, Madsen, and Unger, *Chen Village,* 144.

to use his appeals to virtue as a crude justification for gaining power and seeking revenge—motives that became most apparent in Longyong's treatment of Qingfa.

The Destruction of Human Feeling

While central government officials announced that certain categories of wrongdoing were now to be severely punished, official propagandists preferred explanations for why so much misconduct had occurred in the first place. True to Communist traditions, the explanations claimed that evil came from the influence of reactionary social classes. But the Chen Village leaders turned the official explanation for evil into an indicator of evildoers. Since evil flowed ineluctably from members of the bad social classes, they said in effect that members of these classes should be punished, even though they had done nothing obviously wrong.

Thus, as the campaign began, the village leadership first pounced upon the village's Four Bad Types. As mentioned in Chapter 3, this had become standard practice. The Four Bad Types were the first targets of practically all campaigns. So the six villagers who were considered members of the Four Bad Types were brought before mass meetings and subjected to frenzied struggle sessions. There was no new clear-cut evidence that they were trying to undermine the revolution. But in accordance with the Chinese Communist political tradition, all members of the Four Bad Types were presumed to be engaged in working against the revolution unless proved otherwise beyond a shadow of a doubt. Everything the Four Bad Types did was judged on the basis of this presumption. Thus, if they complained that this year's harvest was not as bountiful as last year's, they could be accused of trying to subvert morale. If they acted in a friendly way toward local cadres, they could be accused of trying to corrupt Communist officials. The Four Bad Types could not win.

Before and after the struggle meetings, the targets of struggle were locked in the dressing room behind the stage of the village hall. This makeshift jail was called the "cowshed," a name derived from the phrase "'cowheaded' demons, freaks, ghosts, and monsters" (*niu, yao, guei, guai*) used during the Cultural Revolution to denote evil persons. The stated reason for keeping the targets in the cowshed was to keep them from contacting friends within the village and developing a strategy for blunting the impact of the campaign. But in effect the cowshed was a jail, and being kept there was a form of punishment.

The presumption that the Four Bad Types were by their very nature guilty of undermining the revolution and thus that one did not have to look for any independent proof of their guilt now provided an important premise for the line of moral reasoning Longyong and his associates used to justify their general approach to the campaign. If the Four Bad Types could be presumed guilty by their very nature, then people closely connected with them might also be presumed guilty, even though there was no clear evidence against them. What type of connection might contaminate someone with the evil contagion of the Four Bad Types? A kinship connection.

Only six villagers were officially designated members of the Four Bad Types. According to government quotas, over twenty individuals should be hit by the campaign. The idea that kinship ties to the Four Bad Types might make one evil provided an important way of increasing the number of targets. The kinship connection was made through a particular interpretation of what it meant to be a hidden counterrevolutionary. As we have said, a hidden counterrevolutionary was a class enemy who had escaped detection when official class statuses were assigned after Liberation and who was now masquerading as a person of the good revolutionary classes. But how was one to discover such people and bring them out of hiding? One way would presumably be to observe their behavior. If they took advantage of confused times like the Cultural Revolution to carry out antisocial mischief, then they would be revealing their true nature. Perhaps this is indeed the way hidden counterrevolutionaries were "discovered" in China's cities after the Cultural Revolution. But the leaders of Chen Village used a different method. Instead of starting with obvious examples of political wrongdoing and working back to connections with bad social classes, they looked first for links of kinship that tied certain people to bad class elements. They used these links to condemn such people as hidden counterrevolutionaries even when they had not done anything obviously counterrevolutionary.

For instance, the husband of a loudmouthed woman in production team no. 6 had been a rich peasant who had hanged himself during land reform. After his suicide, in accordance with the letter of the law at the time, his widow had been classified as a poor peasant. But many villagers thought that since her husband had been a rich peasant, she should also be classified as one. Moreover, she was an acid-tongued gossiper who had irritated a great many villagers. Many poor and lower-middle peasants who disliked her shrewishness felt that in view of her problematic class background she should be a little more humble in her dealings with them. She was arrested and subjected to struggle sessions. The chief evidence brought against her was that she had tried to corrupt teenaged girls by telling them salacious stories. These were stories, it seems, that were traditionally used to provide adolescents with a kind of sex education. By the puritanical standards inherent in official Communist ideology, telling such stories was considered "feudalistic," but it seems highly unlikely that a well-liked villager with an unquestioned poor peasant background would ever have been harshly criticized for doing so. But this widow was, it had been decided, contaminated with the evil of the bad classes, so that anything she did might be interpreted in the worst possible light.

At least three other loudmouthed widows of Bad Types were also arrested and struggled against. One of these, an old woman, went insane from the experience and died soon after. Three other men who were sons of deceased Bad Types also became targets of the campaign.

The villagers could easily be mobilized to attack such persons because these targets were unpopular. The women who were attacked as hidden counterrevolutionaries were all gossipy shrews. Some of the men were insufferably arrogant; others were lechers. But although the peasants might be led to attack such individuals because of their shrewishness, lechery, and other obnoxious traits, these characteristics could hardly be considered counterrevolutionary in themselves. The village leadership had to justify the attacks on other grounds, and their justification was the targets' kinship relation to people who belonged to the wrong classes. Thus Longyong and the other village leaders implicitly affirmed the importance of kinship relations within the village. They tried to justify their actions by saying in effect that the village was not merely a conglomeration of autonomous individuals each of whom should be judged on the basis of his or her own personal attitude toward the village and the revolution. Rather, the village was a pattern of relationships, the most important of which were kinship relationships; individuals were to be judged good or bad primarily according to their particular positions with respect to such a field of relationships.

But even as Longyong and his associates affirmed the continuing importance of kinship relationships, they were identifying them with evil. Kinship contaminated. People who had done nothing counterrevolutionary themselves were besmirched through kinship with the evil class enemies. And to this theory of the propagation of badness, Chen Village's leaders opposed some ideas about the achievement of goodness. Truly good people could not destroy the objective fact of kinship, but they could and should reject the subjective feelings traditionally associated with kinship. They should refuse to allow such feelings to have any place in their world. Thus as the leaders of the campaign conjured up villains for the masses to condemn, they also conjured up new heroes for the masses to admire. The heroes were people who most vigorously rejected any temptation to treat a victim of the campaign as a mother, father, brother, or sister. Thus among the persons most praised by the village's propaganda apparatus during the campaign were the four teenaged girls who reported the rich peasant widow mentioned above for telling salacious stories. (Throughout this region of China, it was the custom in the village for adolescent girls to sleep away from home in the houses of widows and for boys to sleep in dormitories such as the one over the militia headquarters. These homes away from home for adolescents were called "girls' houses" and "boys' houses.")[3] The widow who had told the stories had apparently done so out of a motherly concern to provide "her" girls with some sex education. Normally, such girls would have begun to look upon the widow as a substitute mother. They would have developed human feelings toward the widow that would have been translated into various kinds of loyalties. But these four girls had no kinship connections with people of bad classes. Moreover, they had become fervent activists in the village militia, earning the nickname "The Red Detachment of Women." When the widow first came under attack, they were reluctant to help the campaign leaders "dig up dirt" against her. But the village cadres, with a great deal of effort, convinced the girls that it was their duty to incriminate the widow. Such contributions were expected of a "Red Detachment of Women," and besides, the girls would not want to become contaminated by their connection with the widow, would they? So in the name of revolutionary duty, the girls rejected all human feelings toward the widow, told about the "dirty stories," and thus provided the only specific evidence available about the widow's counterrevolutionary conduct.

The pattern of opposition between good and evil reflected in the confrontation between the four girls and the rich peasant widow repeated itself again and again in the struggle rituals that formed the heart of the campaign. Almost all of the targets of the campaign were related by kinship to members of the bad classes. At least part—and in the case of the hidden counterrevolutionaries almost all—of the targets' political wrongdoing was the result of family ties. The heroes of the campaign were people "without feeling" (*wu renqing*)—people who refused to have any personal sympathy for the victims of the campaign and who struggled against these targets without mercy.

To the extent that Longyong and other leaders of the campaign used kinship ties as proof of otherwise unprovable counterrevolutionary guilt rather than as an explanation for independently proven guilt, they made an even more radical attack on traditional village social order than the Four Cleanups work team had. The Four Cleanups work team had attacked one of the *results* of particularistic relationships based on kinship and human feeling: favoritism. But now the village leaders under Long-

3. For a further account of these living arrangements, see Richard Madsen, "Harnessing the Political Potential of Peasant Youth," in *State and Society in Contemporary China*, ed. Victor Nee and David Mozingo (Ithaca, N.Y.: Cornell University Press, 1983); also see William L. Parish and Martin King Whyte, *Village and Family in Contemporary China* (Chicago: University of Chicago Press, 1978), 231–32.

yong directly attacked not favoritism but the traditional bases for sympathy. A bad village was a village divided into various clusters of loyalties generated by bonds of kinship and extended by good human feelings. A good village was one in which almost all residents were united in anger against a small remainder of internal enemies. In such a village, there would be no expression of personal sympathies, only the collective expression of zeal.

Such a vision of village life was widely plausible among the villagers only during times of crisis, when they faced extraordinary dangers from within or without. Then in desperation villagers might generally allow basic respect for human feelings to give way to collective zeal. By early 1968, villagers shared widespread feelings of anxiety over the restlessness created by the Cultural Revolution. Little mysteries spawned giant rumors: the batteries powering the village's telephone were missing; evil people must have cut the village off from the outside world to prepare to create mayhem! Some guns from the armory were missing: hidden agents of the Guomindang must be preparing an armed insurrection! There were in fact benign explanations for these puzzles: the batteries had been taken by some prankish children, the weapons somehow misplaced. But villagers were ready—indeed almost eager—to believe the worst. The feeling that evil could be hidden almost anywhere within the village grew. "Even in your sleep," one interviewee [an upper-middle peasant] said, "you might make a mistake."

Such pervasive fearfulness made villagers all too prone to attack the scapegoats proposed to them by village leaders. The anxiety made it seem plausible that these targets were truly sinister. And if one did not wholeheartedly attack these people, one's reluctance might conceivably be interpreted as a sign of one's own bad conscience. The peasants could thus, as one interviewee put it, be "led around by the nose" by the village cadres.

Unfortunately, Longyong and the other village leaders were themselves vulnerable to the temptation to abuse their power. Since their power could be enhanced by village fearfulness, they seemed eager to deepen the sense of crisis, using inflammatory rhetoric to concoct threats to village life—like those posed by an old woman telling dirty stories—that did not really exist. And as they increased their power, they tried to extend their vision of a big family united by collective zeal from a vision appropriate to times of extreme crisis to one suited to the full range of ordinary life within the community.

Thus by the fall of 1968, after the phase of struggling against hidden counterrevolutionaries and other supposed class enemies was over, the village leaders began a Three Loyalties movement. The Three Loyalties were loyalty to Mao, to Mao's Thought, and to his revolutionary movement. The peasants were to manifest these loyalties—so the propaganda went—by giving up all their private property: their private plots, their private pigs and honeybees, even their privately owned kitchen utensils. Moreover, they were to make Chen Village brigade—the village as a whole and not the individual production teams—their principal accounting unit for production. This meant that each household's income depended entirely on the collective productivity of the village as a whole rather than on the productivity of any smaller unit. No longer could individuals express their loyalty to their families by putting an extra amount of effort into their private plots or private sideline enterprises. No longer could the group of twenty-five or thirty neighboring families that formed a production team receive extra economic benefits from better organization and harder work than other production teams. All particularistic loyalties smaller in scope than loyalty to the village as a whole were to be abandoned. The village was to become, as the saying put it, "a single beehive," and loyalty to the village as a unit was to be equated with loyalty to Mao, to his Thought, and to his revolution.

This loyalty was to be sustained by communal worship of Mao. In place of the old ancestor tablets, each house was to erect an altar to the chairman consisting of a small stand decorated with pictures of and quotations from Mao and flanked by the little red book of Mao's sayings. The walls of the village were festooned with pictures of Chairman Mao and quotations from his works. Before meals, each household recited one of Mao's quotes and sang a few stanzas of "The East Is Red." Before political meetings, the peasants sang a hymn expressing loyalty to Chairman Mao and, joining hands in a circle, danced a simple dance in honor of the chairman. Mao's words and his image were presented as sacred symbols expressing the basis for a zealous life devoted not so much to China as a nation but to the village as a whole.

This Three Loyalties movement was not devised by the village leadership out of thin air. The leaders were responding to directives sent down by officials at the commune and county seats. (This movement, however, was not a policy of the central government; it was not carried out in the majority of counties in China but was spontaneously initiated by officials in scattered counties throughout China.) But Longyong and his associates were not reluctantly following orders. They developed this movement with tremendous enthusiasm. Longyong seemed to leap at this opportunity to make the moral zeal generated by the Cleansing of the Class Ranks campaign into the moral basis for a village united forever like a big family. But the attempt to make this vision into the primary basis for village life did not work. Collective zeal quickly waned. Productivity dropped. Private property was soon returned, and production teams were again made the basic accounting units. The contempt for particularistic human feelings and the zeal for collective village welfare that were such important themes during the Cleansing of the Class Ranks campaign could not by themselves provide an adequate basis for ordinary village life.

The Attack on Heresy

In addition to claiming that the village was contaminated from within by the ties of kinship that connected villagers to the village's own Four Bad Types, the village leaders guided and justified their conduct by asserting that the village was contaminated by heretical ideas transmitted by outsiders. The outsiders in this case were the rebellious urban youth. Their "heresy" consisted of new ideas incompatible with the orderly operation of the community.

Responding to urban political currents, the rebellious urban youth had preached that the highest form of political morality consisted of rebellion against authority—against village authority. They had shown contempt for local social customs and disregard for local order. Even the outside work teams that had directed campaigns like land reform and the Socialist Education Movement had never done anything so drastic. They had indeed introduced foreign ideas into the village and had criticized some local authorities. But they had always said that they were committed to working with the peasants to serve the peasants. When they tried to teach Maoist ideology, they attempted to make that ideology a living reality within the village and had even been willing to modify that ideology to allow it to resonate with local traditions. They had mobilized poor and powerless villagers to attack rich and powerful ones, saying that they were helping villagers themselves take control of their lives. And the goal of their efforts had always been to create a stable new village social order. The urban youth who joined the Maoism Red Guards, on the other hand, had in effect claimed that they knew more than any of the peasants. They had petulantly demanded that the villagers learn to think like city people and join the confusion sweeping the cities. They were critical of all authorities within the village, even those duly established by the Socialist Education Movement work team. They had no positive political or economic program for the village, only negative criticisms of village life. This was heresy: a body of ideas unacceptable to villagers' conceptions of themselves. In the Cleansing of the Class Ranks campaign, the village leaders moved with great gusto to punish those who had advocated such heresy.

One group's heresy is often another's common sense. The urban youth who belonged to the Maoism Red Guards had not thought that they had done anything very wrong. They simply echoed what hundreds of thousands of their urban peers were saying throughout China. Mao himself encouraged them to dare to rebel. Compared to the ideas of many of their urban peers, their views were in fact relatively mild. Most of the sent-down youth who had returned to Canton had actually lived fairly quiet lives during the Cultural Revolution. They stayed at home and minded their own business while other urban Red Guards conducted pitched battles in the streets. Even while they were in the village, they never advocated physical violence against any of the village powerholders. If they could have remained in the city during the Cleansing of the Class Ranks campaign, they would not have been severely punished. Many people in the cities were worse than they.

But urban authorities forced them to return to their village. There, a rude welcome awaited them. The village leaders were ready to include about ten of them among the top three categories of targets for the campaign: persons who had spoken out against Chairman Mao; persons who had spoken out against Vice-Chairman Lin; and bad Cultural Revolution leaders. In the eyes of the village leaders, the rebellious urban youth fit these categories precisely.

They made popular targets. Without the rebellious youth, the village would have sailed calmly through the storms of the Cultural Revolution. The urban youth had fomented unrest from the autumn of 1966 to the autumn of 1967. Most ordinary villagers were angry about that. Their anger was enhanced by a general fear of outsiders, a fear that spawned rumors that—if not in Chen Village, at least in other places—sent-down youth had poisoned village wells. The villagers were happy to attack them. Besides, the more of them who were made campaign targets, the less ordinary villagers had to fear that the campaign would turn against themselves. Moreover, Longyong and the other cadres were angry at the urban youth for toppling them from power. Now was a good time for revenge.

But the desire for revenge and irritation at the rebels for having voiced criticisms that caused local unrest were not in themselves morally adequate reasons to attack the youth. It had to be shown that they had perverted the purposes of the Cultural Revolution, that their criticisms were utterly without merit, that they had an utterly wrong and reprehensible vision of the good life in a socialist society, and that they were guilty of heresy. To develop this argument, Longyong and his village henchmen needed the help of people better versed in Maoist ideology than they were. So Longyong relied on Ao Meihua and Su Liai, two of the sent-down youth counselors who had rejected the rebellious youth from the beginning and had stayed behind to work in the village.

If the behavior of the rebellious youth had been disturbing to the masses and threatening to the local cadres, it was utterly infuriating to people like Ao Meihua. She and her counselor colleagues who stayed in the village during the Cultural Revolution had worked furiously to uphold local order by invoking the Thought of Chairman Mao against all deviants. They did not *think* about Mao's Thought; they proclaimed it. In this way, they rose to power and glory in the village. When their rebellious urban comrades started to assert, on the basis of Cultural Revolution pronouncements, that Mao's Thought provided a justification for *dis*order rather than for order, Ao Meihua and her counselor colleagues were outraged. Such thinking contradicted everything they stood for and threatened the foundations of everything that was most meaningful to them. When they later heard some of the rebellious urban youth actually *questioning* the wisdom of Mao's Thought, they regarded this as proof that the rebellious urban youth had fallen into an utterly reprehensible heresy. Those youth had to be punished without mercy. As Ao Meihua explained, "We had been thoroughly educated in Communist ideology; we stopped having pity."

Longyong made Ao Meihua and Su Liai his chief inquisitors for prosecuting the rebellious urban youth during the campaign. Both of these young women had worked closely with Longyong during the restless days of the Cultural Revolution. In return, Longyong made them members of the "special materials small group" responsible for compiling evidence against potential targets in the Cleansing of the Class Ranks campaign. Ao and Su went to work with tremendous, self-righteous enthusiasm gathering materials against campaign targets, especially the rebellious urban youth. "Without us," Ao told me later, "the brigade wouldn't have gotten as much material [on the rebellious youth]. We knew their thoughts, their feelings."

As the youth who had returned to Canton trickled back into the village—having been forced to leave the city by the Canton police—those who had been among the leaders of the Maoism Red Guards were brought to brigade headquarters for questioning. Sometimes these initial interrogations lasted several days. The young people were pressured to "confess" their own misdeeds and to inform on their friends. Information other persons had given about them was used as leverage to extract further confessions. Then Ao and Su tried to raise the mistakes they had discovered to "the level of principle and line." They tried to show how all the faults of the campaign targets were part of a general pattern of fundamental opposition to the highest ideals of Maoist thought.

The main "crimes" thus discovered were the following: destroying the "grasping of revolution and the promotion of production" by leading the sent-down youth to Canton; listening to foreign radio broadcasts; spreading antisocialist rumors in Canton by repeating to friends the contents of Red Guard wallposters that said that some city people were suffering economic hardship in China; and calling the beloved leader Chairman Mao "Old Fatso" (an apparently popular sobriquet among rebellious young people in Canton).

In the eyes of people like Ao Meihua, these were horrible crimes. To call Mao "Old Fatso" was not just a juvenile irreverence but an outrageous blasphemy. To pass on rumors about poverty in China was not just gossip but a denial of the goodness of socialism. To listen to foreign radio broadcasts was a manifestation not just of undisciplined curiosity but of a lack of faith in Mao. The rebellious sent-down youth thus did not believe in the goodness of Mao's Thought. They preached false doctrines, and one of the worst effects of their false doctrines was leading the youth back to Canton. That was thus not just an act of youthful rebellion but part of a commitment to heresy—an act of faithless defiance of the wisdom of Mao Zedong.

About ten of the urban youth were interrogated about such "crimes" and forced to confess complicity in them. In the process many of them were frightened into informing on their fellows. Then, after having been duly terrified, most of them were released, so that the leaders of the campaign might concentrate on a few outstanding targets. Special punishment was reserved for three of the urban youth who had played the leading roles in organizing the Maoism Red Guards, seizing power from the cadres, and then preparing the exodus of the sent-down youth to Canton. They were locked up in the cowshed and underwent fearsome struggle sessions day after day and week after week. After a month and a half, one of them was released. But the other two spent a full year in that tiny makeshift jail.

The struggle sessions against the youths were truly frenzied. There was more physical violence in these sessions than there had been during the Socialist Education Movement. Young militiamen rose from the assembled crowd and beat the struggle targets. Many ordinary villagers seemed genuinely infuriated at the youths. As one of the targets later told my colleague in Hong Kong, when asked why the peasants expressed so much rage against him: "First, the peasants said whatever the cadres said. Second, they thought we were malcontents, were mischievous, created chaos, were disobedient to the brigade cadres. Sometimes they looked on the Party as very sacred. . . . You should not anger [the cadres], should know your place, obey the rules, not create a lot of trouble. . . . They were genuinely struggling against us."

But there were clear differences between the cadres and the ordinary villagers with respect to how seriously they took the youths' heresy. These differences became evident when it came time to decide how much punishment the youths should receive. Longyong, the other peasant leaders, and Ao Meihua and Su Liai all seemed to want to get the maximum possible punishment for the three city youths who were the principal targets of the campaign. But most ordinary villagers were willing to be much more lenient.

After the youths had been struggled against for about a month and a half, they were brought before mass meetings to be sentenced for their crimes. Although the decisions about their sentences were supposed to come directly from the people, the village leaders suggested what kinds of sentences they should give. One urban youth "confessed" to all his crimes: "I said I was a counterrevolutionary, the filial son and grandson of the bourgeoisie. . . . Whatever you said I was, I accepted." Because he confessed, he was then released. But the other two, being more obstinate and having played a larger role in the Cultural Revolution, were led before mass meetings to receive sentencing. The village leaders suggested that they each receive fifteen years in labor reform camp.

But the sentencing did not go altogether smoothly. One of the other people to be sentenced was a village barefoot doctor who had confessed to sexually molesting a young girl patient while she was under anesthesia. Panicked at the thought that his crime would be found out, he decided that under the policy of "leniency to those who confess, severity to those who are obstinate" it would be better to confess than to be caught. Since he had confessed, the brigade leadership suggested that he only be sentenced to two years in labor reform yet recommended that the two sent-down youths who had refused to confess get fifteen years. But when the peasants discussed this, many of them were confused. They thought that the sex offender's crime was a "vile thing" (*chou shi*) and deserved the maximum penalty, whereas the sent-down youths had only done a "bad thing" (*huai shi*) and should be punished only insofar as they had actually disturbed social order in the village. "And so some women yelled: 'No, the worst thing in the world is doing this kind of thing. . . . He *must* have ten years.'" But the sent-down youths "only talked with their mouths. Two years. Just let them know that they shouldn't do such things again." But for Longyong and his associates, the sent-down youths had breached a fundamental, sacred moral norm by preaching a heresy that legitimated rebellion against local authority. This was worse than a sex crime and deserved an extreme penalty. In the end, the cadres got their way. The sex offender got two years. The two sent-down youth rebel leaders received ten-to-fifteen-year sentences.

It was in Longyong's interests bitterly to attack the rebellious youths' heresy, because, I would argue, it was in his interests to strive for a village in which everyone worked hard under a strong central village authority for the common good of the village. In such a village, Longyong would be the perfect person to play the role of the strong central authority. But a truly intense collective village life and a truly steadfast submission to authority could not exist if people carelessly criticized accepted sacred symbols and invoked the name of Mao to justify chaotic, undisciplined forms of rebellion. A dispassionate scholar might say that such rebellious vocations were quite compatible with certain themes in Mao's own thought, but Longyong was not a dispassionate scholar. He was passionately committed to making the village like a big family, and he interpreted Maoism to support this vision. When he ordered the arrest of one of Stocky Wang's sent-down youth friends with the words, "There are people who want to protect this rotten Wang, who want to obstruct the revolution!" he was obviously not talking about obstructing a revolution that would radically change the power structure of the village, but of a revolution that would *maintain* that power. If some of the sent-down youth were revolutionary rebels, Longyong was a revolutionary conservative. And to equate revolution with rebellion was for him a dangerous heresy.

People who owed their position to Longyong had an interest in supporting his position—especially sent-down youth like Ao Meihua. These individuals had risen to power not by being practical politicians but by being ideologues who preached a version of the Maoist gospel that was useful to Longyong. If they could not vigorously defend that ideology, their positions might become very tenuous indeed.

But the rhetoric employed by Longyong with the aid of Ao Meihua, Su Liai, and his other associates was not simply a mask for naked ambitions to power. In the beginning of the campaign at least, it was partly an expression of moral sentiments shared by many of the villagers. Our interviewees—even those who had been harshly punished in the campaign—stressed that the peasants were angry at the rebellious youth because of their "freshness." The villagers generally seemed to believe that the urban youth had been disrespectful of local authority and irreverent toward Mao. Such action and such talk created needless confusion and unrest. The villagers agreed with the general idea that the youth should be prosecuted for heresy.

However, Longyong's interest in making such an extreme case against the educated youth caused him and his associates to pull away from the moral discourse of ordinary poor and lower-middle peasants. The more he and his associates talked in extreme terms about the need to crush ideological dissent without mercy, the more they removed themselves from any real dialogue with the villagers and the more their actions became strictly manipulative. As this happened, the temptation increased to use their power—power gained partly through their appeal to genuine local moral ideals—to satisfy purely personal ambitions and personal interests. Longyong seized upon the almost hysterical atmosphere he had helped to create to become more of a local emperor than ever before. He and his associates enjoyed the pleasure of their near absolute power and reveled in the satisfaction of revenging themselves on those who had once been their enemies. Their obsessive appeals to good political morality resulted in a higher immorality.

Crushing Rivals and Enjoying Revenge

The desire to crush rivals and enjoy revenge seems to have been an important force throughout the campaign. In addition to fitting into official government categories of campaign targets in a rough way and to being disliked by many ordinary villagers, many of the campaign targets had personally displeased the campaign's leaders. In fact, the individuals who suffered the most in the campaign were people toward whom Longyong held special grudges. The husband of the old widow who went insane from her treatment and then died had deeply angered Longyong in the early 1960s. Both of the sent-down youths who were given fifteen years of labor reform had personally angered Longyong before they had become involved with the Cultural Revolution. And one of those sent-down youths had jilted Ao Meihua after a romance had begun to develop between them. This certainly did not help them during the Cleansing of the Class Ranks campaign, although it is difficult to determine exactly how much of their suffering was due to a simple desire for revenge on the part of the village's local emperor and his court.

Where Longyong's revenge motive showed through most clearly was his treatment of Qingfa. Qingfa was one of the first persons to be arrested during the campaign. He fit the category of Cultural Revolution "black hand," a discontented fallen cadre who used the Cultural Revolution to manipulate events from behind the scenes. He was charged with encouraging his production team to resist the authority of the brigade and with attempting to buy votes to ensure representation for his political faction on the new Revolution Leadership Small Group, a move that had been blocked by Longyong's ability to mobilize his own political faction more astutely under the circumstances. Longyong had been no less guilty than Qingfa of working behind the scenes through informal groups before the election to secure a position of dominance on the Revolution Leadership Small Group. But it was not Longyong's style to organize factions by directly promising favors. He tended rather to mobilize supporters by appealing to their righteous desires to secure a place of dominance in the village. Longyong could claim that his way of organizing people was more correct than Qingfa's. He could also claim that since Qingfa had been deposed and not officially reinstated after the Four Cleanups campaign, Qingfa had no right to try to get a place for himself on the new brigade administration. Indeed, government directives explicitly stated that it was a crime for cadres who had fallen during the Four Cleanups campaign to try to use the confusion of the Cultural Revolution to "reverse their verdicts." And Longyong now had the power to use these claims as justification for attacking his old rival. In the process Longyong could perhaps remove Qingfa from the village political scene once and for all and richly repay him for the suffering Longyong had endured during the early part of the Socialist Education Movement.

So Qingfa was dragged into the cowshed and subjected to struggle sessions again and again. But he was a less popular target than most of the others selected for attack. He had, after all, been a powerful and respected leader in the village for a long time, and many people were in his debt. And although his father had been a small landlord, he had been a young boy when his father had squandered his family's money and died. Before Liberation the teenaged Qingfa had been genuinely destitute. For all his adult life, he had worked with the poor and lower-middle peasants of the village to advance their welfare. These peasants thought of him as one of their own. Moreover, though not a few people disliked Qingfa, all but the most fervent supporters of Longyong felt that his "crimes" were natural failings for a leader in the Chinese countryside. He did not deserve to be treated like one of the Four Bad Types nor even like one of those close relatives of the Four Bad Types who had made no positive contributions to the village. Nor did he deserve to be treated like one of those strange rebellious urban youth who had brought all sorts of useless, troublesome ideas into the village. The poor and lower-middle peasants struggled against Qingfa partly because they believed that what he had done was wrong and partly because Longyong said to and Longyong had power. But many of them could not forget that Qingfa was one of their own. The ordinary peasants' general attitude toward Qingfa was a mixture of indignation and respect, with some individuals having more indignation and others more respect.

But Longyong, with the help of people like Ao Meihua, painted Qingfa's "crimes" during the Cultural Revolution in the most lurid light possible. Developing the theme that counterrevolutionary conduct sprang from kinship connections with the bad classes, they made a great deal out of the fact that his father had been a landlord. They were determined to push the attack against him without mercy "until he collapsed and until he stank."

After about three months, the Cleansing of the Class Ranks campaign began to quiet down. The villagers had exhausted themselves physically and emotionally from struggling against the various targets; moreover they had to return to the business of planting the spring rice. Most of the targets were then released from the cowshed. People were only supposed to be kept in the cowshed while they were being interrogated and publicly struggled against. The average stay in the cowshed was about a month for most targets. But Longyong kept Qingfa—together with the two urban youths who had been sentenced to fifteen years—there after the struggle phase of the campaign had been completed. These three major campaign targets remained in the cowshed for a full year. The reason the village leaders gave for keeping them there was the lack of clear instructions from above about what to do with them. And indeed, in those troubled times, power in the commune seat kept shifting among various military and civilian factions, so that no clear orders were coming down to the village at all. But if Longyong and the other village leaders had really wanted to release Qingfa and the two urban youths, they could have found an excuse to do so. To ordinary villagers, it began to seem more and more that Longyong was being purely vindictive.

Culture, Politics, and Character

In the Cleansing of the Class Ranks campaign, the worst potentialities of Longyong's character were realized. Longyong was capable of great generosity and great courage. But now he was manifesting a terrible meanness and cowardliness; he was revenging himself on his enemies and grasping for more and more power. With the help of his colleagues, he was persecuting basically innocent old widows and other defenseless people in order to further his hopes for the village and his own political ambitions. To call his behavior bad is not to apply inappropriate Western concepts of morality to a Chinese context. Revenge, the unprincipled lust for power, and the persecution of innocent people are contrary to the moral ideals of both Chinese traditional culture and Mao Zedong's Thought.

Longyong's attempts to "jump very high" and to crush his rival Qingfa were made possible by the village's political situation immediately after the Cultural Revolution: the lack of supervision of village affairs by commune level authorities, the exclusion from the new village government of practically anyone not loyal to Longyong, and so forth. The virulence of the campaign can be partly explained by the general anxiety the villagers felt in the wake of the Cultural Revolution, an anxiety that created a need for emotional catharsis. But Longyong could not have taken advantage of the political opportunities to turn himself into a vengeful village dictator unless he had an ideology to justify and give direction to such conduct. And the nature of the moral ideology Longyong used to justify and direct his actions shaped the way the village masses poured their pent-up emotions into the campaign. Let us examine the cultural "maps" Longyong used to pursue the path he followed.

The central idea was that of class struggle. The official government directives called for a new phase to the war between the classes. For a person of poor and lower-middle peasant status to participate in this struggle was the greatest of goods. According to this idea, people of bad classes were qualitatively different from people of good classes. The latter need not and should not show any compassion for the former. The bad classes were to be treated absolutely without human feeling. Their members deserved such merciless treatment because of their complicity with the centuries old, brutal "feudalistic" system of oppression of the poor. Such notions formed the cornerstone of the official rhetoric during the Cleansing of the Class Ranks campaign.

The ideas about the moral nobility of class struggle may indeed have guided oppressed peasants toward genuine heroism in the earlier phases of the revolution. When landlords and rich peasants tightly controlled village life, the idea of the nobility of class struggle may have guided poor peasants to suppress their fear and overcome their passivity and to struggle for equality and dignity by becoming masters of their own fate. But once the old classes had been overthrown and the peasant economy socialized, the idea of class struggle began to lose its relevance to local political action. The Socialist Education Movement had tried to revive the notion of class struggle by claiming that the thought of the old classes still existed and was manifested in the speech and action of cadres who sought out special privileges and treated ordinary peasants unfairly. The call to class struggle challenged poor and lower-middle peasants to assert their dignity by fighting against the privileges and prejudices of a new village elite. There could be something morally uplifting in that, although, as we have seen, the Socialist Education Movement led to many unprincipled attacks on basically innocent cadres.

But now in the Cleansing of the Class Ranks campaign, the idea of class struggle was totally inadequate to define the nature of the challenges facing the people of Chen Village. There was perhaps a genuine need to tighten up local discipline and to reassert the necessity of law and order. But this was not class struggle. To rally villagers with the cry of continuing the class struggle was to call them to attack fellow villagers without mercy even though those objects of attack had not been implicated in any system of oppression against the poor of the village. It was thus to tempt village leaders with opportunism rather than to inspire them with courage.

The government's ideology of class struggle had always been interpreted by the villagers in the light of their own local world views. "Classes" had never been vast arrays of people spawned by nationwide economic forces but groups of individuals within the village. The struggle against classes was less a part of a vast movement of world history than an aspect of a local struggle to realize local community hopes. Village leaders were not so much members of a national Communist movement as members of the village. Villagers judged their cadres not on the basis of how well they obeyed Party discipline but how well they contributed to the glory of the village and how well they respected local conceptions of decent conduct.

Thus, during the Cleansing of the Class Ranks campaign, Longyong's conduct seemed to be justified as much in terms of the idea of treating the village as one's big family as in terms of the official government ideology of class struggle. But this local, tradition-based conception of the behavior appropriate to a good revolutionary concerned with class struggle was becoming increasingly inappropriate to current realities. It suggested that the leader of a village should be a tough, authoritarian, patriarchal figure who could inspire villagers to disciplined zeal. In a poor, loosely organized village, such a person might have indeed played a positive role in rallying villagers to respond to outside threats or to seek justice against oppressors. But now the Communist government had given the village a tight political organization. Village leaders had at their disposal unprecedentedly powerful tools of coercion and communication. An unprecedentedly effective organizational apparatus was available to conduct systematic inquiries into villagers' private lives and to set up intense struggle sessions against deviants. Without these "organizational weapons," the harshness of an authoritarian, patriarchal leader could be a beneficial antidote to weak community solidarity. With those weapons, that harshness could be a terrible, destructive force. If the new forms of government imposed upon the village were not to become oppressive, they needed to be controlled by some form of participatory democracy— the "mass line." But the culture of the village did not provide models of democratic leadership.

By the time the Cleansing of the Class Ranks campaign began, the villagers were angry and anxious. The Cultural Revolution had brought considerable confusion into their lives. They were ready to accept strong, single-minded leadership that could help them focus and control their anger and anxiety. They needed someone who could pull them together. Longyong's style was right for such a crisis situation. When the government began to call for renewed class struggle to combat class enemies who had crept into the good class ranks, many poor and lower-middle peasants were in the mood to struggle. It was difficult to understand just who the campaign targets should be, but the villagers went along with the decisions of the village leadership, especially if the leadership picked as targets people who were generally considered obnoxious. Thus, Longyong and his people could attack almost anyone they wanted. With a general mandate to be fierce and wide discretion regarding whom to be fierce toward, Longyong was tempted to satisfy his urge for power and revenge to the limit, and he began to do so. As he picked on targets whom many villagers sympathized with—like Qingfa—and as he extended the terms of punishment beyond reasonable limits, he lost touch with ordinary villagers.

The result was bad for Longyong, for his close associates, and for the village as a whole. Longyong began to become a very mean, vindictive person, a local tyrant. Close associates like Ao Meihua were also becoming cruel, self-righteous fanatics. The villagers had been led to participate in acts that they had reason to regret when their passions cooled down. Moreover, the villagers, seeing the vindictiveness of Longyong and his associates, now began to lose respect for their leadership. This resulted in widespread apathy.

We have already seen how the zeal that made possible the short-lived economic reforms of the Three Loyalties movement quickly burned itself out and thus caused the reforms to be abandoned. This apathy extended to all areas of village public life. Villagers failed to show up for public meetings of any kind. As Ao Meihua put it: "The human feelings of the villagers were all messed up." There was a great general listlessness.

Not until an outside work team entered the village in 1969 to settle the cases of those in the cowshed and to hold elections for a new village leadership did the listlessness abate and a new sense of collective purpose begin to assert itself. But the great amount of distrust and disillusionment generated by the Cleansing of the Class Ranks campaign seemed to deal a final blow to the moral basis for political activism in Chen Village. To be an activist now became less and less a matter of being a leader—a person who embodied and brought into focus the moral ideals of the community—and more and more a matter of being an administrator.

8 Liuist Morality

A CURE FOR MORAL
DISINTEGRATION

The argument of this chapter is an ironic one: Mao's Great Proletarian Cultural Revolution handed an ideological victory to Liu Shaoqi, and not necessarily to the real Liu Shaoqi, the Chinese patriot whose reputation was blackened by Maoist caricature, but to the caricature itself: Liu Shaoqi, the "renegade, traitor, scab," the bête noire of the Maoists' darkest dreams. Liu Shaoqi was so evil, so "revisionist," the Maoists claimed, because he was an ethical utilitarian. He allegedly believed that humans were primarily driven by individual material self-interests and that government policy should mainly focus on accommodating such interests. Thus, the Maoists said, the revisionist Liu believed that the government should only attempt to carry out social changes that were manifestly in the self-interests of a majority of the Chinese population. For instance, peasants should not be forced to work in large-scale agricultural collectives unless it could be demonstrated that such collective work would increase the standard of living for most of them. This would not happen until China's "productive forces," that is, its agricultural technologies, were sufficiently advanced. Then the peasants would see that to reap the benefits of the more productive technologies, they would require a more complex division of labor, and they would gladly join collective production teams. But as long as peasants used primitive, labor-intensive farming methods that required little division of labor, it was foolish to force them to work in large-scale collectives. Moral spirit could not transform matter. Moral appeals could not change objective economic laws. Passionate appeals to selflessness could not overcome the natural pull of self-interests.[1]

1. The ideas in this paragraph are based mainly on Lowell Dittmer, "The Radical Critique of Political Interest: 1966–1978," *Modern China* 6, no. 4 (October 1980): 363–96. See also Lowell Dittmer, *Liu Shao-ch'i and the Chinese Cultural Revolution: The Politics of Mass Criticism* (Berkeley: University of California Press, 1974).

In fact, Liu Shaoqi does not seem to have believed that people were inevitably motivated only by short-term, material interests. In his famous book *On the Self-Cultivation of a Communist Party Member*[2] (denounced as "eyewash" advocating "bourgeois individualism and enslavement" during the Cultural Revolution), Liu clearly stated that: "At all times and on all questions, a Party member should give first consideration to the interests of the Party as a whole, and put them in the forefront and place personal matters and interests second."[3] A good Party member could and should develop an enlightened attitude of mind that would enable him to see that his truest interests were those of the Party, and thus he should be willing to "sacrifice his personal interests without any hesitation or reluctance."[4] It was the duty of the Party to help the Chinese people cultivate this kind of moral enlightenment. Yet, unlike Mao, Liu Shaoqi did seem to believe that altruism had its limits. Ordinary citizens could not be expected to have the moral enlightenment of a well-cultivated Party member; therefore their immediate material interests should be respected. Thus, Liu once said, "It is perfectly justifiable and necessary to demand, on the basis of developed production, an increase in one's income and improvement in one's living standards. Only in this way can the enthusiasm of the workers be continuously promoted and the outstanding workers' movement acquire a solid foundation."[5] As Lowell Dittmer explains, Liu "attempted either to reinforce [altruism] by augmenting it with some material incentive (such as salary or posi-

2. The title given here is a literal translation of the Chinese title of Liu's book. The title of the official English translation is *How to Be a Good Communist* (Beijing, Foreign Languages Press, 1951 and 1964). This official translation, however, fails to capture the Confucian flavor of the original. *On the Self-Cultivation of a Communist Party Member* was originally published in 1939. In 1942, it was one of the main documents used in the Chinese Communist Party's first major internal rectification campaign. In 1962, it was republished (in a revised form) with much fanfare. Its republication coincided with the major effort to promote the veneration of Mao's Thought undertaken by the propaganda apparatus of the People's Liberation Army, under the direction of Lin Biao. In retrospect, it appears that these two events inaugurated one of the earliest public phases of the ideological struggle that culminated in the Cultural Revolution. After the fall of Liu Shaoqi, his book was, of course, vehemently condemned as a prime indicator of his reactionary thought. (The quote about "eyewash" comes from *Hongqi* [Red Flag], no. 5 [March 1967].) For commentaries on Liu's thought, see Dittmer, *Liu Shao-ch'i*; and Howard L. Boorman, "How to Be a Good Communist: The Political Ethics of Liu Shaoqi," *Asian Survey* 3, no. 8 (1963):372–83.

3. Liu Shaoqi, *How to Be a Good Communist,* rev. 4th English ed. (1964), in *Collected Works of Liu Shao-ch'i,* 3 vols. (Kowloon: Union Research Institute, 1969), 1:249.

4. Ibid.

5. Liu Shaoqi, "Message to Outstanding Workers" (April 30, 1956), *Collected Works,* 2:334. As quoted in Dittmer, "Radical Critique," 367.

tion) or to assure altruists that they were bound to draw reciprocal benefits: 'If you suffer hardships to let others have a better life, they will appreciate it and look after you.'"[6]

This sensitivity to the need for revolutionary leaders to respect the economic demands of their constituencies was damned by Mao's followers as "revisionist." Yet Liu's moral discourse was at least as consistent with the moral spirit of Marx's own writings as Mao's was. Marx had emphatically claimed to have written a scientific theory for explaining how class struggle would lead to revolution. The mode of moral discourse suggested by this theory was utilitarian: individual human beings are motivated by self-interest; in a class society, the interests of certain categories of individuals are fundamentally opposed, so that the members of society's dominant class achieve their interests at the expense of other, exploited classes; the structural dynamics of economic systems, however, eventually make the dominant class vulnerable to the system's main exploited class, and a revolution occurs; this process will eventually lead to a final revolution that will usher in a classless society, a society based on an economic system in which no class of individuals will be compelled to or in fact able to pursue their interests at the expense of members of other classes. Liu was being faithful to Marx the scientific socialist even as he echoed themes from Marx the morally enraged prophet who gave up the possibility of a comfortable academic career to promote the revolution of the proletariat.[7] Liu was aware that people could not be motivated to undertake the painful, dangerous business of leading a social revolution if they were concerned only with their own immediate material interests. The realization that a revolution could further these interests might initially lead members of the exploited classes to take part in the revolution. But such concerns had to be expanded into a broad conception of the ultimate goodness of fighting for the overall benefit of the Party and of the people of China.

Throughout most of his career, Mao too had been sensitive to the need to base Communist policies on the perceived interests of China's exploited poor. But Mao's experience had been different from Liu's, and the difference in experience helped develop a difference in moral emphasis. In the 1930s, Mao rose to the supreme leadership of the Party through his experience as an organizer of peasant partisans. He had defied the orthodoxy of scientific Marxism, which held that peasants, precisely because of their material interests, would not make good revolutionaries. He had

6. Dittmer, "Radical Critique," 367. The quote from Liu is from *On the Self-Cultivation of a Communist Party Member.*

7. For one well-known account of this ambiguity in Marx's writings, see Daniel Bell, "Two Paths From Marx," in *The End of Ideology* (New York: Free Press, 1966).

led his peasant armies on the extraordinarily painful and dangerous Long March and directed them in protracted guerrilla warfare during which life was extraordinarily hard and "death [was] a common occurrence." Such heroic struggles helped to evoke a vision of moral heroism, a vision in which soldiers should be asked to deprive themselves, to suffer and die, not because this would soon make them rich, but because self-sacrifice in the service of the people was good in itself, a transcendent moral duty that made one's life worthwhile and one's death "weightier than Mount Tai." Liu on the other hand had spent his early revolutionary career as an underground organizer of urban workers. From the point of view of scientific Marxism, such work was a much more orthodox undertaking than Mao's. And although it involved great personal danger, it entailed the careful quiet building of Party organizations rather than the heaven-storming heroism of guerrilla warriors. Hence, perhaps, Liu's lesser emphasis on the absolute imperative of total moral heroism.[8]

After the Communists' accession to power in 1949, their task involved less of the heroic bravado of the guerrilla fighter and more of the practical organizational ability of the urban Communist organizer. The Party had to manage a complex economy and govern a huge nation composed of many people who had not directly taken part in the Communist revolutionary struggles. Under such circumstances the practical emphasis of Liu Shaoqi, based on ''an attitude of practical conditions," made more sense than the heroic idealism of Mao. As de Tocqueville once said: "After the battle comes the lawgiver. The one destroys; the other builds up. Each has his function."[9] Mao was more a warrior than a lawgiver, and his warrior's ethic began to seem out of place in the new political situation. In the late 1950s, Mao discredited himself in the minds of many of China's top leaders when he pushed through rapid collectivization and then the Great Leap Forward—economic policies based on his assumption that moral enthusiasm for collective living could form the basis for economically productive cooperative enterprises rather than, as Liu Shaoqi would have tended to argue, the other way around. In his attempt to reassert his power, Mao came to contrast his moralistic approach to public policy with Liu's more pragmatic position. But by pushing his appeals for moral heroism to extremes in the Cultural Revolution, he helped destroy the moral foundation of Chinese politics.

We have seen how this demoralization of politics came about in Chen Village during the Cultural Revolution and its immediate aftermath. Peo-

8. This discussion of the personal background for Liu's ideas is based mainly on Boorman, "How to Be a Good Communist."

9. Alexis de Tocqueville, *Democracy in America*, trans. George L. Lawrence (Garden City, N.Y.: Doubleday, 1964), author's preface to the 12th ed., p. xiv.

ple were urged to dedicate themselves to absolutely selfless service of the Chinese people when they needed to be concerned with producing enough food to eat and to struggle passionately against class enemies when there were no clearly threatening class enemies around. This destroyed the climate of trust and the spirit of commitment to common endeavor that could have helped the villagers partially to transcend their individually perceived short-term economic interests in the name of a common public interest.

Thus, in the 1970s the victory belonged to the Maoist caricature of Liu Shaoqi. If people could no longer trust each other, there was no longer any basis but self-interest for political action. The only possible moral basis for political order was utilitarian. As we shall see, cadres came to justify their behavior and to be judged by their constituents solely on the basis of their competence in managing Chen Village's economy. This was not simply because the cadres who had been associated with Liu Shaoqi were beginning to fight their way back into power at the national level. Political morality within Chen Village took on a decidedly utilitarian cast even when Mao and the Maoist Gang of Four were still in power in China. Politics at the village level steadily turned utilitarian not so much because the highest levels of national government authority wanted it that way but because there was no other viable basis for political order at the local level.

The real Liu Shaoqi—who died in prison in 1969—would perhaps have been sorry to see the triumph of extreme utilitarianism attributed to him. While he seemed to believe that the short-term economic self-interests of China's peasants should be accommodated, he also believed that those interests needed to be constrained and transcended, through a process of disciplined political education, by an identification of narrow self-interests with the interests of the nation as a whole. He might well have been sad to see how the utilitarian politics that characterized Chen Village in the 1970s left a vacuum of meaning in its wake, engendering the kind of aimless public listlessness that comes from the absence of a common purpose.[10]

Economics in Command and Managers in Power

In the fall and winter of 1968, two new work teams came to Chen Village. They each gave long bombastic speeches about the glorious progress realized by the Cultural Revolution and the brilliant contributions that

10. The social and economic changes taking place in Chen Village are analyzed in more detail in Anita Chan, Richard Madsen, and Jonathan Unger, *Chen Village: The Recent History of a Peasant Community in Mao's China* (Berkeley: University of California Press, 1984), chaps. 7 and 8.

China—although faced with severe challenges from American imperialism and Russian revisionism—was making to the world revolution. To consolidate these national and international victories, the work teams promised to examine Chen Village's affairs and adjust local policy. They hinted that Longyong and his associates had gone too far in the campaign to cleanse the class ranks. But before either of these work teams had a chance to accomplish anything, they were abruptly recalled.

The abrupt coming and going of these different work teams was a symptom of a general instability in the provincial and county governments. Factions formed during the Cultural Revolution were still fighting each other, and power was still shifting from side to side. This situation was confusing and depressing for both the cadres and the masses of Chen Village. Longyong and the other brigade cadres were filled with fear and anger over the fact that they might be criticized for doing what they had believed to be their duty during the Cleansing of the Class Ranks campaign. Some of the ordinary peasants welcomed this new possibility; others were appalled by it. But everyone was insecure about the future. No one knew which way the wind was going to blow next. Morale among the villagers plummeted. People arrived late for meetings or did not show up at all. Productivity declined. Cadres, not daring to make stiff demands on villagers for fear of being subjected to subsequent criticism, went about their jobs in an apathetic way.

Then, in the early spring of 1969, a new work team entered the village. This work team called a brigadewide meeting for 9:00 A.M. on the day after it arrived. But at 9:00 A.M. hardly anyone had arrived at the meeting hall. People gradually sauntered in, taking seats with circles of good friends as far away from the front of the hall as possible, bringing along snacks to eat, and obviously hoping to return home as quickly as possible. The casual, indifferent atmosphere was just the opposite of the intense participation that had characterized the meetings of the Cleansing of the Class Ranks campaign. Even at 11:00 A.M. the whole village had still not completely assembled.

Finally the spokesman for the work team arose to speak. "He was short, carried a book bag and wore sandals. He spoke in such a soft voice that the masses in the back couldn't hear him, so he had to stand in the middle of the hall. After ten minutes, he said: 'Meeting adjourned.' We thought this was strange. The previous work teams were not like this! Seeing this, the peasants said all of a sudden: 'This person has some ability.'"

A modest, low-key work team! This was something new and different. Practically every previous work team had been sent to launch a great moral crusade against bad people, bad classes, bad ideas, bad customs, with the promise that such a crusade would bring about glorious progress toward a glorious socialist village and a glorious socialist China. This new work team, however, was doing no such thing. It was lowering expectations, dampening passions, promising no great leap forward into a new era, and claiming only that it wanted to "put policy on a solid footing." As it went about its work, it gave the impression that although many people in the village might have committed mistakes during the preceding tumultuous years, those mistakes were not hideous crimes but understandable errors committed by people of basic good will.

The work team was the harbinger of new government policies that brought about a new era in Chen Village life. No more would the villagers be encouraged to engage in impassioned crusades against internal class enemies. In the early to mid-1970s, there were still, of course, frequent political campaigns: the One Hit Three Anti Campaign (1971), the Criticize Lin Biao, Criticize Confucius Campaign (1973), the Study the Dictatorship of the Proletariat Campaign (1975).[11] These campaigns were launched by Maoists—the now infamous Gang of Four—within the Communist hierarchy; their high-level promoters hoped they would revive the spirit of class struggle, condemn traditional values, and discourage petit bourgeois economic activities like private plots. In Chen Village, the One Hit Three Anti Campaign produced at least one struggle session against a hapless scapegoat, and the other campaigns produced their share of confusion and anger. But none of these campaigns produced the wide-ranging, systematic struggles characteristic of the campaigns of the 1960s. Compared to what the villagers had experienced in the past, the new policies were practically irenic. This was partly because cadres who had been deposed by the Maoists in the Cultural Revolution were now returning to power at the provincial and national levels and were blocking the implementation of the Maoists' directives. (The decisive turn in Guangdong came at the end of 1971, when Lin Biao's associates were cleared out of the province, leaving only relative moderates in control.) But this was also because the Maoist crusades lacked social support among peasants in places like Chen Village. This lack of support set the stage for the final repudiation of the whole idea of class struggle by the government led by Deng Xiaoping, the close associate of Liu Shaoqi who eventually came to power after the death of Mao and the overthrow of the Gang of Four in 1976.

The coming of the low-key "readjust policy" work team was the beginning of the end of the era of heroic politics in Chen Village. The villagers were no longer much inclined to view local political life in terms of desperate battles against Good and Evil. Thus it would be extremely difficult

11. For more detailed accounts of the effects of these campaigns on Chen Village see Chan, Madsen, and Unger, *Chen Village*.

for the government to incite them to imagine and rally around grand new visions of the good political life. The goals of village collective life were now modest: the villagers were supposed to cooperate to raise or at least maintain the general level of material prosperity. Village leaders were supposed to encourage this to happen in the most efficient possible way. That is what they were judged on. They were increasingly becoming managers—"peasant technocrats"—rather than leaders and moral teachers. And ordinary people were inclined to cooperate simply as collective producers, not as sharers of revolutionary hopes.

Although provincial government policies helped this moral spirit become a dominant part of the village's political life, they did not of course create it out of thin air. The moral themes that dominated village public discourse in the 1970s had also been invoked in the 1950s and the 1960s. But they had been mixed in with traditional values such as the importance of good human feeling in politics and with official ideas about the importance of class consciousness and class struggle. But now both traditional and Maoist ideas about the moral basis of public life were receding into the background and the belief that the moral basis of political life was simply determined by the technical requirements of increasing collective material prosperity was rising into prominence.

Changes in the government propaganda reaching the village and in village political and economic institutions provided the context that evoked and supported this new spirit of politics, even during the first half of the 1970s when Maoist officials in Peking were pushing to renew the spirit of the Cultural Revolution. This new spirit of politics helped shape the characters of the village's leading activists and finally began to lead to new moral crises in the village.

A New Context for Political Morality

The first element in the new context for political morality during the 1970s in the village was a change in the government propaganda aimed at the community. In the early 1970s it was not so much a difference in the actual wording of the propaganda messages that flooded the countryside through radio and newspapers. The words remained essentially the same, though subtle changes of phrasing hinted at new themes. The main changes in the propaganda came from the way these words were spoken at the local level and the way official propagandists linked these words to actions. The readjust policy work team was the first official group entering the village that clearly struck the new propaganda notes. The work team used the standard revolutionary rhetoric, but it uttered that rhetoric in a new tone of voice. And its actions dissipated the self-righteous passions that the words had so recently inflamed. Let me briefly recount what the work team did. Then I can explicate the propaganda message that the work team's actions, gestures, and rhetorical style conveyed and show how that message increasingly became the dominant ideological theme of the 1970s.

After its initial speech, the two-person work team quietly went about talking to as broad a range of villagers as possible. The work team took pains to start its inquiries with the village's leading cadres. It did not give the cadres the assurance that it would back up every decision that they had made, but by its calm sympathy with their side of the story, it tended to reassure them that it would not totally repudiate them. In interviewing disgruntled villagers, including the three persons still locked up in the cowshed, the work team also projected a sympathetic attitude. It gave the overall impression that it would improve the position of the disgruntled villagers, even though it would not go so far as to lead them to attack the brigade's cadres.

The first order of business for the readjust policy work team was to settle the affairs of the persons still imprisoned in the cowshed. After an investigation, the work team announced that Qingfa and the two rebellious youth still in the cowshed should be released from their makeshift jail and should not be punished again as long as they sincerely confessed their guilt. They could live and work in the village, and their ultimate fate depended on the rectitude of their deportment. Qingfa responded to this opportunity with an especially spectacular confession of guilt.

> He wept and cursed himself. He apologized with shame to Chairman Mao. He said that Liu Shaoqi had harmed him, that he had become gravely individualistic. He hadn't been able to get rid of his individualism. When he had fallen, he had been very discontented and had wanted to harm other people, so that he would have a chance to "ascend the stage" again. He said he hadn't realized the extent of his wrongdoing before. Only when he had received this shock had he realized what a bad role he had played in the village. He expressed his shameful apologies to the poor and lower-middle peasants, to the Communist Party, and to Mao Zedong. Then he wept and wailed some more.

From the point of view of the commune's leaders, Qingfa's performance was so articulate and sounded so sincere that they decided to make him a model of repentance. He was taken around to all the villages in the commune to confess his guilt and give witness to his conversion. He also gave his declaration of contrition before a mass meeting at the commune center and another meeting at the county seat. His display of repentance paid off. When the Communist Party authorities reviewed his Party membership, he was not expelled but simply put on probation. Within a year he was reinstated as a Party member in good standing and he was ready to "ascend the stage" in Chen Village once again.

The two rebellious youth also made sincere-sounding confessions of guilt and were released from the cowshed. The records that had been drawn up against the other targets of the Cleansing of the Class Ranks campaign (with the possible exception of those against the Four Bad Types) were burned. The Cleansing of the Class Ranks campaign was officially over.

Thus the work team, following general policies set by higher-level authorities, confirmed the correctness of Maoist thought in word but modified it in deed. It made Qingfa and the others give abject confessions of guilt and thus affirmed the basic rightness of the moral standards in accordance with which they had been judged. But if those persons were really as bad as Longyong and the others had said—and indeed as they themselves admitted in their confessions—they should probably have gone to labor reform camps. By letting them go, the work team said in effect that they were basically good people who had made some mistakes and were not dangerous enemies of the people. It also implicitly criticized Longyong for the way he had treated them. And it told everyone that now was the time to accept, tolerate, and learn to cooperate with one another in spite of everyone's faults and mutually held grudges.

Most villagers seemed happy with this message. The general opinion seemed to be that the readjust policy work team was an exceptionally good one and worthy of a great deal of respect. One major exception to this was Longyong. He was apoplectic. "The brigade chief was *terribly* angry. Whenever he would get mad, he would break out in a fever. He couldn't control himself. . . . He was very fierce at that time. He used to call himself 'bullheaded' and be proud of it. He made the fact that he was extremely poor and the fact that he couldn't read a single character into a kind of capital. . . . He was very savage during this time." Longyong was angry because the work team had challenged the way he had handled the Cleansing of the Class Ranks campaign by its actions. More than that, the work team had also rebuked him verbally, although not, it seems, at a public meeting of all the villagers. The work team members had accused Longyong of having a "warlord work style." Longyong was criticized for running the village as his independent empire and for not paying enough attention to higher-level political authorities. This rebuke was not only a blow to Longyong's pride but an inroad into his power. It signified that the style of politics that had enabled Longyong to "jump so high" was no longer officially approved. All of Longyong's rage and all of his appeals to villagers' native moral sentiments were not enough to offset the blow to his power given by this shift in government standards concerning the proper behavior for a village leader.

As the 1970s continued on, the propaganda message implicit in the work team's combination of word and deed continued to emanate from authorities at the provincial, county, and commune levels. The appeals for self-sacrificing participation in the glorious Chinese Communist Revolution were balanced by policies that rehabilitated leaders who had once been declared enemies of the revolution. (In 1979, even the Four Bad Types were declared rehabilitated and allowed to function again as full-fledged citizens of the polity.) No attempts were made to whip up peasant emotions into a revivalistic fervor. The official propaganda had always said that good Communists were supposed to do two things: "grasp revolution and promote production." In the late 1960s, the emphasis had all been on revolution. Now, in the early 1970s, as much by deed as by word, the government was putting the accent on production.

Besides subtly shifting the meaning of their propaganda messages, government authorities were taking measures to modify the political and economic institutions of the village. Again, the readjust policy work team began this process. After settling the affairs of the targets of the Cleansing of the Class Ranks campaign, it organized elections for a full-fledged revolutionary committee, to take over from the provisional Revolution Leadership Small Group. The basic functions of this revolutionary committee were the same as those of the small group and, for that matter, of the old brigade management committee. But under the direction of the work team, there were important changes in the personnel of the new village governing body. Most of the people who had been elected to the Revolution Leadership Small Group were elected to this new revolutionary committee, receiving almost exactly the same number of votes as they had received in the earlier election. There were, however, a few significant exceptions. Three of the people who had been Longyong's close supporters during the Cleansing of the Class Ranks campaign failed to be chosen. They were replaced by individuals who were more independent of Longyong. As the result of these moves, Longyong's ability to impose his particular vision of the world on the village was weakened.

In 1971, after having been on probation for a year, Qingfa was rehabilitated. He was once again made a party member in good standing and soon after was given a post on the revolutionary committee—first as militia chief, then as public security head. There was now more of a balance of power on the revolutionary committee than ever before. One result of this was that the revolutionary committee could no longer speak with a single clear voice about the grand moral goals to which the villagers were to aspire. People like Longyong and Qingfa had built their careers on very different ideas about these matters. They had to seek more modest goals on which to cooperate—the goals of providing for a decent level of public order in the village and for a steady degree of economic development in the immediate future.

Besides overseeing personnel shifts in the village's government, authorities at the county and commune seats made some important changes in the structure of the government itself. At the time of the readjust policy work team, procedures were initiated that linked the local village government more firmly to the bureaucracies at the commune and county levels. The number of meetings village cadres had to attend at the commune and county seats was greatly increased. More written reports were required than ever before. New regulations were instituted specifying how public security measures were to be reported to and reviewed by higher-level authorities. Through all these measures, local cadres like Longyong lost some of their power independently to dominate the affairs of the village. And the state gained a new measure of ability to supervise and control the political life of Chen Village brigade.

Thus, the choice of personnel for the new village political organs, together with the new regulations and procedures linking the organs more closely to higher levels of bureaucracy, helped to create a new era of politics in which the emphasis was on local balance and harmony and dutiful obedience to the bureaucratic regulations issued by higher-level authorities. The energies of village cadres were coming to be directed not at transforming the village's social relations but at making the village work, not at uplifting the moral consciousness of the villagers and committing them to new levels of self-sacrifice but at facilitating their ability to produce material goods collectively.

A final important factor in the changed context for political morality was the development of new village economic institutions. In the 1960s, the slogan that had epitomized central government economic policy toward the rural economy was: "Grain as the basis and multiple undertaking." The meaning of this was that rural collectives should concentrate on producing grain and should carry on other "multiple undertakings" such as pig raising, vegetable growing, and handicraft production only to the degree that they did not interfere with the primary business of producing grain. But now, around 1970, the slogan changed to: "Grain as the basis and overall undertaking."[12] The meaning of this shift was that it was now permissible for rural collectives to carry out rather ambitious large-scale enterprises in addition to grain production. In particular, the way was now open for the establishment of a great variety of small-scale manufacturing industries at the level of China's production brigades.

In Chen Village, as in villages throughout China, this change in central government policy led to a spectacularly rapid development of small-

12. For the effect of this slogan, see Byung-joon Ahn, "The Political Economy of the People's Commune in China: Changes and Continuities," *Journal of Asian Studies* 34 (1975):656.

scale industries. Up until 1969, the only manufacturing industries in the village had been a small brickworks and a small sugar refinery. Now the brickworks was expanded into an operation employing forty workers full time. (Brick making was a natural industry for Chen Village because the village had access to plentiful supplies of burnable grass from the hills behind it to fuel the brick kiln.)

In the early 1970s a new complex of factory buildings began to be constructed in the western corner of the village. By 1973, these buildings housed a peanut oil press; a rice-mill; a new, expanded sugar refinery; a distillery (using waste from the sugar-refining process to make alcohol); an agricultural implement factory and repair shop; and a crude laboratory for developing new fertilizers. Most of these factories manufactured goods or provided services for the use of the villagers themselves. Thus, before the erection of the rice-mill, oil-press, and sugar refinery, the villagers had to bring their grain, peanuts, and sugar cane to the commune seat to be processed. Now this processing could be done locally, saving villagers the effort of transporting their unprocessed products and keeping the processing money within the village. With the exception of the brickworks, the new brigade industries employed persons mostly during the agricultural slack seasons. During the slack seasons, over one-sixth of the village's able-bodied laborers were employed in the brigade industries by the mid-1970s.[13]

Construction of these new small-scale industries helped to create a new relationship between the brigade and the production team levels of government in the village.[14] As we noted in Chapter 2, the brigade level of government in the 1960s was in a relatively weak position with respect to the production teams. The production teams—based upon neighborhoods within the village—were the main units of production. Each production team owned its fields and major agricultural tools. Under the leadership of the production team management committee, the team members tilled their collectively owned land and at the end of the year divided among themselves the net profit of the team. Control over collec-

---

13. For analyses of the role played by small-scale industries on the development of rural China since the Cultural Revolution, see Ahn, "The Political Economy of the People's Commune in China," 652–55. Also see Jon Sigurdson, *Rural Industrialization in China* (Cambridge, Mass.: Harvard University Press, 1977); and Sigurdson, "Rural Industry and the Internal Transfer of Technology," in *Authority, Participation, and Cultural Change in China,* ed. Stuart R. Schram (London: Cambridge University Press, 1973), 199–232.

14. For a discussion of the interrelation between small-scale industrial development and the increase in the power of brigade cadres, see Marianne Bastid, "Levels of Economic Decision Making," in *Authority, Participation, and Cultural Change in China,* ed. Stuart R. Schram (London: Cambridge University Press, 1973), 179–81.

tively produced wealth was vested in the production teams, as was control over the collective agricultural labor that occupied most of a peasant's life. The brigade was that level of administration which took in the affairs of the village as a whole. But the brigade governing body had little wealth. In the 1960s, its work was financed by a small tax levied on each of the production teams. The brigade's income was barely enough to pay for the salaries of its cadres. The brigade government had little public money to use to gain power over members of production teams. Moreover the brigade's authority was limited only to those activities that took place outside of the time peasants spent on productive labor. We have seen how Qingfa at one time used carefully cultivated loyalties based upon good human feeling as a means of gaining a modicum of brigade control over the production teams and how Longyong used the force of his personality, the righteousness of his public image, and his ability to link his personal righteousness with the symbols of orthodox Maoism as a means of controlling the production teams. Both Qingfa's and Longyong's ways created a number of problems for both leaders and led. But now the brigade cadres had another way of gaining control over the production teams. The could regulate the money and work of a significant number of villagers.

The new industrial enterprises were directed by the brigade, and they were very profitable. The brigade cadres used the money from the industries to create as many new industries as possible. When the limits of this expansion were reached, they invested the money into public works projects, such as a new village school and a new village meeting hall. This control over money and labor power, brought about through the expansion of the brigade industries, gave the brigade an economic leverage over the village that it had never had before. The brigade cadres were able to decide who would get the desirable jobs in the new industries and perhaps to some small extent which sectors of the village would benefit most from this expansion. Possession of wealth changed the nature of the political challenge facing the brigade.

Moreover, the task of expanding the small-scale industries gave the brigade cadres something to do besides politics. In the past, to lead a meaningful life as a brigade cadre, one had to be involved in the process of creating power by gaining the loyalty of various groups of villagers through appeals to the villagers' moral sense of the right requirements of social order. If one did not do that, one had nothing to do. Now, however, one could busy oneself with plans for improving the village through economic development. One could justify one's work as a cadre, to oneself and to others, by one's competence in bringing about economic development, rather than by one's ability to develop loyalties through the moralistic arts of politics. Competence in managing production was always the main criterion for evaluating the worth of a production team cadre. Now a similar ability, but exercised on a larger scale, tended to become the measure of worth of a brigade cadre.

In summary then, changes in the government's official propaganda, modifications in local political institutions, and the development of brigade-controlled, small-scale industries all combined to encourage the village's leading cadres to adopt a new moral posture in their political conduct. This in turn set the tone for general attitudes in the village about the meaning and purpose of participation in public life.

Managerial Ethos as the New Moral Basis for Political Activism

In the 1970s, the moral basis for political activism in the village was shaped by a new concept of the proper goals of political conduct. In the 1960s—since the Socialist Education Movement at any rate—the Chinese central government had preached that the goals of politics were transcendent, the process of politics apocalyptic, and the means of politics heroic. The goal of politics was a grand world-historical redemption that would be achieved through cataclysmic class struggles conducted by people engaged in heroic acts of self-sacrifice. If my analysis is correct, the natives of Chen Village (as opposed to some of the urban youth sent to live there) did not fully understand or accept this grand challenge of the official propaganda. But under certain circumstances some of them reinterpreted the official propaganda in terms of local hopes for a glorious future for the village, hopes that had their own transcendent, apocalyptic, and heroic dimensions. In the 1970s, however, the ends of politics became modest and concrete, the process regular, and the means pragmatic. Government propaganda increasingly preached and village public opinion accepted the notion that good cadres and responsible citizens were to work for the short-term material betterment of the village. This was to be accomplished through careful, patient, persistent work, rather than through earth-shattering struggle and was a job that could best be accomplished by pragmatic people, working out of an enlightened self-interest.

The main goal of public life became the economic development of the village. The ability of the brigade government to fulfill economic goals became the primary measure of its goodness. When political goals were more transcendent, a government's goodness could not be judged according to its ability to fulfill those goals, since it was impossible to discern unambiguous progress in their realization. The goodness of a government had to be judged on the basis of the *means* it employed and on the character of the persons employing the means. Good cadres and good citizens were people who fearlessly engaged in struggles against class enemies and who lived a rigorous, abstemious style of life. When devotion to class struggle seemingly produced a spurt in agricultural production, as it did in the latter part of the Socialist Education Movement, this was seen as a good by-product of the revolutionary struggle and a sign that the struggle was heading in the right direction. But it was not seen as something that in itself validated the struggle. If a person had made some clear contributions to village productivity—as Qingfa had done during the course of his career—but was connected with the bad classes or manifested aspects of their thought, then he should be attacked without mercy, for the goal of life was revolution not mere production. But now that the goal of politics was the tangible one of a short-term rise in production, the means employed and the life-style adhered to by the villagers—cadres and citizens alike—were less important than their ability to further the progress of the village toward such a goal.

As a result, the qualities of the good cadre became those of the good manager. By "manager," I mean a person whose job it is skillfully to direct an enterprise to achieve its established goals rather than to lead it to discover new goals. The main criterion for judging the worth of a manager is effectiveness: does the manager make a profit, compile a winning record, and so forth? In the 1970s, Chen villagers increasingly judged their cadres purely in terms of their effectiveness in increasing the village's prosperity. Administrative skill, not virtue—whether traditional or revolutionary—provided the measure of a cadre's worth.

Effective management of the village's new political-economic order required a variety of skills, some traditional, some more modern. First, cadres needed the ability to carry out simple cost-benefit analyses to determine what kinds of projects the village could feasibly undertake in order to improve its economy. Second, they had to have the capability to develop adequate plans to execute the projects. Third, they had to be able to motivate villagers to support those plans and participate in them. Given the low level of technology being introduced into the village, such abilities did not require any sophisticated scientific knowledge but merely a native shrewdness and the skill to apply an intimate experience of the village to estimating the capacities of its human and natural resources and to bringing those capacities into full play. Longyong, for one, possessed qualities like these in abundance.

But in addition to the qualities Longyong possessed, the modernization of the village required abilities more like those Qingfa demonstrated: the ability to forge personal connections with people both inside and outside the village in order to gain needed resources for the village's development, for example. It was important that good relations be established with bureaucrats in charge of allocating scarce supplies like lumber and nails. Also good human feelings had to be developed among certain strategic segments of the village's population so that they would loyally cooperate with the new projects. Human relations management techniques were at least as important in Chen Village as they are in Western organizations!

Furthermore, new skills that the old-style leaders did not possess were also becoming important to the management of Chen Village in the 1970s: the ability to read and write and to understand the subtleties of fairly complicated official regulations. Such qualities were needed not so much for ensuring that the simple plans for the new economic development projects were carried out in the village as for bringing the management of village affairs more closely into line with official government regulations. As we noted above, government bureaucrats insisted on more and more written reports and required more and more meetings between commune- and county-level cadres and brigade-level cadres. The village's welfare was becoming increasingly dependent on higher levels of government, and it was important that upper-level bureaucrats think highly of the village's administration. For this reason, it was important for the effective management of the village that the village government have some cadres from a younger generation who had a higher "cultural level" than the cadres of Longyong's generation.

Thus, to manage the village effectively, a variety of cadres with different personality characteristics, intellectual abilities, degrees of experience, and kinds of social contacts were required. In the past such different qualities were sometimes interpreted as signs of the presence or absence of particular degrees of moral righteousness, and thus one type of person could justify the political condemnation of another. Now these different qualities were interpreted not in moral but in technical terms. They were all useful for solving particular facets of a managerial problem. They were what was needed for a well-balanced managerial team.

As gaining and maintaining a cadre position became increasingly based on possession of effective managerial skills, the cadres themselves took on more and more of a technician's mentality. They carried out their work not as a moral endeavor devoted to fighting evil and realizing good but as a job concerned with solving problems through expert ability. An indication of this change in orientation is the way they began to separate their private lives from the performance of their public jobs. In the past, for instance, Longyong had lived a spartan private life to correspond to the rigorous moral demands he placed on people in his public life; Qingfa had made the human relations cultivated in his private life into loyalties important for the conduct of his public life. But now, both of these cadres began to modify the tenor of their private lives slightly so that their lifestyles began to converge somewhat. Longyong became a little less abstemious but still remained proudly aloof from other people in his private life. Qingfa retained his love of good food and comfort but became less involved in the cultivation of private networks of loyal supporters. As for the new generation of literate cadres, a common term used to characterize their private lives was selfishness: these people did not care about anything outside of the circle of their own small families. Thus all cadres began (in varying degrees) to withdraw into a somewhat isolated, self-indulgent private life after competently performing their public jobs. They could do this because success in the public sphere was based more on competence and less on a reputation for any kind of total moral commitment.

Another indication of the "technician's mentality" that began to take over the cadres in the 1970s was that they saw more of a need to attend meetings and less of a need to engage in physical labor among ordinary peasants. The number of meetings that cadres held with one another and with their superiors at the commune and county levels greatly increased. Some of the peasants derisively began to call some of the cadres "meeting specialists." And the time spent at meetings was subtracted from the time that had been spent on manual labor in previous years. Very few top cadres now spent the requisite 100 days a year laboring among the ordinary peasants. In the past such labor had been important not so much for its economic contribution to the village's agriculture as for its symbolic contribution to the village's morale. The village leaders were supposed to share the toil and sweat of ordinary people. Now, however, village leaders felt less compelled to make a contribution to village morale. They could do their job by contributing their skills to the management of the village. To do an expert job one had to attend plenty of meetings with other cadres. Thus, the cadres developed a mentality that helped them continually invent new reasons for more meetings: the mentality of the technocratic manager.

Many of the peasants interviewed in Hong Kong seemed to think that quite a few of the village cadres were not earning their keep. They were getting too soft, not working hard enough, attending too many meetings. Most of these interviewees were peasants of bad class backgrounds who had been very happy to leave the village for Hong Kong, so perhaps they were more cynical about the cadres than other villagers. But I would not be surprised if cynicism about cadre meeting specialists were quite widespread among the villagers. Cadres did seem to attend an extraordinary number of meetings, more than were probably necessary for the efficient running of the Chen Village brigade. But interviewees generally seemed happier that cadres were wasting their time on meetings than spending their time conducting moralistic crusades against class enemies. That too was probably a widespread attitude among the peasants of Chen Village. The days of heroic politics had, finally, brought out the worst in the village's powerholders and in contending groups of villagers themselves. By the end of the Cleansing of the Class Ranks campaign, the villagers had every reason to be deeply cynical about anyone's claims to being morally superior to anyone else. Such claims did not offer a very effective basis for new village authority.

But now, village expectations were lowered. Now all a good official had to be was a capable manager. Now all villagers had to do was to work for the prosperity of the village; they no longer had to help redeem the village. This was something the villagers could agree upon. It was a workable solution to the disintegration of morality produced by the explosions of morality in the 1960s.

But the dominance of the new managerial ethic among the village's cadres eventually began to create its own moral problems. The village peasants were most assuredly practical people who usually concerned themselves with the down-to-earth tasks of eking out a living rather than with grand visions of the meaning of life and the nature of goodness. When they chose production team heads, they always looked for good managers, not moral exemplars. They were happy that the brigade cadres were now like the production team heads—interested not in preaching but in managing the village and increasing its wealth. They were pleased when the new brigade enterprises began to bring a better standard of living to the village in the early 1970s—better food; somewhat easier work; more bicycles, wristwatches, and sewing machines; better hygiene; sturdier houses. But this new wealth whetted their appetites for more wealth. And then, as was inevitable given the rudimentary nature of the village economy, the rate of increase in their standard of living began to level off. The result was a great deal of dissatisfaction, especially among the village youth. What was the good of continuing to work hard in this little village if one's standard of living failed to improve? The old reasons for working hard had been replaced, and now the new ones were beginning to fail.

At the end of this chapter, we will return to a discussion of the ideological problems created by the rise of the new managerial ethos in the 1970s. But first let us explore how the rise of the new managerial ethos was reflected in the character development of the political leaders whose careers we have followed throughout this study and in the moral character of some new "revolutionary successors" who began to rise to prominence on the village's political stage.

Longyong

After the readjust policy work team of 1969 had completed its work, Longyong remained in power, a somewhat weakened and somewhat chastened local emperor. He now turned his attention to the task of building up the village's new industrial sector. He had the natural shrewdness, devotion to hard work, knowledge of human character, and imaginative daring of an excellent entrepreneur. He did a good job. He can be credited with much of the success of the village's small-scale industries.

Longyong still maintained a relatively austere life-style, and thus came to stand in clear contrast to most of the other village cadres. Most cadres became careless about spending all of their required time on manual labor and seemed to enjoy taking advantage of their increasingly frequent meetings to eat especially good meals paid for by the brigade. Unlike in the past, most brigade meetings now began or ended with a meal. Good food—plenty of fish or meat—was still a luxury in rural China, the most important luxury available to cadres. Many peasants seemed quite irritated by the fact that their cadres took advantage of their position to enjoy such luxuries. But they could not have been too irritated at Longyong, because he usually refused to participate in cadre meals.

Longyong constantly criticized his fellow cadres for using their positions to eat well on brigade funds, and he used to mutter to friends like Ao Meihua that "bad things are coming back." Part of this criticizing and complaining must have come from personal conviction, but another part came from his desire to maintain a grip on his subordinates. As one interviewee suggested, Longyong used his personal austerity to gain political leverage over the other cadres. They knew that if a political campaign came along, they could be vulnerable to criticism for their laxity from the austere Longyong. To forestall such a possibility, they were more inclined to keep Longyong happy by obediently cooperating with him.

Yet while remaining relatively austere and relatively incorrupt, Longyong began to relax some of his standards. Those of our interviewees who disliked him liked to tell stories about his lapses. He was not above accepting some gifts of hard-to-get herbal medicines from urban youths applying to leave the village, and in return for this he was especially helpful in expediting their applications. He began to improve his house in the 1970s and turned it into a building of a little above average quality for the village. His diet improved. He took care to see that his home production team was especially favored when the brigade industries were constructed: the site chosen for the industries was the western part of the village—*his* part of the village. And a person who used to work in the brigade sugar refinery told how Longyong used to come by and demand that the sugarcane harvested by his production team be processed before the others. Many interviewees recounted such incidents with gusto, because they loved to puncture Longyong's image of righteousness. But they all had to admit that he was still more austere and less corrupt than most cadres.

Longyong may have been mellowing as he got older, but he may also have been realistically calculating how much moral rigor was really necessary for him to maintain his political leverage over other cadres. As long as he was *relatively* incorrupt, he could use the issue of his incorruptness as a lever to enhance his authority. Whatever the depth of his moral convictions, he knew how to use his personal virtue as political capital.

Moreover, he did not have to maintain a high absolute level of personal rigor, because his power and prestige were coming increasingly to depend on his planning ability. Even those interviewees who enjoyed puncturing holes in his image of righteousness had to admit that he was the best economic planner and manager in the village and to concede that they should, after all, respect him for that.

His managerial ability had limits, however. He was perhaps the perfect man to initiate the fairly simple projects that began the village's small-scale industrial expansion. These required an abundance of basic shrewdness and raw enthusiasm. But as matters became more complicated, as prudent economic development came to require a keen sense of limits and effective management to require a detailed knowledge of government regulations, Longyong began to make blunders. He did not know when to stop expanding the brigade's industries. In 1972, he pushed through a plan to build a paper factory that would use the waste from sugarcane processing to make crude paper. He had apparently heard that such factories had been successfully established in other parts of China, but he failed to appreciate the difficulties of finding a market for such a product in Chen Village's region. The factory was a costly failure for the village. Villagers used this blunder to criticize Longyong's managerial ability, and younger, better educated, less headstrong cadres began to contend for his power.

Longyong, however, pushed on. When he was forced to recognize that it was not practical to establish any more small-scale industries at the present time, he urged his fellow cadres on the revolutionary committee to go along with his plans to carry out new public works projects: improved roads, a new school house, and a big new village meeting hall. These projects were completed, but to finance them, the brigade had to take out loans, and these became a severe liability by the end of the 1970s.

Qingfa

After Qingfa had been rehabilitated and given the posts first of militia chief and then of public security head, he and Longyong dared not fight each other anymore, but there was obviously no love lost between them. From the point of view of many of the villagers, however, the unenthusiastic nature of their cooperation brought its own benefits. The posts of both militia chief and public security head were crucial for carrying out attacks against class enemies. When the brigade's militia chief and public security head were working in close, enthusiastic cooperation with who-ever happened to be Chen Village's local emperor, this collaboration could produce powerful struggles against individuals whom the local emperor had defined as "reactionaries" or "class enemies." In the first part of the Four Cleanups campaign, Qingfa had used his control over the militia and public security apparatus to attack Longyong. In the Cleansing of the Class Ranks campaign, Longyong had used *his* control over militia and public security to denounce Qingfa and a host of other "reactionaries" and "class enemies." Now with Longyong's old enemy Qingfa in charge of first the militia and then public security, Longyong, though still the most powerful person in the village, had no way of wag-ing a major political campaign against people whom he disliked. Qingfa, on the other hand, had no way of attacking Longyong's supporters. As long as this situation persisted, the villagers did not have to worry that their tranquility would be disrupted by the "wind and waves" of a major political campaign.

Qingfa went about his militia work and later his public security work in a routine, competent, but uninspired manner. The militia was given the proper paramilitary training, but it was not often used to whip the villagers into patriotic fervor. The public security committee did not con-cern itself with vestiges of counterrevolutionary evil in the village. It spent most of its time protecting villagers from petty criminals in their midst—mostly chicken thieves and dirty old men. In a novel by Nicolas Freeling the hero says, "There is crime, which is a technical infringe-ment of a formal code. It can be combatted by technology, a technician's men-tality. And there is evil, and technicians . . . cannot cope with an ethical abstraction."[15] Qingfa busied himself with the technical task of keeping local crime under control. He did not worry about combatting revi-sionist Evil. The technical task was less strenuous and much safer than the moral one.

Although Qingfa's new posts did not carry the same amount of author-ity his old job of Party branch secretary did, the new jobs were perhaps even more rewarding than his old position of power. The new jobs—especially the public security position—required a great many meetings because the government was now concerned to have such work done according to proper rules and procedures. Qingfa seemed to relish the meetings, especially those at the county seat and, occasionally, the pro-vincial capital, since they usually provided especially good meals and comfortable lodging in hotels. Qingfa became one of the village's meet-

15. Nicolas Freeling, *Sabine*, as quoted in *Newsweek*, October 22, 1979, 122.

ing specialists. Meetings were a good way for a person who liked life's small luxuries to enjoy such amenities. It was safer to get good meals that way than to get them from local villagers in exchange for promises to do them favors. That was officially disapproved of and could get one into trouble. But it was one's duty to go to meetings, and if the officials who convened the meeting provided a good banquet, it was one's duty to take part.

Back home, when he was not attending meetings, Qingfa was the very image of affability. In the days when he was Party secretary he was, as one interviewee put it, "fierce as a tiger." But now he was "gentle as a lamb." Before, in order to exercise his power, he had to intimidate people who were not his friends. Now, he did not have to bolster his authority but only do a routine job. He could afford to be affable to everybody, and besides, there was no point in making unnecessary enemies.

Never a proponent of rigorous austerity, Qingfa used his reacquired status to make himself as comfortable as possible. With some help from money sent to him by relatives in Hong Kong, he built his family a two-story brick house, one of the finest houses in the village. He flaunted his love of good food and comfort. Some interviewees recalled him telling a group of young people that they should relax and enjoy themselves rather than be so concerned about working hard, for life was to be enjoyed. This was Qingfa's way of irreverently making light of the official Communist ethic and of the austere ethic of Longyong. As the 1970s progressed, Qingfa could begin to afford to say this. The government stressed competence over ideological purity. Qingfa was competent and increasingly secure in his position. He was perhaps tired from his years of struggle in the 1960s; even though he was only in his early forties, his hair was prematurely grey, probably as a result of the hardships he had experienced. Now was the time to relax and enjoy himself and to be proud of the fact that other villagers admired and envied his life-style.

Qingfa was not directly responsible for the expansion of the village's small-scale industries. But his work in the militia and as public security head helped provide the calm stability that was necessary for such enterprises to flourish. Moreover, the example he provided of competence, a relaxed personal style, and a frank desire for an increase in the material standard of living offered a paradigm of the skills, moods, and motivations appropriate to the village's new emphasis on economic development. Also, his attendance at all those meetings and his apparent ability to impress officials whom he met there helped bring Chen Village favorable attention from bureaucrats at the county and commune levels, attention that may have helped the village in its quest for economic development.

The late 1970s were kind to Qingfa. Officials at the county seat were impressed enough with his performance to give him a job in the bureaucracy there. He was now no longer a village cadre but a functionary in the commune bureaucracy, where for doing relatively routine work (he was in charge of the commune's warehouses) he got higher pay and more prestige than he would have received in the village. From being a traditional village leader, expert in playing the politics of patronage and good human feeling, he had partly changed into a modern bureaucrat and seemingly managed to gain from this a considerable amount of personal satisfaction.

Bengua — a Revolutionary Successor

In the 1970s, practically all the village cadres began to adopt the elements of a technician's mentality to guide and justify their public life and work. But as the character portraits given above suggest, older cadres like Longyong and, in a somewhat different way, Qingfa retained a measure of older moral styles based upon old habits and commitments. Longyong still retained many of the elements of his old asceticism and rigorous devotion to duty; Qingfa retained some of his ability to weave webs of human feeling. The purest examples of a moral character shaped by a technician's mentality were to be found among the younger generation of cadres who gained positions of authority *after* the Cleansing of the Class Ranks campaign.

One such revolutionary successor was nicknamed "Bengua." The nickname, freely translated, means "foolish." (Younger villagers often possessed playfully used derogatory nicknames; older people had more respectable nicknames.) But Bengua was in fact by no means foolish. He was one of the best-educated young men in the village. He had completed an upper-middle school education in the agricultural middle school at the commune seat. He was one of only two young villagers with such an education. He had participated in fairly respectable Red Guard activities in his middle school during the Cultural Revolution and had just returned to the village shortly before the readjust policy work team had arrived there.

Bengua's mother was a well-respected old Communist Party member and was the poor peasant representative of her production team. Her husband had deserted her just before Liberation, and Bengua was her only son. He was about twenty years old in 1970.

The fact that Bengua came from an impeccable class background and had such a politically prestigious mother ensured him of great respect on the part of the poor and lower-middle peasants of the village. But throughout middle school, Bengua had hardly lived in the village. He had boarded at the middle school and returned home only during vacations.

The villagers were not closely familiar with him. Also, since he had been a student all his life, he was not proficient at agriculture. The villagers had nothing against him; but although they respected him because of his background, they did not feel close to him. Because of his lack of farming ability, they were not especially impressed by him. Unlike Longyong and Qingfa, he did not fit traditional village conceptions of a natural leader.

But Bengua was the type of young person whom provincial and county policy was now in the early 1970s promoting as revolutionary successors. Communities like Chen Village lacked people with "culture," people who could read policy documents, understand the intricacies of official directives, and appreciate the need for systematic planning to carry out economic development projects of even moderate sophistication. So when the readjust policy work team supervised the elections for the brigade revolutionary committee in 1970 they encouraged Bengua's election to a place on the brigade's governing body. Bengua ended up becoming the brigade's deputy Party branch secretary.

Villagers had no great enthusiasm for Bengua, but no great hatred either. As one interviewee put it, "The masses' opinions of Bengua are average." Most of our interviewees commented favorably on the fact that Bengua could give good, clear, sensible speeches explaining policy decisions, and they respected the fact that he could read and understand fairly complicated policy documents. His education gave him what several interviewees called "flexibility"—the ability to understand the underlying principles behind government regulations and thus to apply the spirit of the regulations to local circumstances rather than simply adhere rigidly to the letter of the law. But in the early 1970s at least, this kind of competence was not greatly beneficial—at least not in a direct and obvious way—to the villagers. Bengua was not nearly as good as someone like Longyong at planning and organizing economic development projects. Such work required an intimate knowledge of the village and its people rather than book learning. Bengua was not seen as making much of a contribution to the village.

However, villagers' estimation of Bengua's ability to make a positive contribution to the village's welfare rose somewhat several years after he had taken office, because he demonstrated that he had a better sense of the limits of economic development than Longyong did. Since Bengua was not dependent on Longyong for his job and since his appointment to that job was the result of his "cultural level," he was in a position to stand up to Longyong. He could say that Longyong did not understand the meaning of certain official policies or that Longyong's plans for village economic development were ill-conceived. So he and Longyong often quarreled. "They would yell at each other, pound the table. [Bengua] dared to 'nail' [Longyong]. The brigade chief really hated him. No one else dared to 'nail' him." In particular, Bengua vigorously criticized Long-yong about the plans for the paper-manufacturing plant that eventually failed. Longyong made some other blunders that Bengua opposed, one of the most egregious being a costly, unsuccessful attempt to use hired tractors to level some village fields. (In levelling the fields, the tractors removed the topsoil.) While Longyong's reputation was damaged by those blunders, Bengua's was furthered. But it was not helped enough to make villagers think he was better than Longyong in planning production. Longyong and other dynamic cadres of his generation knew how to mobilize villagers to get projects started. Bengua could not do this. He could only warn people to stop.

The villagers' lukewarm attitude toward Bengua was based only in part on his lack of extraordinary ability to initiate economic development projects; it was also based on his personal character traits. The term *selfish* was consistently used to describe Bengua. Indeed, our interviewees generally seemed to agree that almost all of the cadres of Bengua's generation were more selfish than those of older generations. This selfishness was a trait manifested not so much in the way the cadres carried out their public work as in their conduct of their private lives. One example given by several persons of Bengua's selfishness was the addition he built onto his house in the mid-1970s. This extension protruded into the lane running by the dwelling. Longyong tried to oppose this. If everybody built out into the lane it would make the village too congested. But by the time Longyong complained, Bengua had already started the project, and since Bengua was a cadre in good standing, Longyong could not force him to stop. In the minds of many villagers, this showed that Bengua did not care about the general welfare. Longyong, or even Qingfa, would never have done anything like that. They would have been more sensitive about the concerns of their neighbors. This lack of sensitivity to the interests of his neighbors in his private life caused the villagers to consider him selfish. The villagers could respect Bengua as a cadre for his basically competent, honest, and fair work. But because of his selfishness in private life, they could not respect him as a person.

Another of Bengua's traits that the villagers held against him was his haughtiness. He appeared distant and aloof. "You very rarely saw him smile. He was very severe. He would say, 'I ought to go out to the masses to have a good time, but I'm too busy with my work.' . . . This was an example of the way he put on airs. He made himself something special. He placed himself above the masses. 'I ought to *come down* with you to have a good time. During work time, you have to obey me.' It was not a good outlook."

Bengua's particular blend of intellectual capabilities, attitudes toward public duties, and personal character traits made him the very image of a technocratic manager. This is not to say that in the early part of his career at least, he was already a good *technician*. He was not yet as good as many of the other cadres in planning and organizing the village's economic development projects. Indeed, his main work as a cadre was not directly concerned with the brigade's small-scale enterprises but with the general political management of the village. But he brought a technician's mentality to the job. He got his job on the basis of his intellectual competence, his ability to read policy documents, to discuss government regulations articulately, and so forth. His job did not depend on an ability to inspire villagers or to weave networks of loyalties from the village's social ties. He made a sharp distinction between the moral bases of his public and his private lives. His duties in public life were to do his work competently, honestly, and fairly and to manage the village's affairs so that the village would be a stable place steadily prospering through prudent economic improvements. His private life was devoted to pursuing the welfare of his family, even where this conflicted with the interests and sensitivities of his neighbors. So long as his private conduct did not involve flagrant violations of local standards of human decency, he deemed that conduct irrelevant to judgments about his public work. In public life he was an "expert" too busy for ordinary dealings with common people because he was occupied with matters they were incapable of comprehending.

In fairness to Bengua, it must be said that his approach to his work was shaped as much by the political and social circumstances in which he got his job as by any personal conviction about the goodness of such an approach. When he got his job, he was a young man with a relatively high cultural level who had left the village in his late teens. Government propaganda and local political, economic, and cultural realities were leading all cadres to take a managerial approach to their work. He was selected because of his potential managerial abilities, not because of his abilities to mobilize people in the manner of traditional village leaders. He himself realized, however, that to be a truly effective manager in the Chen Village of the early 1970s, he could not simply be coolly competent but had to have some of the ability to inspire and capture loyalties that the older cadres possessed. Several years after he assumed his post as deputy Party branch secretary, he decided that he wanted another job, one that would give him more time to become proficient in agricultural labor and to cultivate friendly contacts with ordinary villagers. He thus asked to step down to the post of village militia head. A militia head would normally do about two hundred days of agricultural labor a year, as opposed to only about one hundred days for a top-ranking cadre like a deputy Party secretary.[16] Bengua felt that if he had more time to labor side by side with ordinary peasants, he would develop a more solid following. But the revolutionary committee, probably at the direction of Longyong, who had no interest in seeing Bengua develop a mass following, refused to grant his request at first. Finally, however, in 1974, he got his wish. But his stint as militia chief lasted only two years, after which he was transferred to a post at the commune seat. Interviewees suggested that Longyong helped to arrange to have him "kicked upstairs" so that he would not be a bother to Longyong. In any case, he spent most of the rest of the 1970s working as a minor bureaucrat at the county seat.

Pigskin

The other young revolutionary successor chosen to the brigade revolutionary committee in 1970 was a young man about twenty years old nicknamed "Pigskin." The nickname was given because of his extraordinarily thick-skinned personality. He exemplified many of the same managerial traits as Bengua. But he exhibited to a somewhat greater degree the less edifying characteristics of the managerial style of life and work.

True to his nickname, he had an exceptionally insensitive manner of relating to people. "He wasn't courteous to people. He could practically bump into you, and he wouldn't pay any attention to you. If he were just an ordinary person, no one would have minded. But since he was a cadre, a lot of people complained about him. They said that he was putting on airs, that he didn't care about people. But to be fair about it, he wasn't putting on airs. He just had a bad personality. No politeness. He had always been like this." Pigskin was simply not interested in people. When young men his age were anxiously looking about for a wife, he was indifferent to such pursuits. "He had his own interests, like raising bees, catching sparrows, and other hobbies. Anyway, he didn't like girls. He seemed to be very arrogant. He couldn't be courteous." No one seems to have had any deep feelings about Pigskin, one way or another. "He didn't hurt people, but he didn't attract any human feeling either."

Although no one seems to have deeply hated Pigskin, most seemed to agree that he was even more selfish than Bengua. Villagers thought that this selfishness was especially manifested in his general disinclination to participate in ordinary collective physical labor. As one inter-

16. For a more detailed account of the role of militia head, see Richard Madsen, "Harnessing the Political Potential of Peasant Youth," in *State and Society in Contemporary China,* ed. Victor Nee and David Mozingo (Ithaca, N.Y.: Cornell University Press, 1983).

viewee put it: "Pigskin didn't labor much at all. He mostly attended meetings at the brigade and commune levels. Qingfa labored more. . . . Most cadres didn't labor much, but Pigskin even less than the others. The peasants really did not like his work style. . . ." Here his attitude was interpreted not as laziness—Pigskin seems to have worked hard enough at his cadre job—but as selfishness: an unwillingness to go out of his way to bear villagers' collective burdens. Pigskin was one of the village's biggest meeting specialists.

Ironically, Pigskin had gotten his job partly because of an officially created reputation for selflessness. He had been his production team's warehouseman in the late 1960s, when a severe flood struck Chen Village. The flood water poured into his family's house, into the enclosure where the family pigs and other animals were being kept, and they made a terrible racket. His mother called to him to come and save the animals and the things in the house. But he did not come. Instead he worked to do his duty as a warehouseman, to protect the production team's grain from the flood waters. After the water had subsided, the brigade propagandists "summed up the experience" of the flood and spent a great deal of time singing Pigskin's praises for having been so selflessly concerned for the collective rather than for his own property. Pigskin thus became an official political hero, and when shortly after this incident, the readjust policy work team was helping to pick revolutionary successors, they chose him. He became a Communist Party member without even having been in the Young Communist League.

When Pigskin became a member of the brigade revolutionary committee, he did not necessarily change his character and become selfish. But once he became a cadre, his peculiar ways of dealing with people began to be interpreted as selfishness. He had been praised by the propaganda apparatus for his willingness to fulfill his duty as a warehouseman in an emergency. But he had never shown outstanding leadership abilities or outstanding zeal for taking up political causes. If he had, he would have been encouraged to join the Young Communist League as a teenager. Now as a cadre, he dutifully did his job. He worked hard and did what he was told by his superiors. But the older cadres had a special sensitivity to people. Even when they were harshly overbearing like Longyong, they somehow communicated the impression that they were devoted not just to their jobs but to the village as a whole. Even when mildly corrupt like Qingfa, they still conveyed their special concern for widely ranging networks of loyal villagers. But when villagers saw Pigskin, this new cadre, simply doing his job with no feel for the people of the village, they interpreted that insensitivity as selfishness. However, the requirements for being promoted by higher-level government authorities were different than they had been in the past. In the new political world, good cadres followed regulations and did their duty, and their ability to relate well to people, to inspire or edify them, was a matter of no concern. What the government wanted now were cadres who were managers with a technician's mentality and a technocratic morality. The government got what it wanted in Pigskin. The villagers got someone whose personal peculiarities irritated them a bit, amused them occasionally, but who basically left them indifferent. At least he was not a corrupt person or a fanatic who made some people love him and others hate him. The villagers had had enough of that for awhile.

Pigskin was not as well educated as Bengua. He had only completed primary school. But he seemed to be a fairly intelligent person with basic literacy. He could read and understand Party documents and give articulate accounts of Party policy in public speeches. In the early 1970s, he became Chen Village brigade's representative on the commune Party committee. (One member from each brigade, usually a deputy Party branch secretary, sat on the commune Party committee, which was chaired by a Party secretary sent into the commune from the county seat.) As such he played an important role in linking the village's government with that of the commune. It was not a role much appreciated by the villagers because it did not bring the village any immediate economic benefits. But given government insistence that the village be more closely linked with higher levels of bureaucracy, it was probably an important role for providing a foundation for the village's development.

Ao Meihua and the Urban Youth

The new political and economic situation in Chen Village had perhaps its most dramatic effect on the urban youth counselors who had begun to ascend to the heights of power and glory in the village through their rigorous self-denial and furious revolutionary enthusiasm. All of these urban youth counselors lost their power, and many lost their revolutionary faith.

The loss of power and faith were interconnected but not in a straightforward, unidirectional way. They lost their power because government propaganda declared their faith invalid, and local economic and political realities rendered it irrelevant. They lost their faith because the exercise of political power was necessary for maintaining that faith.

As the Chinese government began to restore peace and order in the country in the wake of the Cultural Revolution, its propaganda, as we have seen, began to deemphasize the revolutionary faith that manifested itself in zealous commitment to the grand Maoist vision of a new society founded on a totally selfless commitment to the common good. The image of the ideal revolutionary increasingly came to be that of the competent manager rather than the fervent prophet. The importance of having the proper socialist consciousness was still stressed in the official ideology, but fanatical zeal was now held to be an improper expression of that consciousness. But if the ideal sort of revolutionary was now a manager, how was one to know if anyone had the proper socialist consciousness, the correct revolutionary faith? Anyone with a modicum of competence motivated by an enlightened self-interest could become a good manager. There were no special works that could validate the existence of a revolutionary faith. So the existence of a proper socialist consciousness had to be inferred by other means—by the possession of a proper class background. We have seen how during the Cultural Revolution in the village, contending factions tried to legitimate their claims by the possession of heroic zeal on the one hand and the possession of a proper class background on the other. These struggles over revolutionary legitimacy in the village were indeed a pale reflection of similar struggles taking place in China's cities during that time. We have also seen how in the Cleansing of the Class Ranks campaign, there was a great emphasis on the automatic transmission of evil through family connections. By 1969 or 1970, the idea that one's revolutionary virtue was almost automatically determined by one's class background had become the reigning orthodoxy.[17] But this doctrine was used not to seek out enemies for punishment but to determine who was worthy of having first choice among the scarce managerial jobs bestowing power and prestige.

As a result, the zeal of urban youth counselors like Ao Meihua was now officially considered misplaced and an invalid indicator of proper socialist consciousness. Ao Meihua and most of the other urban youth in the village came from impure class backgrounds. Ao's father had been a physician, and most of the other urban youth came from similarly nonproletarian and nonpoor peasant backgrounds. This meant that when the time came to choose people for leadership positions in the village, Ao and the others were to be left out. Such jobs had to go to pure poor or lower-middle peasants. The veto of Ao's election to a post on the brigade revolutionary leadership group at the beginning of the Cleansing of the Class Ranks campaign hinted at this change, and as the 1970s began, this trend became unmistakably clear. Official government propaganda suggested that Ao and most of her urban colleagues might not have real revolutionary faith, and this official suggestion had concrete consequences for their careers.

Moreover, as the promotion of stability and economic development,

17. See Stanley Rosen, *The Role of Sent Down Youth in the Chinese Cultural Revolution: The Case of Guangzhou* (Berkeley: University of California Center for Chinese Studies, 1981).

rather than the "grasping of revolution" became the village's primary concern, it became clear to Ao and the remaining urban youth counselors that the villagers no longer needed their political work. As Ao Meihua put it: "The cadres in Chen Village could handle things themselves when they weren't using politics to take command, but when *everything* was politics, they needed us." The counselors' hunger for power and glory, together with their lack of local kinship ties and of economic responsibilities, made them ideal agents for ruthlessly smashing social ties based on human feeling, ideal collaborators in Longyong's revolutionary program for the village. But now that that program had built a base for the economic development of the village, the services of the fervent urban counselors were no longer needed. There were enough local people around to fill the major roles of planning and managing the new enterprises, and the villagers wanted to give these jobs to their own youth rather than to those from the city. As Ao Meihua said: "We were like silkworms spinning cocoons and thus destroying ourselves because of the product we made."

Besides not having any real need for the urban youth, the villagers came increasingly to perceive them as a troublesome nuisance. The villagers were unhappy with the disruptions the rebellious Maoism Red Guards had caused during the Cultural Revolution. Their unhappiness with these rebellious youth tended to make them a little suspicious of all urban youth. Their suspicions were deepened when a new group of about fifty urban youth was sent to the village in the fall of 1968 to join the group that had come in 1964. Unlike the 1964 contingent, this new group did not come under the illusion that they had an almost sacred vocation to build socialism in rural China. They came because they were forced out of the city by a government eager to solve its urban population problems and to disperse juveniles who had caused trouble during the Cultural Revolution. The members of the 1968 group were even more restless and less willing to adapt to village life than the 1964 group had been. Seeing this, the villagers' antipathy toward urban youth deepened. Under these circumstances, there was little power and little glory available within the political context of Chen Village for Ao Meihua and the other original urban counselors.

The loss of an opportunity to continue advancing in power through the exercise of revolutionary zeal was devastating for these young people's revolutionary faith. It was not simply that that faith was a cloak for personal ambition; the faith had helped to define that ambition. This faith held that the most important thing in life was the realization of revolutionary glory and that one knew one was on the way to achieving such glory if one continued to advance upward politically. Young people like Ao Meihua had sacrificed everything to their hopes of achieving revolutionary glory. Now that there was no way for them to attain that, they were left without any of the things that might make life meaningful for ordinary city people: no chance for continuing their education, no chance for a quiet, reasonably comfortable career in an urban government agency, not much chance even for a normal family life lived with an urban spouse in proximity to one's relatives with hopes for a modern education and comfortable urban future for one's children. The only way to make this situation bearable was to change what one believed in and hoped for.

Fervent young Communists like Ao Meihua gradually lost their commitment. That commitment may have been founded on their hopes for achieving political power and glory, but it had been fortified with massive investments of emotional and intellectual energy. Those investments kept it from crumbling immediately, even when its foundations had disappeared. Ao Meihua bears this out.

Ao Meihua continued to be very Red throughout 1969. Her Redness was bolstered by the fervor of Red Cheng, who had become her fiancé just before he had left to join the People's Liberation Army. In the summer of 1969, Ao was summoned to Beijing to visit Cheng in a hospital there. Since she was his fiancé and he was gravely ill, the army paid for her trip to see him. In Beijing, Cheng downplayed his illness, tried to tell Ao Meihua that it was nothing serious and that he would soon recover. He would not talk about death and never expressed any sorrow for himself. He asked to see Ao's personal diary. "But I hadn't brought my diary, I had just brought my Mao study notes. After looking at the notes, he said: 'That's great. You're not writing about romantic things, about petit bourgeois feelings. You're studying Mao's works.'" After a week in Beijing, Ao returned to Chen Village. After she returned, Red Cheng wrote her several more letters. The last letter said: "I can't die on a sickbed. I certainly will continue to struggle. I will never forget the class struggle, the dictatorship of the proletariat, the liberation of the people of the world. The Chinese revolution is part of the world revolution." His last words were: "May you become even firmer than before." Soon after that letter, three months after Ao Meihua had visited him, Red Cheng died.

The memory of Red Cheng's exhortations kept Ao Meihua's zeal alive into 1970. But with her hopes for achieving revolutionary power and glory gone, her view of the world slowly became less rigid and the scope of her sympathies more diffuse. She gradually began to think of Marxism-Leninism-Mao Zedong Thought less as a doctrine to be blindly believed and vigorously proclaimed and more as a theory to be rationally understood and flexibly applied. She began to associate with, sympathetically understand, and eventually to like persons whom in the heyday of her political fervor she would have shunned as politically impure.

By the end of 1970, she had fallen in love with a youth from Canton who had an exceptionally bad class background: his father had been a minor functionary in the Guomindang and his mother was classified as a "rightist"—one of the Bad Types. Because of this man's bad class background, Ao Meihua had kept her distance from him during the days of her extreme Redness, even though he was generally well liked and respected by the villagers as a hard worker with good political behavior. But now Ao dared to draw close to him, at first with the rationalization that she would be able to increase his political fervor and lead him to draw a clear line between himself and his parents. After a romance had developed between the two of them, her boyfriend, encouraged by members of his family, decided to escape to Hong Kong. Ao Meihua was horrified to hear this. She did not feel ready to "betray" China in such a way herself, but she was unable to persuade him to stay and unwilling to report him to higher authorities.

Her boyfriend was caught trying to escape to Hong Kong. Since the authorities correctly surmised that she must have known about her boyfriend's plans and been unwilling to report them, she came under suspicion. In late 1971, a campaign was launched in the Guangdong countryside to persuade sent-down urban youth who were likely to have thoughts of escaping to Hong Kong to "volunteer" to go to remote Hainan Island to build socialism gloriously by working on state banana farms there. Ao did not want to go, but after much resistance, she was forced to "volunteer." This policy of sending youth to Hainan was later reversed and Ao did not have to go. But because she had resisted the efforts to send her there, she was looked upon as a "backward element" by local authorities and lost all of the positions of responsibility she had held in the village. For her part, she felt that she had been rejected by the village and thus began to feel less and less committed to staying there. Her boyfriend successfully escaped to Hong Kong in the middle of 1973. Afraid of the dangers of trying to escape and still possessing some residual commitment to the village and to China, she did not go with him. But her courage to escape continued to wax and her commitment to the village continued to wane, and she made the dangerous swim to Hong Kong in the spring of 1974.

She and her husband live in the United States now and struggle to maintain a decent lower-middle class life in a large city. Ao's belief in grand revolutionary visions is gone, but marks of her old zeal and discipline still persist. The life she and her husband lead is characterized by a greater than average desire to work hard, to be satisfied with simple pleasures, and within their limited means to help friends in need.

The other urban youth counselors who had risen to power and glory with Ao Meihua also left the village political scene. Su Liai, Ao's colleague during the Cleansing of the Class Ranks campaign, did not lose her Redness but did lose her desire to continue working within the village. At one point she was engaged to marry Bengua, the young revolutionary successor; but to his great anger and consternation, she broke off the engagement because she knew that if she remained engaged to him she would certainly spend the rest of her life in Chen Village. Her continued Redness and her proletarian class background paid off. She was one of the first urban youth recalled to Canton to take a job in a factory there. Two of the other urban youth who had worked so furiously with Ao Meihua as counselors, married each other and settled down to a relatively quiet life in the countryside; the woman works as a village storekeeper, the man as a schoolteacher.

Stocky Wang and Overseas Deng, whose stars had burned so brightly and whose revolutionary fervor seemed so strong in the first year of their stay in Chen Village, but who ran afoul of Longyong, led many of the urban youth back to Canton during the Cultural Revolution and paid the penalty in the Cleansing of the Class Ranks campaign, both left China: Stocky Wang left illegally, and Deng successfully applied to return legally to his native Indonesia. Besides these people, six other members of the cohort of urban youth who came to Chen Village in 1964 left for Hong Kong, most illegally. Ironically, most of these were precisely those young people who had showed the most promise and the most commitment during the first year or two of their stay in the village. Five of these six had been Young Communist League members and four had been the main counselors for their production teams. Those who were the most committed to revolutionary idealism when they came to the village were in general those who most thoroughly rejected communism and life in China in the end.

Most of the other urban youth from the 1964 cohort had also left Chen Village by the late 1970s. The majority found ways to get transferred to jobs back in Canton. A half dozen of them got into political trouble for one reason or another, were not willing or not able to escape to Hong Kong, and volunteered to go to Hainan Island in the hope that they might rehabilitate themselves politically in that new context. The dozen others who remained in the village were women who married local peasant youths and have become just like ordinary peasants' wives.

By the mid-1970s the job of counselor, which was once mainly performed by the most zealous of these urban young people, was now primarily held by young peasants. The new counselors were people who could preach the goodness of Mao's Thought without stepping on too many toes, without getting people too disturbed. The sound of Maoist rhetoric was still heard in the village, but it had lost its moral sting.

Morality and Utility: the Fate of Public Spirit in Chen Village in the 1970s

The managerial ethos that began to direct the conduct of the village's leading cadres was linked to the growth of a utilitarian ethic that directed the cooperation of ordinary citizens with one another. The motivation behind the pursuit of collective work was an ever purer form of economic self-interest. The goal of collective cooperation was increasingly seen solely as the attainment of collective wealth. Of course in the past self-interest had always been an extremely important part of peasant motivation. And villagers were always very interested in increasing their wealth. But self-interest had been modified by loyalties to networks of kin and neighbors with whom one had cemented bonds of good human feeling and by general commitments to the glory of the community that was the village as a whole. It had also been colored by visions of Maoist ideology as refracted through the local loyalties and understandings of the village. These loyalties, commitments, visions, and hopes did not disappear immediately, but they steadily began to fade in importance. What was left was more of a pure utilitarian ethic based upon the calculation of self-interests than had existed before.

By the early 1970s, the attacks on human feeling had broken many of the bonds of loyalty between relatives and old friends. Ever since the Socialist Education Movement, villagers had been wary of giving any concrete economic and political support to relatives or friends in need—especially if those relatives or friends were in need because they had been politically compromised. When there was a marriage or a death in a family or when yearly festivals came around, relatives and old friends met to participate in appropriate rituals, but these networks of relatives were of little use to a family in economic or political trouble. When villagers entered into cooperative relationships outside the scope of their immediate families, the most important set of these relationships was with the production team. Of course, most of the members of one's production team were neighbors, and many of them were likely to be relatives and old friends, and those bonds could strengthen the economic ties that linked members of production teams together. But now one had little to do with relatives and friends who were not members of one's production team. These purely economic bonds superseded the bonds of loyalty traditionally created through human feelings.

At certain relatively brief periods of time, as in the Mao Study campaign of 1965 and 1966, villagers were impelled by moral pressure to work hard to fulfill their economic duties to their production teams because of the very goodness of collective work and perhaps because of a sense that they were contributing to the collective glory of their community as a whole, not because such work would bring them any immediate personal economic rewards. But that kind of motivation had almost disappeared by the mid-1970s. Villagers worked to the extent that they received economic rewards for that work. And were they good at calculating those rewards! The sent-down urban youth marvelled at how well the villagers could calculate economic things: how many dollars and cents were owed them, how many catties of grain they had coming to them for their work points, what the relative advantages were of putting some extra energy into their collective work as opposed to their private plots. Even illiterate villagers could perform the lengthy arithmetical calculations necessary to answer such questions in their heads, and they could often make these computations more quickly and more accurately than the educated urban youth.

The new emphasis on the economic welfare of one's individual family as the basis for collective cooperation led to the abandonment of the most important economic experiment of the latter half of the 1960s: the Dazhai work-point system. According to that system, one was paid for collective work on an hourly basis; the value of one's working time was determined by one's peers in the production team, and the difference between the highest and lowest paid laborer was relatively slight. The Dazhai system stressed egalitarianism and cooperative work for the good of the collective as a whole rather than for one's individual profit. But now in the 1970s with the emphasis on the economic betterment of each individual family, the Dazhai system became unworkable. Production team meetings to determine who would get how many work points degenerated into bitter arguments. Strong, skilled workers failed to work as hard as they could because they resented the fact that their hard work brought them only slightly more income than the work of weaker, less skilled laborers. Similar problems with Dazhai work points cropped up throughout Guangdong Province, and in 1972, provincial authorities encouraged production brigades to abandon the Dazhai system. The villages around Chen Village quickly did so, but Longyong resisted, still clinging to his dream of an egalitarian village committed to selfless collective cooperation. But even Longyong could not stem the tide forever, and the Dazhai system was abandoned in Chen Village in 1975, giving way to a piece-rate system.

Villagers continued to work outside their own production teams to cooperate on brigadewide projects, but this cooperation was motivated not so much by moral pressure, political zeal, or community pride as by the desire for the comfortable jobs and good pay provided by the new brigade industries. But while making a contribution to the solidarity of the village as a whole, the brigade industries also generated centrifugal forces. For instance, the brickworks was a profitable enterprise because there was a plentiful supply of burnable grass on the hills surrounding the village. The burnable grass was cut by villagers working privately in their spare time, usually during their lunch periods. The brickworks paid one yuan per hundred catties of grass. Usually, the most one could make in a day of collective labor was also one yuan. And if one worked extremely hard in one's spare time, one could gather a hundred catties of grass in a day. So during their lunch hour, instead of resting, the villagers dashed up the hillsides to gather grass. They returned exhausted and at best worked lethargically until quitting time. The new collective brigade enterprises created new opportunities for private industry, but these opportunities distracted the villagers from collective labor.

Thus, because of the new emphasis on economic gain as the prime motivation for collective collaboration, new problems were created for the village economy. Many of these were technical problems that could be solved by managers with a technician's mentality. New regulations and procedures could be instituted to increase the individual's stake in working for the collective economy. The Dazhai work point system could be scrapped in favor of a piece-rate system. If need be, new rules could be established limiting the amount of time villagers could spend cutting grass for the brick factory. (This was not in fact done, because the success of the brick factory was deemed more important than the attainment of maximum efficiency in collective agriculture. Besides, cutting grass was a very popular way of earning extra income.) Most of the new regulations and procedures increased the level of inequality in the village, but up to a point they kept the village economy functioning at an acceptable level of efficiency.

But the new economic problems could only partly be solved by technical manipulation of the village economy. The new shift to a strictly economic motivation began to create a crisis of meaning, and that crisis could only be solved by moral leadership not by technical management. If villagers were now to work together simply because they could increase their individual prosperity (or more precisely the prosperity of their own households) by cooperating, the question of the value of economic prosperity would begin to arise. In the first stages of economic development, the answers to this were simple. Basic physical needs could be satisfied better than before. In the early 1960s, villagers' diets had been meager with barely enough rice to satisfy hunger and very little meat or other protein to provide variety to the diet and to satisfy basic nutritional needs. Now by the early 1970s, their diets had vastly improved; they had more than enough rice to eat, plenty of vegetables, and more meat than ever before. In the early 1960s, housing was ramshackle and crowded. Now houses were increasingly being made of brick, with cement floors and more space than ever before. Health care and hygiene had been very poor, but now the filthy village streets and wells had been cleaned up, there were more medicines and even a barefoot doctor available, and people did not suffer as much from sickness. The only means of transportation used to be by foot, but now more and more villagers had bicycles. Life was still very poor by our American standards, but basic physical needs were being taken care of better than ever before. To strive to improve one's physical condition was self-evidently a good thing.

But there were limits to the extent to which the rural economy could continue to bring about such basic improvements in the standard of living. Further increases in rice yields required improved strains of seed and large amounts of chemical fertilizer. Because of disruptions in agronomic research caused by the Cultural Revolution, no new seed varieties were available in the 1970s. And because of general problems in the Chinese economy, the government was unable to provide artificial fertilizer in the quantities necessary for increased yields.[18] To make matters worse, in the early 1970s China's rigid agricultural bureaucracy handed down a series of commands to plant various crops that were inappropriate to Chen Village's conditions. Cadres like Longyong did their best to avoid implementing such policies and, when forced to comply, to mitigate their impact, but the result of all these factors was stagnation in the village's agriculture.

The rise in the village's standard of living in the first half of the 1970s had come about through the development of the village's small-scale industries, based on the wealth accumulated by the hard collective work of the late 1960s. But by 1975 the effects of deteriorating seed grain, scarcity of fertilizer, and inappropriate bureaucratic policies toward agriculture were becoming apparent. The standard of living began to decline. If the only reason for hard work was individual economic betterment, what was the purpose of hard work now?

Longyong tried to provide one answer to this question. When the brigade industries had expanded as far as they could for the time being, he pushed through plans to use the profits to construct fine new public buildings: a new school building, an improved health clinic, new buildings to house the brigade administration, and finally a new village meeting hall. The new meeting hall was especially impressive, a large, two-story brick structure that looked almost like a theater in Canton. It replaced the dirt-floored shed that had been the previous village meeting place—its "great school for communism," the scene of its struggle ses-

18. Interestingly, similar plateaus in agricultural productivity were reached in Taiwan in the 1970s as the limits of new strains of hybrid rice were reached and the cost of artificial fertilizer rose. (I am indebted to William L. Parish for this observation.)

sions, its political revival sessions, and its general production planning meetings. Ao Meihua and other interviewees mentioned the beauty of this new hall again and again. There was nothing like it in all the rest of Chen Village's commune. Perhaps the meaning behind the construction of that hall was most poignantly expressed in one particular phrase used by Ao Meihua to describe it: "It was," she said, "our village's glory."

Chen Village was still not necessarily any richer than any of its neighboring villages, but it now had a more modern visage. The villagers who had once been looked down upon and exploited by their neighbors could now hold up their heads with collective pride and glory.

But the feeling of community pride and the sense of glory began to fade almost as soon as the hall was finished. The sense of collective hope and purpose symbolized by the building began to deteriorate as the standard of living stagnated and then fell. One could see this especially among the young people of the village. Some of the peasants who began to emigrate from the village in the mid-1970s mentioned again and again how lazy the village's young people were becoming. One interviewee suggested that the reason for this was that the new generation of young people, having had some opportunities for schooling and therefore knowing more than their elders about the outside world, were demoralized by the realization that there was a better life to be had in China's cities but that they had no way of attaining that life. The interviewees enjoyed recounting stories that indicated the selfishly mischievous nature of the new generation. A group of former Chen Village peasants for instance roared with laughter at the story of the young man who purchased a watch—few members of the older generation bothered with such things—and used his watch to convince his production team leader, an older man who estimated time by the position of the sun, that it was quitting time when it was really a few hours early. The story was used as an example of a new spirit among the youth. But not just the young people were affected. A general spirit of lethargy affected large portions of the older generations.

It was Mao's revolutionary vision, refracted through villagers' local hopes, that provided much of the drive which in the late 1960s led the villagers to build a new foundation for their economic development. But this vision had turned out to be self-destructive, ruining the atmosphere of basic trust needed to form the basis of genuinely collective endeavor. This vision of heroic struggle against vicious enemies was self-destructive, I would suggest, because it was adapted to the needs of violent revolution rather than of peaceful institution building. During its struggles for power the Communist Party faced many real enemies, and Mao's vision was an authentic response to grim realities. But by the 1960s, the old enemies had been vanquished and a revivification of the Maoist vision involved the fabrication of new enemies. This fabrication, however, took place with an arbitrariness that offended the most basic principles of human justice. The vision thus tended to produce immorality, not moral heroism. But when the Maoist vision lost its credibility, there was nothing left to take its place as the moral basis of collective endeavor. Social solidarity tended to be based only upon the pursuit of self-interest within a collectivized economy. This was a fragile basis indeed.

Coda

Just how fragile this foundation was became apparent in 1979 in a series of events that I did not hear about until early 1982 after the rest of this book had been written. These events confirm the most pessimistic predictions made in the first part of this chapter.[19] In the spring of 1979 about two hundred young villagers—practically the whole younger generation—suddenly left the community for Hong Kong. A similar exodus took place from villages throughout the border region in which Chen Village was located. The youth were inspired to flee by rumors that the Chinese police were no longer stopping people from crossing to Hong Kong. Though not true, these rumors created such a mass exodus that they proved self-fulfilling: the border guards were overwhelmed. Such a mass exodus was unprecedented in the village since Liberation. Not even during the hard economic times of the early 1960s—when border controls were in fact relaxed—had young people deserted the village in such numbers. The vast out-migration signified a radical extension of the principles of the individualistic ethic: there was no longer any point in working for the good of the community as a whole even out of enlightened self-interest; now it was simply every individual for him- or herself. There is evidence that this lack of commitment to the village, especially on the part of the young, is widespread in China. (A recent sociological survey indicates that only 6 percent of young peasants attending middle school want to stay in their villages; newspaper reports refer to difficulties caused by peasants throughout China—not just in border regions—trying to "jump over the village gate" and go illegally to the cities.)[20]

The task of dealing with this breakdown of commitment to the local community ultimately fell to the government headed by Deng Xiaoping, who by late 1978—less than two and a half years after Mao Zedong had died and his close supporters (the so-called Gang of Four) had been

19. The information on these events was gathered by Anita Chan and Jonathan Unger in January 1982 and is reported in detail in the epilogue to *Chen Village*.

20. Reported in Stanley Rosen, "Education and the Political Socialization of Chinese Youths," in *Education and Social Change in the People's Republic of China*, ed. John Hawkins (New York: Praeger, 1983).

purged from power—had gained firm control over the Communist Party. Deng's policies toward agriculture, formulated in 1979 and 1980, tried not to overcome the loss of commitment but rather to adapt to it. As applied to the region around Chen Village at least, this policy meant the dismantling of the system of collective agriculture.

By 1980 the village's collective land had been divided into small parcels and allocated to each family. (The production teams officially retained ownership of the property, but the responsibility for deciding how it was to be used fell to the families to which it was allocated.) Since the exodus of the young had left the village's households short of labor, they began hiring labor from outside the village—a procedure that was legitimized by the new government regulations. By 1982, a hundred hired hands were working in the village. Moreover, the village's small-scale industries were leased out to local families (and in the case of the brickworks, to a total stranger from outside the village), who hired laborers to run the enterprises for a profit.[21]

Because of the new economic order, nonprofitable public works like the village hall—Chen Village's "glory"—were an economic liability. Debts had been incurred in building such projects, and now there was no collective income from which to repay the loans. The village hall had to be mortgaged to the state to pay the village's debts.

With the disintegration of the village's public spirit, came the end of Longyong's public career. In mid-1979 he had loudly criticized families who encouraged their children to flee to Hong Kong. By the end of the year, however, his own two sons had also fled. With the last shreds of his moral authority gone, he resigned. Soon afterwards, Qingfa was made local Party secretary again. (Bengua had been asked to take the job, but he had refused because he did not want to leave the security and comfort of

21. There has been considerable regional variation in the implementation of the new policies. By the summer of 1981, over 30 percent of the production teams in China had allocated production responsibility to individual households, as in Chen Village; about 40 percent of the teams had allocated the responsibility to small "work groups" of three to five households (most likely neighbors related by kinship); and about 25 percent of production teams still used the system of "unified management" that was employed in Chen Village before 1980. See Jurgen Domes, "New Policies in the Communes: Notes on Rural Societal Structures in China, 1976–1981," *Journal of Asian Studies* 41, no. 2 (February, 1982):253–67. Domes cites a series of regulations broadcast over the Guangxi People's Broadcasting Station (September 29, 1980) clearly forbidding the hiring of farmhands and demanding that "collectively owned local factories and workshops be preserved." Our interviewees clearly state, however, that in the area around Chen Village, the hiring of labor and leasing of local factories was officially approved. Perhaps such approval was due to the fact that Chen Village was becoming part of a "special economic zone"—a development that may make Chen Village atypical of most Chinese rural communities.

his post at the commune seat.) Qingfa enthusiastically set about taking full advantage of his new job to enrich himself and his relatives and friends. He saw to it that a large share of the village's choicest land was allocated to him and hired laborers to till it, and he solicited generous "gifts" in return for granting permits.

Because of Chen Village's special circumstances, the new economic and political order turned out, in the short run at least, to be materially beneficial to the village's families. Their children in Hong Kong sent them money and consumer goods. (Within about three years, about half of the village houses had television sets, specially wired to receive programs from Hong Kong.) Furthermore, in 1980 the village became part of a "special economic zone" that made it possible for villagers to sell their produce to the Hong Kong market. This led many families to enrich themselves beyond anything they might have dreamed of a decade previously. But although families were increasing their individual wealth, the public environment of the village was becoming palpably worse. Petty theft was more commonplace than ever, and now there were even cases of burglary and major theft hitherto unheard of in Chen Village. Nobody even bothered to clean up the smelly garbage that began to accumulate in the village lanes.

9 Conclusion

MORAL CHARACTER AND CHINA'S FATE

A man's character, Heraclitus once said, is what determines his fate.[1] And for Plato, Aristotle, and Confucius—and for that matter Mao Zedong—the character of a polity's citizens was a determinant of its fate. My interpretation of Chen Village's recent history suggests that we can divide China's grass-roots political leaders into four main character types. By understanding the social and cultural origins of these character types, we can gain some insights into the contemporary fate of the People's Republic of China.

Four Character Types

Different kinds of local political leaders develop different characteristic styles of political conduct because they depend on different types of resources to acquire and maintain their power. Among these are moral resources—the ability to live up (or at least pretend to live up) to various kinds of moral expectations. From different sectors of Chinese society come diverse ways of thinking and talking about morality and correspondingly varied moral expectations for would-be leaders at the local level. The moral aspect of the political capital of some local leaders derives primarily from their ability to fulfill the moral expectations of members of their local community. That of other leaders is based on an ability to meet the expectations of officeholders within the government apparatus that attempts to reach down into the community. I will discuss two character types in each of these categories.

As we have seen, the members of rural Chinese farming communities have tended to conceive of their interests and hopes in terms of the con-

1. Quoted in Michael Maccoby, *The Gamesman* (New York: Bantam, 1978), 32.

ceptual idiom of an ethos with deep roots in the Confucian tradition. In this tradition, a good society is a harmonious array of differentiated relationships linking the present with the past.[2] To explain the nature of this vast array of relationships, the Confucian idiom uses metaphors; one of the most apt metaphors is that of the traditional Chinese family. A good family is a harmoniously integrated organic whole composed of individuals faithfully committed to distinct social roles. And a good society is like a good family writ large.

But within the traditional Chinese idiom for understanding the nature of a good society there have been, as it were, different "dialects." One of the main differences in these dialects comes from the way the family metaphor is used in imagining the rest of society. It is possible, I have suggested, to apply the metaphor loosely: the social world outside one's immediate family is only a pale reflection of one's own family. Thus, society is like a federation of small families bound together by attenuated networks of overarching kinship ties. In this vision of social order, individuals conceive of their social responsibilities primarily in terms of their responsibilities to their immediate families and they deem it right and just to put concern for the prosperity and status of their families first, before concern for any larger public good. To safeguard and to further one's own family's prosperity one will of course have to rely on the help and cooperation of certain people not in one's immediate family. To acquire this cooperation one can cement relations with such outsiders through exchanges of favors made with appropriate expressions of good human feeling. Since close family ties are much more important than distant family ties, one will tend to seek and expect help and cooperation from close kin rather than from distant relatives.

However, it is also possible to apply the family metaphor more strictly to the wider social world: one's whole community can be viewed as a single big family bound together by common duties to perform complementary roles (by virtue of the fact that all the community's members occupy a common zone of familiarity). This vision of social order leads individuals to put the good of the community as a whole above the immediate good of themselves or their own small families.

Villagers' subjective commitments to either of these two visions of community order tend to be shaped by their objective position within the village's economic and social structure. Those villagers who belong to families that are part of relatively dense, overarching kinship networks tend to think of the village as a federation of families, because they have

2. Of course, this was an ideal rarely realized. But in traditional Chinese thought it was precisely the *ideal* of what a good family ought to be that has provided the metaphor to be used in understanding the nature of the good society.

access to organizational resources that will enable them to achieve the goals which that vision postulates as good by the means which it postulates as proper. Adult villagers whose families are not strategically located within such networks and adolescent villagers who are growing out of their natal families and have not yet formed families by marriage tend to see the village community as one big family, because they lack the resources to achieve the type of "good life" defined by the village as a federation of families. Commitments to these different visions of the good society are also encouraged by villagers' perceptions of the temper of their times. During times of great crisis for the community as a whole, villagers may reason that their moral responsibilities to the community outweigh those to their immediate families. During times of peace, villagers may feel justified in being preoccupied with the welfare of their own small families.

These different visions of the good society are not, however, merely a mechanical reflection of villagers' interests. Although villagers tend to adopt visions of the good society that correspond to their interests, they arrive at those visions by employing the forms of discourse available in their culture, and as we have suggested in Chapter 3, it may well be that traditionally available patterns of discourse lead to visions that do not correspond to villagers' interests within their contemporary social situation. Moreover, under certain circumstances, villagers may be persuaded that the logic of their moral discourse compels them to take stands that contradict their immediate socioeconomic interests.

Political exploitation of an ability to fulfill the moral expectations of those villagers who see the village as a federation of families tends to produce a type of political leader whom I will call the "member of the Communist gentry." The outstanding example of this type in Chen Village is Qingfa, although the real Qingfa is a complex person whose action can only approximately be explained in terms of the dimensions of this ideal type.

The traditional gentry were landlords; they owned a major part of the means of agricultural production. The member of the Communist gentry is not a landlord, but he (virtually all such people are male) has been given an important measure of stewardship over the collectivized means of production by the Communist government. Although he cannot generally be so crassly exploitative as a member of the traditional gentry, he does have some opportunity to use his stewardship over the means of production for his own benefit and to exercise his control over the allocation of land and supplies as patronage to build up a base of loyal supporters. The member of the traditional gentry built up a base of loyal supporters and tried to ensure social order (and hence his own security) in his village community through the dispensing of patronage. The giving of patronage and the reception of loyalty was justified and guided by the traditional ethos stressing the sacredness of kinship. An important channel for the exchanges through which the member of the traditional gentry acquired loyalty in return for patronage was the extended kinship networks that bound his family to other families through descent from a common ancestor. Because of the sacredness of kinship, these exchanges were not to be made in a crassly utilitarian way but with appropriate expressions of warmth—the flavor of human feeling. When patronage was given outside the channels of kinship ties, it was to be done as if the giver and receiver of the patronage were kin, older and younger brother, with appropriate expressions of human feeling. My research indicates that the traditional Confucian ethos, with its stress on the sacredness of kinship, has remained alive in rural China, so that the giving and receiving of patronage must continue to take place according to its moral idiom. If one is going to buy loyalty or to have one's loyalty bought, the "sale" must be conducted in a traditionally appropriate way.

To acquire and maintain a base of loyal supporters by bestowing the patronage made possible by one's stewardship over economic resources, a rural cadre in Communist China had best belong to a fairly dense network of kin. Patronage politics is, after all, officially forbidden. This by no means makes it impossible, but it nevertheless dictates discretion. If a rising cadre with no close kin in a village tries to build a power base by dispensing patronage to persons who are not his relatives, his behavior obviously smacks of corruption and leaves the cadre politically vulnerable. But if the cadre is well connected with an extensive network of kin, he can gradually build a power base by dispensing the small favors that are still considered natural for a well-placed kinsman to share with his humbler relatives in rural China. Once he has built a solid and secure political base, he can perhaps extend his patronage to other groups.

Belonging to an extensive network of kin does not make it inevitable that a rising cadre will follow a political career based on the dispensing of patronage; it merely offers him a good opportunity to do so. To comprehend fully why certain cadres in Chen Village chose this path we would have to understand the whole complex of psychological forces and moral sensitivities that make up their individual personalities. But I have not been able to probe such personal motivational factors. I have simply been interested in exploring how interactions between the opportunities provided by the Chinese political system and the moral expectations generated by their cultural system encourage political leaders to shape their characters in particular ways.

The Chinese government may also of course make it impossible for a rural cadre to avail himself of opportunities to build a power base through patronage, for the local leader's position depends on the approval of higher-level government authorities. But as we have seen, the Chinese government often condoned at least a modicum of such patronage politics over the fifteen-year period we have recounted. It did so apparently because such forbearance is an efficient way of maintaining social order and productive efficiency in rural China. The building up of power through patronage conforms to the traditional ethos of the Chinese countryside. Most rural people expect it and find it understandable and perhaps even reassuring. Some may not especially like it, but most will not normally object to it unless it is carried to extremes. Moreover, the cadre who depends on patronage politics to build up his power base, precisely because he is vulnerable to charges of corruption from higher-ups, is often disposed to be loyal to his political superiors in matters that particularly concern them. He will ensure that grain quotas are delivered, that village order is maintained, and that at least vigorous lip service is given to official government policies. The government is assured of local order with a minimum of effort. If it wants to clean up cadre corruption and do away with local leaders who rely on patronage, it must employ extensive resources, such as outside work teams, and must create a considerable amount of turmoil, with unpredictable side effects, in the countryside. So the central government has often been content to grant considerable leeway to rural cadres who build up their power through traditional forms of patronage.

If a rural cadre avails himself of the opportunity to build up a political following by dispensing patronage and justifies that patronage by using Confucian moral discourse, his character will take on a particular shape. His lifestyle, his practical goals, and his means of pursuing those goals will all be affected. It will not advance his political ambitions to adopt an austere mode of life; indeed a modest amount of conspicuous consumption may even further his image as someone who is well able to take care of his less fortunate friends. The political goals he pursues among his constituents will likely be conservative ones. Although he may be interested in such things as economic development, he will want to preserve the way of life and the forms of local organization that have traditionally predominated in rural Chinese society, for it is upon these that his career rests. His means to these ends will involve the time-honored methods of compromise, concern for human feelings, and the nuances of face-saving. Since the path to power employed by the Communist gentry is rooted in persistent moral traditions that closely correspond to the rhythms of rural life, the Communist gentry have been a remarkably durable lot. The loyalty of their followers has often endured even after they have been deposed. Their usefulness to the Chinese state in maintaining an efficient rural government has persisted, even though their methods of government have contradicted the norms of the official ideology.

At its best, the character of the Communist gentry leads to a humane sensitivity to the different interests and hopes of the many diverse people who make up a village community and to a relaxed flexibility in exercising authority. The Communist gentleman can be tolerant of the fact that certain people under his authority are more concerned about their private good than about the community's public good. To govern them effectively he does not have to try to "convert" them forcibly. Through a skillful use of patronage politics he can establish social order with a minimum of turmoil and strife. At its worst, however, the character of the Communist gentry leads to personal greediness and a gross favoritism that will inevitably produce resentment on the part of those not favored.

Even at its best, however, the character of the Communist gentry creates fundamental problems for villagers in contemporary China. For better or worse, villagers live in a socialist economy under the domination of a powerful national state. Under such a system, the decisions of local political leaders weigh much more heavily on their lives than in imperial or even republican China. Under such circumstances, even a little favoritism, carried out in the name of "good human feeling" can have very painful consequences for those left out. As long as China's socialist economic and political system persists, the conduct of the Communist gentry will be widely felt to be irritating, even for people who may believe that it is morally natural and good. A corollary to this fact is that the Chinese Communist government will be forced to proceed slowly in promoting radical socialist transformations in the rural economy or risk generating massive peasant discontent. To avoid peasant discontent with "unfair" cadres, for example, the government may have to tolerate more individualistic economic remuneration systems like the piece-rate system, rather than press for more collectivistic ones like the Dazhai system. The more its basic cadres are like the Communist gentry, the less thoroughly socialist the government can afford to make the Chinese countryside.

To help bring about socialist political and economic changes, the Chinese government has relied on a second kind of local leader whom I will call the "Communist rebel." In Chen Village, the prime example of this type was Longyong, although he certainly bursts the bounds of any abstract typology.

The Communist rebel (who, like the member of the Communist gentry, is almost invariably a male) gets and maintains his power through his ability to embody and fulfill to an extraordinary degree the shared hopes of resentful individuals on the margins of a particular rural community, persons lacking the ability to attain power and prestige through the normal channels of a traditional social order—that is, through exchanges based on good human feeling and structured along kinship networks. But the hopes of illiterate, little travelled people on the margins of a rural community in China are not likely to be radically removed from their local experience and from the cultural traditions of their community. Those hopes will be expressed in terms of a permutation of the dominant ethos of that community, like the conception of the village as a single big family. In Chen Village, this vision of the community as a single big family was a radical vision that would transform the normal traditional structure of the village if realized. But it was not an outlandishly new vision that totally transcended the community's dominant world view. This was a vision not unrelated to those that had animated rural rebels and reformers throughout the premodern history of China. Villagers followed Longyong, not because he was a modern embodiment of official Communist virtue, but because he was a traditional representative of a locally comprehensible rebellious enterprise.

To embody the rebellious hopes of the members of a rural community, a prospective activist had best authentically belong to the ranks of its disadvantaged. The disadvantaged must see him as truly one of their own, not simply as someone who achieves his political purposes by coming down to their level. But to be a leader of those on the margins of a village community, it is not enough simply to belong to the ranks of the disadvantaged. One must live a particular type of personal existence; one must stand out in a way that embodies the hopes of the disadvantaged. Thus it was politically important not only for Longyong to live an austere personal life that identified him with the poorest members of his community but also for him consistently to play the role of an effective patriarch of the entire village. For the sake of his political career, he had to excel in the rough brashness that peasants saw as necessary for gaining their hopes and in the single-minded concern for the community that would assure his followers that their interests as a whole were being served. (When, however, a Communist rebel achieves a measure of success and his leadership can be based on his ability to dispense the material resources under his control through patronage, he may be tempted to moderate the austerity of his life-style, as Longyong began to do after he became able to exercise his rulership through control over the profits of the brigade's new industrial sector.)

The Communist rebel's political goals will be relatively radical, but they will be limited by the horizons of his community's social imagination. And members of a relatively poor, isolated farming village are not likely to extend their conception of public responsibilities much beyond the boundaries of their village. Thus, Longyong's political project consisted of making his village into a single, hardworking, relatively egalitarian "big family": a radical goal by local standards, but a limited and problematic goal from the point of view of national political leaders committed to the well-being of the "national family" (*guojia*). And the Communist rebel's means to his ends are limited by the dimensions of the traditional ethos he represents. Thus Longyong achieved his ends by behaving like an authoritarian patriarch rather than following the "mass line" principles promulgated in official Communist ideology.

At its best, the character of the Communist rebel leads to an uncompromising dedication to the good of the community as a whole; it can inspire the kind of selfless discipline among community members needed to advance the public good. At its worst, however, it leads to a power-hungry ambitiousness and an arbitrary, dictatorial rule.

Even at his best, however, the Communist rebel creates fundamental problems for the national government by leading to what the Chinese Communists call the deviation of "localism." The Communist rebel's mode of rule, based on appeals to his community's chauvinist spirit, leads him to resist government authority in the name of serving his community. Indeed, as we have seen, the Communist rebel's hegemony may prove even more resistant to state supervision than that of the patronage politician. When the Chinese Communist government has wanted to promote progress in the socialist transformation of its rural communities—deemphasize private plots and sidelines, tighten collective labor discipline, use Dazhai work points instead of piece rates, increase the power of production brigade organizations relative to that of production teams—it has supported the Communist rebel and given him moral and political encouragement to exercise his particular kind of leadership to the full. But even as it has done so, it has created problems for itself. Localist sentiments have become more virulent. Many villagers have chafed under the rigidity of the Communist rebel's rule. Having used the Communist rebel to move socialism several steps forward, the government has found the costs of this progress prohibitive and has been forced to retreat.

But even when the Chinese government has withdrawn its support from him, the Communist rebel has remained remarkably resilient. With his power grounded more in the sentiments of his community than in the support of the state, he may continue his political activity, even when no longer unequivocally supported by the state.[3]

3. Interestingly, with the relaxation of dogmatic restraints upon Chinese scholars following the fall of the Gang of Four, a vigorous discussion has taken place among Chinese historians about the influence of traditional culture on the revolutionary potential of the Chinese peasantry. Most Chinese historians publishing between 1949 and 1976 emphatically argued for the revolutionary nature of China's peasantry: the peasantry had always been an oppressed class that throughout history had undertaken rebellions aimed at destroying China's "feudal system." Since 1977, however, an articulate group of historians has been arguing that even rebellious peasants were constrained by the limitations of China's familistic culture. Thus, peasant rebellions were never able completely to over-

The political capital of both the Communist rebel and the member of the Communist gentry consists primarily in their ability to meet the expectations of members of their local community. Now I will consider two types of local leaders whose political resources stem from their ability to meet the official moral expectations imposed by the apparatus of the Chinese state.

These expectations are defined by the official ideology promulgated through the government's central propaganda apparatus. The conceptual language of that ideology is Marxist, even though it is spoken with a very heavy Chinese accent. According to the official ideology, a good society is not rooted in the past but anticipated in the future. It will be a classless community of equals who will enthusiastically work together for the common good, because the collective good will be identical with their individual good. The main source of evil in the present society is social class divisions; to bring about the good society, the Communist Party should lead the proletarian class in its struggle against all exploiting classes. A good Communist belongs to the proletarian class and struggles wholeheartedly for the interests of that class. In Chinese communism, however, one does not actually have to be a wage earner to be on the side of the proletariat. One can be on the side of the proletariat as long as one has the class interests of the proletariat at heart. Almost anybody can thus become identified with the proletariat, although in practice the most exploited classes in old China—the poor and lower-middle peasants—were considered the proletariat's natural allies.[4] In Chinese Communist ideology, one of the main metaphors used to depict the struggles between the classes has been a military one: the good and bad classes are like great armies arrayed in battle against one another. But as we have seen, within this sinified Marxist-Leninist framework two dis-

---

throw the institutions and culture of "feudal society." And this new (for Chinese historians) interpretation of the past is clearly no mere academic exercise. It is meant to explain why the leadership style of so many peasant cadres is that of "feudal patriarchy." As Wang Xiaoqiang, a historian who defends this new interpretation, recently noted: "In our country, which has a very deep and long feudal tradition, the serious influences of peasant consciousness both in and out of the Party and especially in the ranks of the cadres, the present condition of the vast peasantry's lacking cultural life and democratic tradition, objectively speaking, have truly created conditions that facilitate feudal patriarchy." (The information on the historians' debate and the quote from Wang Xiaoqiang are taken from Kwang-Ching Liu, "World View and Peasant Rebellion: Reflections on Post-Mao Historiography," *Journal of Asian Studies* 40, no. 2 [1981]:295–326. I am very grateful to Professor Liu for sending me early galley proofs of this article.)

4. On this point, see Benjamin I. Schwartz, *Chinese Communism and the Rise of Mao* (Cambridge, Mass.:Harvard University Press, 1951).

tinct dialects developed: Mao Zedong's and Liu Shaoqi's. The principal difference between the two dialects was perhaps their way of thinking about the structure and function of the class armies.

For Mao, the class armies were at war. Good class soldiers had to be heroes totally forgetful of themselves and ready to lay down their lives at any moment. To ignore their self-interests and achieve this heroism they needed a spiritual motivation. This could only be acquired through a quasi-religious faith in the person and thought of Mao. Only people with this faith truly belonged to the good classes.

But for Liu Shaoqi, the class armies were in a state of watchful peace. The exploiting classes had been vanquished, though not utterly annihilated. Almost everyone in China, except for a small minority of counter-revolutionaries, ex-landlords and the like, now belonged to the good classes. Good class soldiers had to keep their army well organized, ready for defense; but they did not have to be heroes. Each of them simply had to play a small part to ensure that the class army was ready to function well. Having done that, each could look to his or her own interests. The enlightened self-interests of good class soldiers encouraged their cooperation with one another.

The local leader who depends for power and prestige on living up to the ideals propounded by a Maoist-dominated propaganda apparatus I will call the "moralistic revolutionary." The primary representatives of this type in Chen Village were the fervent urban counselors.

The moralistic revolutionary gains his or her power through being part of a formal political organization—the Communist Party or the Young Communist League. Without the validation given to one's personal excellence by admission into such an organization, one has little political power. But to enter such an organization, one has to stand out among those of one's peers who also want to belong, to stand out with respect to one's commitment to Maoist virtue. Whereas the political behavior of the Communist gentry and the Communist rebel embodies and fulfills the ideals and interests of those whom they would lead and thus binds them to their political inferiors, the behavior of moralistic revolutionaries is structured around total conformity to the official ideals of their supreme leader and thus separates them from their political inferiors. For this reason the political fervor of the urban counselors had a peculiarly narcissistic quality. The most dedicated of the urban youth seemed more concerned with their own purity than with their ability to help either their urban peers or the residents of Chen Village. At the height of their zeal, they adopted life-styles that were supposed to embody the essence of poor and lower-middle peasant virtue, but that seemed bizarrely unrealistic to the actual peasants of the village. And their exaggerated attempts to manifest an ideal spirit of helpful service toward one another actually forced them into an alienating competition with one another.

Moralistic revolutionaries possess a breadth of vision that Communist gentry and the Communist rebels lack. Moralistic revolutionaries see themselves as part of a vast historical process transforming all of China and perhaps all of the world. The political goal they pursue is the success of the revolution as a whole. But because they are so caught up in manifesting concern for these broad goals, they often suffer from a kind of far-sightedness. They can see Humanity but not people, Class Struggle but not concrete groups in conflict, Revolution but not the intricacies of the political process. They thus lack the practical means to their political ends. In an effort to achieve their ends, they may thus enter into alliances with characters like the Communist rebel, and because of their insensitivity to concrete political praxis, they may end up being manipulated by such locally entrenched leaders, perhaps without even realizing it.

The moralistic revolutionary is not a very durable character type. A total commitment to dogmatic ideals harmonizes poorly with the practical worries engendered by the need to make a living, with the responsibilities produced by the need to raise a family, and indeed with the compromises demanded by a need to win over and to organize a concrete political constituency. The moralistic revolutionary will therefore most likely be an unmarried young person, separated through some process from dependence on his or her natal family, free from the immediate responsibility of earning a living, and presented with a clear opportunity to advance himself or herself politically through fervent attachment to an official political ideal. Such were the zealous members of the youth brigade during their first year in Chen Village.

But the devolution of the idealistic commitment of the members of the youth brigade after their first year in the village illustrates the fragility of the moralistic revolutionary's character. Once the members of the youth brigade were scattered among Chen Village's production teams, they faced the need to earn a living and to get along with their rustic neighbors. Some of them quickly became like ordinary peasants. Others seized the opportunities presented by the Cultural Revolution to join the Maoism Red Guards and to attempt quixotically to make Chen Village part of a national revolutionary crusade and then quickly gave up any revolutionary concerns when their movement did not meet the test of reality. Others, still maintaining their desire to play a revolutionary political role in the village, allied themselves with Longyong and began to adopt his vision of the world and to work for his limited goals. They maintained some of their idealism by diluting their original, total commitment. But the residual idealism of these latter urban youth was extremely vulnerable to fickle shifts in the government's official ideological line. When the government closed the doors on their opportunity to advance politically through their fervor and when events like the Lin Biao affair brought about drastic shifts in the official ideological line, the residual idealism of these young would-be revolutionaries quickly disintegrated.

During the 1960s, the Chinese government, urged on by Mao, used its educational system and propaganda apparatus to mass-produce idealistic revolutionaries among its urban young. Some of these idealistic revolutionaries bolstered the power and furthered the policies of figures like the Communist rebel in the Chinese countryside. But the moralistic idealism of such urban youth almost inevitably broke down. For some, probably a minority, it developed into a realistic activism that produced faithful bureaucrats (perhaps like some of the members of the work teams that came to Chen Village) or perhaps new types of locally rooted Communist rebels. For others, the idealism devolved into an anomic restlessness, a restlessness that one finds many indications of today, especially in China's cities.

The type of local leader whose power and prestige depends on living up to the ideals propounded by a government apparatus dominated by the ideological heirs of Liu Shaoqi is one I will call the "pragmatic technocrat." This type is approximated in my narrative by the young revolutionary successors, Bengua and Pigskin.

The pragmatic technocrat's political capital lies in his competence in the technical aspects of economic management. He or she (some pragmatic technocrats are women, though in China the majority are men) knows how to manipulate people and things so that they mesh smoothly to produce tangible material goods in an efficient way. The technocrat leads people not by inspiring them, convincing them of their moral duties, or earning their loyalty through patronage but rather by demonstrating that it is in their self-interest to do as he or she directs. The other types of leaders we have discussed appeal in some way to venerable ideals; the technocrat appeals to visible facts: if you organize your work in this way you will produce more and become richer than if you do it in some other way. To get people to accept their leadership, peasant technocrats have to make a plausible claim to know more about the relevant facts than most others. If they are working in a farming village with traditional technology, they might base such a claim on their long experience with village work. If they are trying to get villagers to adopt innovations like collectivized production teams and the new small-scale industries, they might want to appeal to the higher kind of knowledge that comes from modern "scientific" schooling. Thus, it has become very helpful for the careers of many rural pragmatic technocrats to have graduated from senior middle school. That schooling may in fact give them little real knowledge relevant to the problems of economic development in village China, but it may make them appear to know more about such unfamiliar matters than anyone else in the village. Since they can claim to know more, they can also claim to deserve to be obeyed.

Villagers seem to have always respected people who were good at the technical aspects of farm work. But the character ideals appealed to by a local cadre like Bengua come more from the central government's (Liuist) propaganda than from the village's traditional ethos. Pragmatic technocrats lay claim to authority almost solely on the basis of technical competence in economic management; the type of management they claim to be especially good at is that required to make the village flourish in a new world of production teams, small-scale industries, and "scientific" progress. Villagers feel no special loyalty to pragmatic peasant technocrats: they are neither personally indebted to them nor personally inspired by them. They accept them because the technocrats seem to be able to do a good job under the circumstances. Ordinary villagers might be very enthusiastic about technocratic leaders if they could quickly work wonders with the local economy. But for now, the kinds of technical innovations that might create rapid spurts in China's agricultural productivity are very slow in being realized. As we have noted, Chen Village's agricultural productivity actually stagnated in the 1970s, not so much because of the technical incompetence of village leaders as because of unrealistic government policies and falling morale among village workers. Under such circumstances, villagers may not be enthusiastic about their technocratic leaders, but may still consider them less irritating than corrupt Communist gentry and less dangerous than Communist rebels.

During the 1970s, my research suggests, the pragmatic technocrat became the dominant character type among local leaders in the Chinese countryside. Not only were new leaders chosen on the basis of their claims to managerial competence, but older leaders became technocratic in character. If rapid technological innovation were taking place in rural China, this proliferation of peasant technocrats might be a sign of rural China's economic vitality. In the absence of such innovation, it seems to be more a sign of the demoralization of rural China. People are unwilling to listen to leaders who speak to them about common goals for which they ought to sacrifice their immediate interests; they prefer to listen to leaders who only talk about practical means to productive efficiency, even if the means do not lead to any dynamic economic growth. The pragmatic technocrat wins by default.

It will be important for peasant technocrats to adopt a personal lifestyle that is not too self-indulgent because they cannot rely enough on village loyalty based on patronage ties to protect them against routine charges of corruption. But they have no incentive to live an extremely austere life, since their power is not dependent upon disadvantaged villagers being able to accept them as one of their own. They appear to villagers to be basically honest, but strangely selfish.

China's Crisis in Political Culture

The characters delineated above are ideal types that indicate what local leaders might be like if they made a total, consistent effort to shape their lives according to certain moral principles. As presented here, these moral principles are also ideal types—models of clearly contrasted, extreme positions within either a traditional Confucian or modern Communist mode of moral discourse. These ideal types are useful in helping us bring into sharper focus certain tendencies in the action and discourse of grass-roots rural cadres and activists during the last two decades in China. But in reality, of course, the distinctions between the types blur. Local leaders do not commit themselves totally and consistently to a particular set of moral principles; the contrasts drawn here are extreme positions in a continuum of values. Indeed, a blurring of character types *has* to occur if political conduct in China is to have a viable moral basis. It is a tragedy for China that at certain times in the past twenty years it has been easy to find leaders who rather closely approximated one or another of our ideal character types. For under the social circumstances prevailing in China during the past several decades, a "pure" exemplar of one of these types has tended to become both an ineffective and an immoral politician in the end.

If most important local village leaders were ideal members of the Communist gentry, it would be impossible to establish a rationalized system for agricultural production, and economic development would stagnate. If they were ideal Communist rebels, villages would become internally well organized but chauvinistic, and the political integration of the Chinese nation would suffer. If the leaders were perfect moralistic revolutionaries, they would make impossible demands for moral heroism that most villagers could not accept. If they were ideal pragmatic technocrats, they would fail to unite the villagers around any sense of common purpose. If pushed to an extreme within the social conditions of contemporary China, each of the main strands of Chinese political culture leads local cadres and activists into severe moral predicaments. To escape from these predicaments, various traditional and modern cultural strands must be fused into a synthesis. Only such a synthesis, I would argue, can provide an adequate moral basis for the creative local leadership necessary to meet the contemporary needs both of villagers and of the Chinese nation as a whole.

It was perhaps the particular genius of Mao to see the need for fusing his grand vision of national, political, and economic development with the tradition-rooted visions of the good society held by China's peasants and for evoking qualities of character among local leaders that would integrate these visions in practice. But by the 1960s, Mao's genius had led to a kind of hubris, which engendered unrealistic and therefore self-destructive attempts to effect such a moral synthesis.

As we have seen, the essence of the Maoist ethos was encapsulated in the imperative, "Serve the People." The people one was to serve were not simply the individuals in one's family or community but all of the people of China, with the exception of class enemies, and indeed all of the oppressed people of the world. And to *serve* the people was not merely to give them what they wanted, or what they thought they wanted at any given time, but to transform them politically into a classless community of equals. This transformation was to occur not through simple coercion but through charismatic persuasion. The Maoist revolutionary was supposed to have close enough ties to the people to be assured of their respect and trust while constantly helping them to transcend their limited visions and local interests. Thus the Maoist revolutionaries were to structure their whole life and consciousness so as to live in the world but not of it. They were to strive constantly and patiently to transform their immediate social world under the discipline of the Communist Party and the Thought of Mao Zedong.

At the village level, the Maoist vision was, under appropriate circumstances, able to resonate with the more traditional vision of the Communist rebel. As Mao urged, the Communist rebel was dedicated to sacrificing himself in order to transform his world: to eliminate inequality, to curb individualistic selfishness, and to inspire a sense of commitment to the common good. He was, moreover, willing to make hard demands on himself in order to legitimate the hard demands he made on others. The Communist rebel's moral vision differed from Mao's in that it was rooted in a specific, bounded social world. It was a vision for creating strength and glory for his home community as a whole, not for China as a whole.

The very boundedness of this vision is what gave it its strength and the Communist rebel his courage and tenacity. It was a vision generated by the primordial sentiments attached to common ancestry, residency, collective memories and hopes. The Communist rebel came from near the margins of his community, from the ranks of those excluded from the community's normal channels of access to power, wealth, and prestige. Understandably, he wanted to change the community. But he had no realistic hope of leaving it. Thus his hopes for personal prosperity were tied to its prosperity, his prestige to the respect of its members. And the validity of his life was measured by the moral order of that community, by the symbols that bound the community together and mediated its history and hopes. His rebellious vision did not therefore totally reject the community's traditional moral discourse but was based on images—like the village as a big family—that were protesting permutations of the community's dominant mode of discourse.

But the local vision of the Communist rebel could not by itself provide an effective program for radical social change. The traditional structure of communities like Chen Village could never be overturned unless the structure of similar villages throughout China was also transformed through the efforts of a national political organization. This is where the moral imperatives and political vision of the Maoist ethos came to have an importance for the Communist rebel. The vision of serving the people could resonate with his hopes for his community and direct those hopes into involvement with the organizational structure of the new Chinese polity. If enabled to see that his struggles were tied to a great nationwide struggle, the local rebel could become a *Communist* rebel.

During the revolutionary struggles of the 1930s and 1940s, it seems that the Chinese Communist propagandists did indeed learn to make their modern visions of national liberation resonate with the traditional hopes of local peasant rebels. This fusion of moral themes made good sense when both national Communist leaders and local rebels were fighting against real, obviously dangerous, interrelated enemies: Guomindang and Japanese armies on the one hand and local landlords on the other. The danger, the hardship, and the injustice of those times gave plausibility on the national level to an ethic of totally self-sacrificing struggle for the good of the people and on the local level to an ethic of grim struggle against privileged gentry for the good of one's community as a whole. The Maoist moral vision and the rebel vision were fused together in an experience of common combat. During the land reform period, too, national Communist organizers and local rebels felt themselves linked together in common cause.

But when the fighting was over, the strands of moral discourse diverged. The Communist rebel's traditional style of moral reasoning suggested that one forsake the direct service of one's immediate family and close kin to serve one's village as a whole when one's whole community was in a state of crisis. When the crisis was past, and when one stood near the center of the village's new structure of wealth and prestige, one could and perhaps should put the welfare of one's close family above one's community. Thus there emerged Communist gentry leaders like Qingfa. From what we can gather, Qingfa would have acted very like a Communist rebel during land reform. According to my interpretation, he became a member of the Communist gentry not simply because he was seduced by his own greed but because he and his constituents considered it moral that he should do so when the revolutionary struggles were over.

And at the national level, Mao's moralistic revolutionary rhetoric was challenged by the more utilitarian rhetoric of Liu Shaoqi because Liu could argue that his rhetoric made more sense than Mao's for managing a country during a time of peace. There was enough ambiguity in the national and local political situations (Was China truly at peace? Was the local battle for social equality truly over?) that Chinese Communists could argue about which mode of moral reasoning was really appropriate. And there was enough at stake politically for the parties to this debate to argue with fierce intensity.

In the 1960s, Mao tried to revitalize his moralistic rhetoric and to join forces with local Communist rebels. But there was something strained and artificial about the attempt. Mao overextended his ideology. He tried to reinstate in all its heroic purity the ethic of total self-sacrifice developed in the course of desperate military struggles. Without a clear and present danger, this kind of ethic could only be justified through a sacred dogma—Mao's apotheosized teaching. Hordes of urban youth became moralistic revolutionaries passionately devoted to that teaching. But the passion of these revolutionaries was bought too dearly to be an effective instrument for social change. Such enthusiasts gained their peculiar passion at the price of losing their roots in society. They thought it morally inferior to be concerned with making a living. (Thus in their early zeal the sent-down urban youth labored hard, not to make money, but to prove their dedication to Chairman Mao.) They thought it morally inferior to feel any spontaneous sympathy for each other. (Thus the sent-down youth tried to look upon each other and the village's peasants only as revolutionary comrades, not as potential friends.) They even felt it morally inferior to look at the world with the open eyes of common sense. (Thus even after being in Chen Village for several months, the sent-down youth thought they could understand what poor and lower-middle peasants were like by reading official Maoist propaganda rather than by looking at the peasants around them.) Moralistic revolutionaries could live out their extreme ideals only as long as they were young, unmarried, and living in sectarian social islands, like the youth brigade. Separated from normal economic and community ties, it was relatively easy for them to seek the satisfaction of their material, emotional, and moral needs through participation in a political organization devoted to the realization of utopian ideals. They could temporarily pour their whole lives into such an organization, for they had put aside the opportunity to satisfy their needs anywhere else. But their needs inevitably grew. They eventually got married and acquired new economic responsibilities. They got tired and discouraged and required stable emotional support. They came to discern complexities and ambiguities in life that an abstract, rigidly dogmatic ideology could not explain. And thus they quickly lost their zeal and grew bitter and discouraged. Among the urban-born young, sanctified Maoist moral dogma temporarily produced fervent moral zealots, but the unrealistic rigidity of that dogma quickly turned their zeal into bitter destructive cynicism.

In the countryside, in my view, Mao's program for moral revival was more promising than in the cities. In the emotional rituals of the Socialist Education Movement, the morality of the emergent Communist gentry was condemned and that of the Communist rebel reaffirmed and linked in a loose way with an attitude of personal reverence toward Mao and a commitment to the more general themes in his thought. This might have been a good start toward producing the kind of disciplined public spirit needed to form the moral basis of a dynamic socialist economy and society. If the methods of the Socialist Education Movement had been less brutal and its rationale more realistic, this beginning might have led to lasting benefits.

But the rituals of struggle that formed the first part of the Socialist Education Movement were inexcusably brutal. Work teams justified the brutality by saying that China's villages and indeed the nation as a whole were in critical danger because a vicious class struggle was being waged. But the class struggle was an invisible one, and a person could only know who was truly on the good or bad side by listening to the sacred teachings of Mao. In the ritual process of the Socialist Education Movement, the brutality and the dogma became mutually reinforcing. The brutality was justified by the dogma and then tended to reinforce commitment to the dogma: if one had struggled so brutally against the invisible evil classes, then of course the evil classes must exist. Yet the brutality of the first phase of the Socialist Education Movement was somewhat redeemed by the ceremonies of innocence that followed. The incubus of the class enemy, villagers were led to believe, had been exorcised. Most cadres could be reinstated. The villagers could join together in grateful praise of Mao Zedong for giving them the victory. The end result of this was that the villagers' devotion to the welfare of their community as a whole intensified; perhaps the villagers even gained some heightened appreciation for the public interest of the nation as a whole.

If the government had then continued to stress the need for cadres to be fair and for the public to be generally dedicated to the common good but had downplayed the idea that this was necessary because of the continued presence of invisible class enemies, if the government had let Mao be venerated as a concrete symbol for the aspirations of a great nation but had downplayed the idea that his "holiness" came from his infallibility as a teacher, and if the government had continued to praise the goodness of selfless devotion to the public good but had recognized the need for individual citizens to be concerned too about their personal welfare, then the public-spiritedness created through the Maoist rituals might have been consolidated, might have mellowed into a realistic guide for honest politics under practical conditions, and might have persisted as a vital part of the moral basis of political conduct in rural China. But in the Cultural Revolution, the fear of invisible class enemies exploded with new fury, worship of Mao's dogmas was pushed to absurd conclusions, and protests against self-interests were exaggerated to the point where they became a transparent mask for their opposite—the unrestrained expression of the most virulently selfish ambition. It was not the tradition-rooted, community-oriented activists of rural China who were responsible for thus forcing Maoism into absurdity but the young moralistic revolutionaries from the cities, the expert devotees of Mao's Thought, urged on by Mao himself.

When Maoism exploded into absurdity, the moral basis of Chinese culture disintegrated into its diverse themes. The Communist gentry, the Communist rebel, the moralistic revolutionary, and the peasant technocrat emerged in all their one-sided, incompatible purity. Being thus one-dimensionally moral as persons, they became immoral as politicians. And thus Chinese political culture became demoralized—an ironic, tragic end for Mao's attempt at moral revolution.

The present Chinese government, controlled by Deng Xiaoping, is steadily continuing to eradicate the last vestiges of Maoism from public moral discourse. The dominant slogan of the new regime is not "Serve the People" but "Seek the Truth from Facts."[5] This new slogan suggests that the truth about the nature of the good life in the new China can indeed be known simply from a rational examination of empirical data. But the empirical facts can never tell one the truth about the ultimate goals of life. At best, such facts can only tell individuals the means to use to maximize their personal interests. This slogan of a utilitarian moral discourse serves as the basis for discussing the meaning of public life in China. I have tried to suggest why that utilitarian mode of discourse and its corresponding political character type, the pragmatic technocrat, came to fill the moral vacuum created by the Cultural Revolution; I have also stated why I think that it is unable to fill the vacuum by itself.[6] At the

5. "Seek the Truth from Facts" (*shi shi qiu shi*), though found in the writings of Mao, was made into the main slogan of the current Deng Xiaoping regime in mid-1978. Deng Xiaoping himself stressed the phrase in his report to the Army Political Work Conference of April 27 to June 6, 1978. For months thereafter, a host of articles appeared in the official press stressing the importance of the new slogan. See *China News Analysis*, nos. 1128 and 1134 (1978).

6. A vivid example of this crisis of faith comes from the discussion surrounding the following letter supposedly written by a twenty-three-year-old girl, Pan Xiao, and published in the May 1980 edition of the magazine *Zhongguo Qingnian* (China Youth).

village level—and indeed, according to many reports, at all levels of Chinese society—the utilitarian mode of moral discourse seems today not so much to animate brisk managerial efficiency as simply to legitimate the careful cultivation of individual self-interests. There is also, as we have indicated, widespread corruption: officials use the "back door" to give favors to friends and relatives and payers of bribes. This marks a return of the ethic of the Communist gentry, but in its most venal form: particularistic favoritism used not so much to achieve a decent level of social harmony but simply to justify selfishness on the part of officials. To complement the new government's goals of "Four Modernizations" in agriculture, industry, science and technology, and national defense, a fifth modernization may well be required—in political culture. While trying to avoid the mistakes of Mao, ordinary citizens, like those in Chen Village, and national government leaders may have to search

---

My father, my mother and my mother's father are Party members. Naturally as a child I believed in Marxism. I had scarcely entered primary school when the great Cultural Revolution began. I witnessed the ransacking of houses, physical fights, loss of human life, human life taken for no reason. At home there were no more smiles on any lips. Round me young people were using dirty language and playing cards. I discovered that life is not like what is written in books.

My family became poor and money was the centre of much quarrelling. I found a modest job. I was refused admission to the Youth Corps because I had once criticized a local leader. I was looking for friendship, but a friend to whom I talked frankly denounced me. Love? The boy I loved with my whole heart abandoned me; I could not eat or sleep for two days and nights. I was searching for the meaning of life. The revolution? An empty word. Making a name for myself? Who can reach that? Amusement, food and drink? In death one takes with one only one's skin.

I read Hegel, Darwin, Owen, Balzac, Victor Hugo, Tolstoy, Lu Xun, Cao Yu, Ba Jin. I found no answer; but I learned from Darwin that man remains a man and cannot get rid of himself. There is no perfect man. Man is selfish. Propaganda for "man living for others" is a myth. Great heroes, great scholars, teachers, great propagandists—none of them could rid themselves of selfish motives. Formerly I had believed that one lives to make the lives of others more beautiful. Now I came to regard this as ridiculous . . .

Dear Editor, I write you all this, though I do not hope that you can cure me. But if you want to publish this, I hope the youths of the whole country will read it. Many feel as I do. Perhaps I may get help from them.

The editor of the magazine appended a note to this letter encouraging a debate on the "meaning of life." In subsequent issues the magazine published selected letters and some articles responding to the letter. The August issue of the magazine stated that it had received forty thousand letters in response to Pan Xiao's letter, many revealing the personal problems of young people. (Translation of the letter is taken from *China News Analysis*, no. 1189 [1980]; comments on its impact are paraphrased from the same source.) For a translated collection of letters published by *China Youth* on this topic, see *Chinese Education* 14, no. 1 (Spring 1981).

together in traditional and modern moral lexicons to find the words to understand what it would realistically mean to serve the people in China today.[7]

7. In fact, a renewed discussion of morality and ethics is being conducted in official circles. A conference on ethics that attracted scholars from all over China was held in Wuxi, Jiangsu Province, in June 1980. In the same month, *Zhexue Yan-jiu* (Research in Philosophy) published three papers calling for greater attention to the study of Communist morality and ethics. Numerous shorter articles on the subject appeared in the national press. (Philip L. Wickeri, "Morality and Party Reform: A Problem in Chinese Ideology," *Ching Feng* 23, nos. 2–4 [1980]:141–50.)

In late 1981, a campaign was launched to promote "socialist spiritual civilization," and in early 1982 another campaign was conducted to root out corruption among cadres. At this writing, the impact of those campaigns is unclear.

216–217; confession by, 209–210; degradation of his character, 175–176; impact of Maoist morality on, 68, 82–85, 98–99, 157; influence of the Cultural Revolution on, 171–174, 193–194; leadership style of, 157, 158, 172–174, 175, 246, 259; as a manager of economic growth, 216–217, 217–218, 221–224; Maoist criticism of, 88–89; Maoist morality rejected by, 98–99; patronage politics used by, 50–51, 65, 89, 99, 171; political capital of, 65; political persona of, 89; political power struggles of, 34, 64–66, 84–85, 172–173, 193–195; politics of human feeling practiced by, 171, 175; public good disregarded by, 172–174; punished by his rival, 193–195; rehabilitation of, 211, 221; social background of, 49, 64–65; social morality of, 172–174; strategies used in the small Four Cleanups, 82–85; struggle sessions against, 194; and vision of village order as a federation of families linked by the flavor of human feeling, 54, 60, 64, 99, 173–174, 175, 246

Chen Village, xiii, xiv, xv; Communist Party branch in, 178; departure of sent-down youth from, 234–235; modernization of, 239–240; poverty of, 36, 41–42, 45; social geography of, 42–46 (*see also* Lineage organization); social prestige of, 36, 52–54; socioeconomic and political change in, 2–3, 41, 141–144, 168–169; as a "special economic zone," 242*n*, 243

Chen Village: The Recent History of a Peasant Community in Mao's China, x–xi, 177*n*, 180*n*, 205*n*, 207*n*, 241*n*; characters in, x, 33*n*; Cultural Revolution described in, 154*n*; Mao Study campaign described in, 130*n*; norms on criticism of friends described in, 172*n*; research for, x–xi; sent-down youth discussed in, 105*n*; Socialist Education Movement described in, 68*n*, 72

Chen Yongguei, 61*n*
China Youth, 262*n*, 263*n*
Chinese Communist ideology, 52–54; attitudes of village leaders toward, 52; and the "Communist rebel" character type, 250–251; compared with lineage organization and the concept of "humanity," 60, 62; concept of the good society in, 252; conflicts with peasant moral evaluation of cadres, 76–80; conflicts with traditional peasant morality, 8, 60, 62–63, 64; liberal policies in, 52; moral discourse in, 14–18 (*see also* Liuist moral paradigm; Maoist paradigm of moral discourse); on revolutionary "glory," 110, 161–162; rival factions in, 66, 69–70, 72; universalistic morality in, 58; vs. the peasant understanding of social class and class struggle, 75–76

Chinese Communist Party, 68, 229; and the concept of a good Party member, 202; and the Cultural Revolution, 155; Maoist criticism of, 69; political power from membership in, 92, 94, 253; village branch of, 178; village brigades managed by, 46–47, 84, 94; village leaders in, 46, 49, 171, 209

Chinese folk religion, 95
Chinese government, 2; class labels assigned by, 41; and the "Communist rebel" character type, 250–251; patronage politics condoned by, 248; power struggles in, 153; rituals devised by, 23. *See also* Rituals of struggle

Class background: as the basis for moral authenticity, 164–165; punishment for bad class backgrounds, 179, 181–185, 194, 196; power of urban youth counselors limited by, 231; of revolutionary successors, 224

Class status and class labels, 15, 94; and criticism of Mao Zedong Thought Counselors, 146, 147; vs. lineage solidarity, 2 (*see also* Lineage organization); marital choice influenced by, 121; and moral behavior of rural cadres, 78;

Designer: Marilyn Perry
Compositor: Innovative Media
Printer: Vail-Ballou Press
Binder: Vail-Ballou Press
Text: 10/12 Palatino
Display: Palatino